DAVID DIMBLEBY

HOW WE
BUILT
BRITAIN

DAVID DIMBLEBY

HOW WE BUILT BRITAIN

Special photography by
Paul Barker

BLOOMSBURY

PREVIOUS
The two fine arches
of Holdenby House
in Northamptonshire.

NEXT PAGE
Burghley House's
spectacular rooftop.

First published in Great Britain in 2007

Text © 2007 David Dimbleby
Specially commissioned photography © 2007 Paul Barker
For picture credits see page 286
Map on pages 10–11 by Reginald Piggott

By arrangement with the BBC
The BBC logo is a trademark of the British Broadcasting Corporation
and is used under licence.
BBC logo © BBC 1996

Bloomsbury Publishing Plc, 36 Soho Square, London W1D 3QY

A CIP catalogue record for this book is available from the British Library.

ISBN 978 0 747 58871 9
10 9 8 7 6 5 4 3 2 1

Editor: Steve Dobell
Design: Grade Design Consultants, London. www.gradedesign.com
Photographer: Paul Barker
Picture Researcher: Anne-Marie Ehrlich
Indexer: David Atkinson

Printed in Great Britain by Butler and Tanner Ltd, Frome

All papers used by Bloomsbury Publishing are natural, recyclable products
made from wood grown in well-managed forests. The manufacturing processes
conform to the environmental regulations of the country of origin.

www.bloomsbury.com

This book has been printed, using vegetable inks, and bound
by Butler and Tanner Ltd, an ISO 14001 accredited company.

This book is dedicated to my wife, Belinda, whose encouragement and steadfast support made it possible.

Introduction

BUILDINGS HAVE ALWAYS FASCINATED ME. From the grandest to the most humble they seem to send out a message about how and why they came to be built. Often we do not have time to notice that they tell a story. We can live in them or use them without looking at them, without even thinking about them. It does not mean that they do not affect us. Our surroundings always affect us, even if we are not fully aware of their impact. A moment's pause to stand and stare is always rewarded because buildings provide so many pleasures, not least the fact that they help us understand who we were and who we are.

As physical objects all buildings are intriguing. The materials that are available to their builders and the way they use them determine their appearance. It is as true of primitive cottages built of stone and mud and roofed with turf as it is of the latest gleaming glass skyscraper in its polished steel frame. There is no other form of human creativity so constrained by practical limitations. The writer or poet has none. The painter or sculptor is relatively free. The musician can conjure up spells from his imagination. The builder has first to look at what he has and then work out how it can be put together to achieve the effect he wants. For me the first pleasure of looking at a building is finding answers to obvious questions. How is the roof supported? How do these walls stand up? What is the purpose of this beam or that girder? How can that arch soar so high without collapsing?

Then there is the pleasure of discovering what the building is trying to say. Is it trying to impress me with its grandeur or intimidate me with its power? Is it wanting to welcome me or excite me? Is it friendly, even cosy, or cool and aloof? And does it achieve its aims? Buildings that are meant to look grand can sometimes look embarrassingly overblown. Others, completely unpretentious, can inspire by their very simplicity. Every building is designed for a purpose, but finding out that purpose is another journey of discovery, particularly in old buildings whose use is long forgotten.

Then again, buildings display our aspirations. There are cathedrals and churches that seek to enhance religious experience. There are schools and libraries hoping to encourage learning. Railway stations and airport terminals try to arouse us to the excitements of speed and the freedom to travel. These buildings are signposts to our history. Through them we can discover what mattered most to previous generations, and where they found their inspiration and their solace.

The greatest delight always comes when buildings are also works of art. The thrill of coming into a place which makes one catch one's breath with excitement or gasp with pleasure is as powerful and moving as that inspired by any other form of art. Its magic is if anything enhanced by a sense of wonder at the ingenuity and daring of its builders. The impact is various. It can come from the graceful use of stone, from the majesty of colonnades and porticoes, or from elegant marble or plaster work that seems to be alive. It can also come from the other dimension of a building: not the walls and ceilings that define height and breadth, but the space that they create.

We are lucky that so much remains to provide us with clues to our past. The great buildings that we enjoy today tell us who was influential in each era. It is usually only the powerful who are rich, and only the rich who build with the best materials. The Norman invaders raised their castles, the Church its monasteries and cathedrals, the merchant class and the courtiers of Elizabeth the great houses of the sixteenth century, the owners of new wealth the fine Georgian cities, and the thrusting industrialists of Victorian times the icons of their age. And today? Today power lies with the great financial and commercial institutions. It is they who are commissioning the super-architects to embody in glass and aluminium, plastic and steel, their world-wide aspirations.

I am not an architectural historian and I have tried to avoid using technical language and jargon. These are my personal impressions of a voyage of discovery to find out what links our buildings to who we are. I have been helped along the way by many experts in their fields who have given generously of their time and their knowledge. With their help I came back with this tale to tell.

David Dimbleby
Folkington, East Sussex

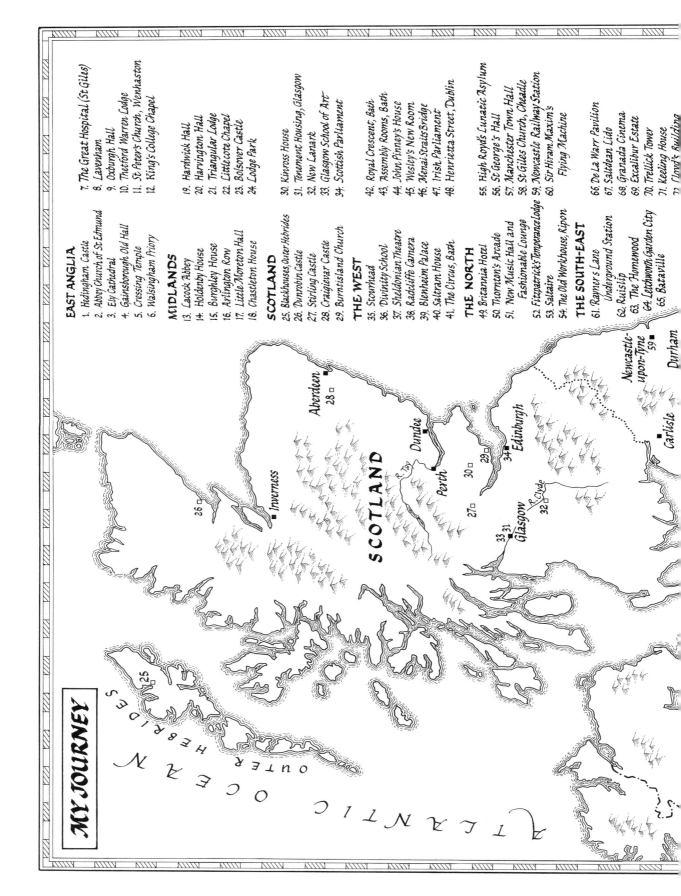

MY JOURNEY

ATLANTIC OCEAN

OUTER HEBRIDES

SCOTLAND

Inverness

Aberdeen

Dundee

Perth

Glasgow

Edinburgh

Newcastle-upon-Tyne

Carlisle

Durham

R. Tay

R. Clyde

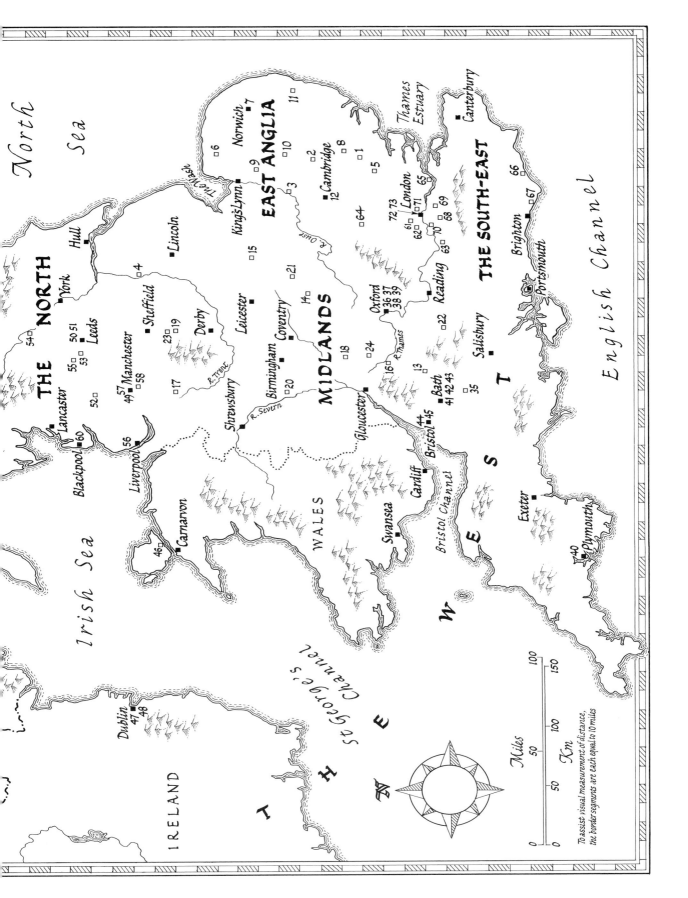

Medieval
Britain

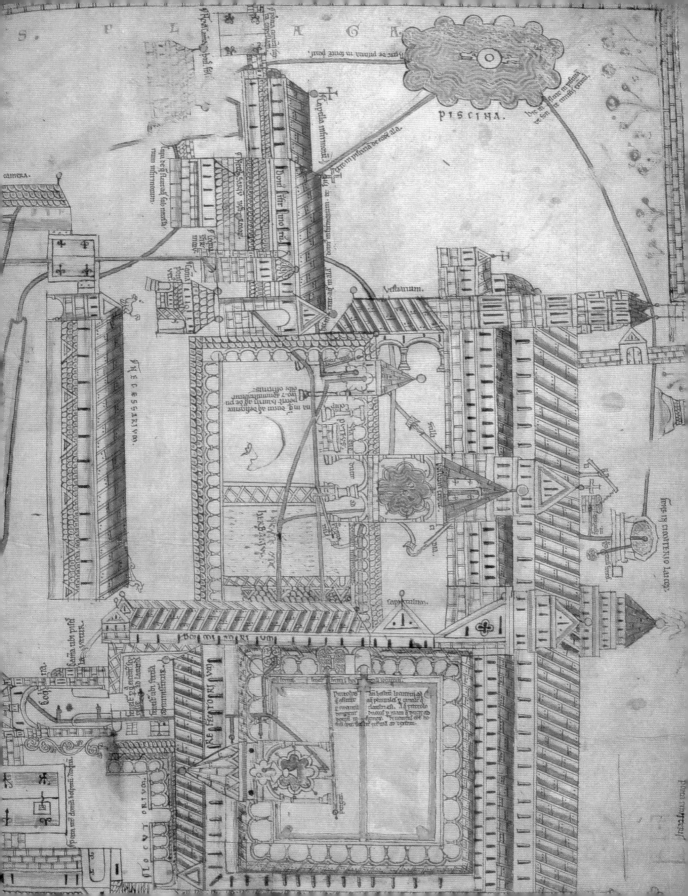

The East
A New Dawn

I WOULD BEGIN AT THE BEGINNING – IF THERE WERE A BEGINNING. Neolithic burial mounds or Stonehenge, remains of Roman villas, or the few traces of Saxon building would all qualify. But the origins of the Britain we know today really begin with the year zero of the Norman invasion in 1066. No single event has had a greater impact on the building of Britain than this victory and the construction programme that followed it. To see its impact I chose to travel to East Anglia, where it is possible to trace the course of medieval architecture in all its glory.

But first I have a confession to make. I have a quirky hostility to William the Conqueror. His victory at Hastings rankles with me even though it was nearly 1,000 years ago. I cannot count the number of times I have tramped across that battlefield in snow and drizzle and summer heat. When I was seven I was sent to boarding school on Telham Hill, near Battle in Sussex. The school gave us a view across the country to the south. Battle Abbey, which stands just behind the spot where Harold received the unwelcome arrow, was just out of sight to the west. On wet days or Sundays when we could not play games we would be sent on a 'road' walk. These often took us down Powdermill Lane, which runs exactly between the Norman and Anglo-Saxon lines of the battle – between Telham and Senlac. It was from Telham that William first caught sight of Harold's army marshalled opposite. I never thought of that day without sadness. Harold, exhausted after his long march from the north, and William, in my childish imagination, cockily invincible, trampling across our playing fields to steal our country from us.

We know enough now about wars of conquest to imagine what it must have been like in the years after 1066, when the Normans started to impose their rule on England. The established order was overturned, old families were disrupted, their lands seized and redistributed to William's followers. Within a few years he had crushed all opposition and his supporters had taken over by conquest more than half the landholdings in the country. When people boast that their families 'came over with the Conqueror' I sometimes wonder whether they have any idea of the havoc they caused. By the time the Domesday Book was completed in 1086, only two of the 170 big landowners in Britain were English. The other 168 were Norman invaders.

PREVIOUS
A plan of Canterbury Cathedral Priory in Kent, dating from the 1150s. The red and green lines mark out the courses and pipes of a complex water supply system.

A new aristocracy had been founded from William's upstarts. In return for guaranteeing that the King's writ would run, and for providing the troops to enforce his will, they received swathes of land, not concentrated in one place, but spread throughout England, to make insurrection harder.

The Domesday Book itself, with its obsessive recording of every detail of life so that, as *The Anglo-Saxon Chronicle* puts it, 'not a yard of land, nay ... not even an ox nor a cow, nor a swine was there left, that was not set down in his writ', sums up my fervent dislike of Norman rule. They were the original control freaks, the creators of modern bureaucracy. Their obsession with documentation has been cleverly tracked by a study of the increase recorded in the purchase of sealing-wax, for without a royal seal no official edict was legal. I have to admit an anarchic prejudice against providing information to the state. I cannot even fill in a census form. It does not mean I do not like Norman buildings, though, which is odd, since buildings spring from the character of those who build them.

I live not far from Battle now, close to Pevensey Marshes, which in 1066 were still all sea. They were drained in the Middle Ages and are now criss-crossed by channels just wide enough to take a canoe. As you paddle gently along this flat water you can see in the distance, across the banks of sedge and the rough pasture where the cattle mooch, the outline of the crumbling ruins of Pevensey Castle. Pevensey was built by the Romans in the third century as part of a chain of forts to protect the coastline. When William the Conqueror landed here 600 years later, he gave the remains of this castle to his half-brother with instructions to restore it. It was one of the first of many. Within two decades 500 castles had been built to keep the English in submission.

Norman castles: the domains of power

Castles are an acquired taste, like battlefields. I once picnicked on a hillside above Marrakesh with Field Marshal Sir Claude Auchinleck, the commander of the Desert Army before Montgomery. I was there to interview him about his life as a soldier. While the rest of the party drank wine and absorbed the scenery, the Auk was working out his defensive strategy for the heights on which we sat: where he would deploy his guns, where the greatest danger lay. It is the same with castles. For some people they come alive only when seen as military installations, with all their ingenious devices for protection from siege. Never having been a soldier, I find this does not come naturally to me. One arrow slit seems much the same as any other.

My first stop in East Anglia was at Hedingham Castle, one of the most striking of Norman castles with an austere and threatening appearance. You can find it just off the main Cambridge to Colchester road. From its battlements flies not the red criss-cross device of English Heritage but the red and yellow flag, adorned with a star, which is the banner of the de Veres. Needless to say, the de Veres arrived with the Conqueror. Aubrey de Vere was given land by William in various English counties. His son, also an Aubrey,

built Hedingham around 1140. The family prospered throughout the Middle Ages. They were created Earls of Oxford. The second Earl was a crusader, fighting alongside Richard Coeur de Lion. The third Earl was one of the barons who forced King John to sign Magna Carta and for his pains found himself besieged at Hedingham by the King, a siege only lifted, it was said, after his men threw fresh fish down on their attackers from tanks on the roof. This evidence that they had enough food to survive, despite being surrounded, so demoralised their opponents that the siege was lifted.

They were in trouble again in 1498 when Henry VII came to stay. He counted the huge number of retainers paraded by the Earl, decided they amounted to a private army, and promptly imposed a heavy fine on his host for breaching the statute of retainers, a law passed to limit the powers of barons. Back in the monarch's good books under Elizabeth I, the sixteenth Earl escorted the young Queen to her coronation, and his son, the seventeenth Earl, became one of her favourites. It was this seventeenth Earl who famously broke wind in front of her and was so mortified that he left the court and went travelling for seven years. On his return, according to Aubrey, writing in his *Brief Lives*, the Earl was greeted by the Queen with the immortal words: 'My Lord, I had forgot the fart.'

I arrived at Hedingham late on a hot summer's afternoon. It was an idyllic scene. The thick walls of the castle, each stone immaculately cut to make

Hedingham Castle: a formidable Norman fortress. The 'fighting' de Vere standard still flies here.

perfect corners, still retained the heat of the day. In a similar way the building itself seemed to retain the imprint of its own history. It is one of the attractions of old buildings that they do not just look exciting but have the power to recreate the past for us. This impact can be created by quite ordinary effects of passing time. The deep grooves made by the wheels of carts in the streets of Pompeii are as exciting as the grandest of the villas unearthed after the eruption. The very ordinariness of the sight brings it alive. I stand in reverie, mesmerised by the thought that the cart track was actually made by the Romans.

The walls at the base of the castle are twelve feet thick. The entrance is through an arched doorway with zigzag carving over it. It is well fortified. Grooves on either side of the door held a portcullis that could be lowered for protection. Two huge rooms one above the other dominate the keep. The first is said to have been a guardroom, where soldiers would eat and sleep. A spiral staircase leads from this room to a hall above. This room, with a gallery around it, is dominated by a huge arch, the widest Norman arch in England, twenty feet high and twenty-eight feet across. Today, with its small windows, large enough to fire an arrow from but not so wide that an arrow could enter, the hall has a gloomy mien. But in its heyday it would have been furnished with tapestries hung on the walls and would have reverberated to the noisy babble of the de Veres holding court.

These halls, a feature of all castles and great houses in the early Middle Ages, are by far the most important rooms. They stood at the heart of the system of feudalism by which, to put it simply, everyone owed a duty of loyalty in return for protection. William I divided his spoils, the land taken from the conquered Anglo-Saxons, along strictly feudal lines. The barons and earls who were given land became tenants-in-chief of the King, swearing loyalty and promising to provide military service, either enlisting themselves or providing their knights when it was required. The knights in their turn were sub-tenants of the baron, to whom they promised loyalty in return for land. They too had beneath them those who worked the land in various capacities, either as free men or as serfs.

These complex relationships needed to be established publicly by acts of homage. The hall at Hedingham would have seen knights who were in thrall to the de Veres coming to do homage, and to discuss their problems, make their complaints and no doubt inform their lord about the political mood of the people on their land. This hierarchical system was enforced by a strict code of etiquette, of procedure and precedence which in modern form we still see enacted each year when HM the Queen comes to the Palace of Westminster to open a new session of Parliament. She has her court around her, Ladies of the Bedchamber, Masters of the Horse, and all the rest of the rigmarole. The State Opening is now symbolic, but I have seen a court that was in its own way not unlike the court held by the de Veres. It was the court of Bin Laden.

In the mid 1960s I was filming in Saudi Arabia, the first time the secretive house of Saud had allowed a television crew into their country. A few days before I was due to leave, I was invited to meet a building contractor who wanted to make a film record of his work in the Middle East and wondered whether I could help. Early the next day I left Jeddah in a small plane, and we landed on a roadway high up in the hills at Taif, between Jeddah and Mecca. The contractor was none other than Osama bin Laden's father. Osama, incidentally, was only ten at the time, and not in evidence. His father was one of the richest men in a country of rich men. He had made his money building roads, mosques and airports throughout the Middle East. It was said that his first fortune was acquired when he built the highway across the desert from Jeddah to Riyadh. He laid the tarmac narrower than the contract stipulated, pocketing the savings for himself. The road was famously dangerous, being just a little too narrow for lorries to pass in comfort.

I was taken into a marquee where the Sheik was holding court. The floor was covered with carpets. Bin Laden himself was at one end, with what the de Veres would have recognised as his steward beside him. Bin Laden himself being illiterate, all his deals were made verbally and recorded by this steward. I sat a few places away to his left, drinking tea and eating dates, waiting my turn. Everyone in this huge tent, sitting cross-legged on the floor, was a supplicant of one kind or another. Bin Laden himself sat in state, ordering his domain. I do not think a day at the court of the de Veres in the Middle Ages would have been much different: the same patient waiting, the earnest entreaties, the assurances given, the promises made.

Religion and rebellion

Apart from the power of the monarch and his barons, the most powerful force in pre-Reformation Britain was the Church. Of all the land redistributed by William after the Norman Conquest they received a third. It was not just as landlords that bishops, abbots and other clergy exercised their power. In Bury St Edmunds, for instance, the abbot of the monastery, one of the richest in Britain, controlled many other aspects of people's lives. He laid out a new town on a grid system with streets running parallel north to south with two main cross streets. He owned the market, the mills, the hospitals and the inns, and raised rents, market fees and tolls. He also appointed the bailiffs who oversaw justice. Little wonder that this autocratic power irritated the townsfolk. Whenever they sought greater control over their own lives, the abbot's response was to introduce further legislation to curb the citizens' freedoms.

There were a number of riots and protests over the years, but in January 1328 they took a more serious turn. A group of rebels conspired to destroy the abbey. With 3,000 supporters, they forced their way into the monastery, plundered the Treasury, imprisoned the prior, beat up the monks and locked thirteen of them in the Guildhall. The monks responded in kind, attacking men, women and children when they were at prayer in the parish church. The town's response was to launch another attack on the monastery, in which the abbey gates were burned down. Only when the sheriff had sent in soldiers did the violence subside.

The gateway to the abbey at Bury St Edmunds, built to protect the monks from the citizens of the town.

A year later it erupted once more. This time the abbot was captured, had his head and eyebrows forcibly shaved so that he would not be recognised, and was shipped out of the country to Brabant in the Low Countries. When he was discovered and brought home, the abbey reasserted its authority by rebuilding its main gate. This gate is a symbol of monastic power. It stands a little apart from the busy streets of the city with their elegant houses and busy shops. It is built of fine stone two storeys high, with elegant arches and niches for statues. If you look closely you can see that to the side of the niches there are arrow slits, half hidden. The wide welcoming doorway has a portcullis ready to be dropped at the first sign of trouble. This gateway, with its high walls enclosing the monastery grounds, seems benign enough, even welcoming, but it had a deadly serious purpose. Many monasteries and abbeys were fortified in this way, to protect the monks from those they purported to serve.

The monastery at Bury predates the Norman invasion by over 400 years, as did the monastery at Ely, founded in AD 673. Ely, in the middle of the fen country, held out against the Normans long after the rest of England had been subjugated. Hereward the Wake led the resistance from the marsh land, countryside so wet and boggy that Fenmen have always been said to be born with webbed feet. Long before Darwin it seems our ancestors understood the theory of the survival of the fittest. After the surrender of Ely, William the Conqueror appointed a new prior, a relation of his called Simeon, to take over the monastery. Simeon began an astonishing and typically Norman project: the building of a new church at Ely. In 1109 it was designated a cathedral, but it took another eighty years to complete. It dominates the horizon from miles around, and is romantically known as 'the Ship of the Fens'.

I have climbed to the top of the tower at Ely. I have taken off in a balloon at dawn and floated up past it. I have seen it from a punt on a far-away canal. The impression it makes is always the same: that quite apart from its great beauty, its fine skyline, its delicate carving, it is a statement of Norman power and domination as much as of religious devotion. Even today, as you walk around Ely, a small city with few if any tall buildings, you marvel at the scale of the cathedral. The impression on the recently subjugated people of the Fens must have been overwhelming. If it towers over Ely now, it must have seemed incredible then.

When you stand in the nave you do not need to be a believer to be thrilled by the scale of the building and by the harmony of its design, despite its use of different styles at different periods, as one technique for making an arch or a window succeeded another. The cathedral is one of the longest in Britain, over 500 feet from end to end, and half of this is taken up by the nave. It was once painted red and blue, and traces of pigment remain, but to our eyes the simple warm limestone, brought here by barge from Stamford, has its own lyrical beauty and harmony. The nave is made up of three long arcades, or rows of arches, one above the other. They are strongly built, with two firm legs to stand on and a rounded top, a design that is satisfying to look at because it is so simple and so old. Before builders worked out how to make a pointed arch, this

Ely Cathedral, towering over the town. Imagine how astonishing it must have seemed to Fen dwellers in the twelfth century.

was the standard way of bridging a gap to make doors and windows or to support a roof. Other parts of the cathedral, built later, show advances in technique. The entrance porch, for instance, which was added in the early thirteenth century, has delicate thin pillars supporting extravagantly shaped arches so ornate you cannot quite believe the pillars can hold them up. Even more delicate and complex is the choir at the end of the nave.

The miracle of Norman building is that so much of it stood and still stands. These days we build with the help of architects, surveyors and structural engineers. Then there were just master masons evolving their techniques from experience, and passing on their knowledge from one generation to the next. Remedial work still needs to be done, but the basic structures are sound as long as they are maintained. In 1989 the walls of the south transept, one arm of the design that forms a cross with the nave, were seen to be buckling. They look like solid stone, but in reality they have just a skin of stone inside and out, with the cavity between filled with rubble. This rubble, a kind of medieval concrete, was made of bits of unusable stone packed down tight and then wetted with lime water. In 1989 the collapsing walls were bound together using a new stitching technique: steel wire was driven through the fabric and held in place with resin. In 1991 the central part of the cross, the octagon and the ceiling above it, were also restored in this way after storms showed that they too were at risk.

This year masons are working on the east face of the cathedral. I climbed the scaffolding to watch. This outer wall had not been touched for several hundred years, and judging by the quality of the stones that were being cut and the care with which they were being slid into place, it will not need to be repaired for another few hundred. It is thrilling to watch stone carvers at work, carving faces, or leaf-shaped patterns that are placed so far above the ground that they will never be seen by the naked eye.

Some of those working on Ely have been involved with the building for up to twenty years. They are full of admiration for the original builders but are also a little surprised that it is still standing. Modern techniques allow much smaller stones to be cut with little extra effort. In medieval times the stones were bigger and had to be winched into place with ropes to the top of precarious wooden scaffolding towers. I saw the small holes cut into the outer walls that held the scaffolding poles. This labouring work was carried out by unskilled workers drafted in from the local community. They were often unpaid, doing the work as part of their obligation to their lords.

For the complicated decoration the mason relinquishes the stone to the carver – 'the arty farty bit', as one of the masons working at Ely called it. The carver, Tim Crawley, had also worked on the site for many years and had carved thirty or forty bosses and gargoyles. He admired the medieval workmanship for its life and vigour: 'It's very quirky often, medieval carving, and if you walk round the cathedral there's just no end of little details to see that will always surprise you. However long you look you'll always find something new. And the quality of some of the work is just superb.'

There is an old tradition among masons of leaving in their work reminders of their own time for future generations to find. Usually it is a coin, but today it can be something rather more pretentious: a time capsule. I was invited to make my own time capsule to place in the rubble and chose a few objects to put in a box that I thought would puzzle the masons a few centuries hence. There was a packet of cigarettes marked 'Smoking Kills', which I chose because I assumed that a few hundred years from now no one would know what these strange tubes of paper filled with tobacco were. I tore out a BBC 1 television schedule for the day, included a receipt for a week's shopping from a local supermarket and added a Mars bar with a note saying, 'You will probably be living on Mars by the time you find this.' The box was ceremonially put in place, embedded in mortar, and sealed with a heavy slab of stone.

During the building of the cathedral many workers would have been maimed or killed. Things were always going wrong. The great drama of 22 February 1322, however, seems miraculously to have killed no one, though it nearly destroyed the cathedral. On that day the clergy heard a rumbling that they thought was an earthquake. The tower at the centre of the cathedral collapsed. Alan of Walsingham, the monk responsible for the maintenance of the church, was according to a fellow monk 'devastated, grieving vehemently and overcome with sorrow. He knew not which way to turn himself or what to do for the reparation of such a ruin.'

PREVIOUS
Ely Cathedral's octagonal lantern at the crossing point of the nave and transepts. Not part of the original design, it was built to replace the central tower that collapsed.

Alan recovered and resolved to repair the damage. His brilliant solution was not to rebuild the tower on foundations that were now clearly suspect. Instead he cut back the columns that had been supporting it to create a huge open space at the crossing point of nave and transept. New arches were erected in the shape of an octagon, something never before seen in church building. This stage of the restoration lasted six years. King Edward III's master carpenter William Hurley was then enlisted to devise a way of roofing the new space. It took him fourteen years to execute his ingenious solution to the problem. He built a wooden dome, or lantern, to cover the space. It weighed 200 tonnes, and its weight was spread evenly around the edge of the octagon. The dome was decorated with carving, and paintings of the saints completed a complex design. The result is a work of genius. The sun floods down on to the transept floor, which glows with light. The nave now leads to this great open space where the eyes of the worshipper lift upwards as though to heaven itself.

The ceremony of the hall

There was a reverence for ritual in medieval times. The life of Ely with its clergy was as formally organised as the life in the castle at Hedingham. Everything was done to emphasise the power of priest and lord. In the life of the landed gentry it was particularly expressed in the great care and attention to detail that was taken about eating. This is so different from our present-day habits that it is worth exploring. Today many families eat in haste, without even the ceremony of sitting down together at table. Food is often no more than a necessary interruption to a busy day. Not so in the Middle Ages. Food itself was precious, and often scarce, so it merited attention, and its preparation and serving determined the kind of homes the rich built for themselves.

The Old Hall at Gainsborough in Lincolnshire is a timber-framed building of the mid fifteenth century, with six bays supporting a high, arched roof miraculously held up not by beams crossing from one side wall to the other but by naturally curved oak trusses that stretch from the top of the walls to the centre of the roof. The kitchen is almost as large as the hall from which it leads, separated by a wooden screen.

There is a wide serving hatch for the delivery of food, but access to the kitchen itself is only possible past the clerk's office, so that he could keep an eye on everything that went in or out. Two huge fireplaces face each other across the kitchen. One was used for boiling water and meat, the other for roasting on a hand-turned spit. The heat here was so intense that spit-turners worked naked. Leading off the kitchen were rooms for storing meat and game, a brewery, and an area for making bread, pastry and pies with its own bread oven. This oven was not unlike a modern pizza oven, a hot cavern with a fire lit beneath it. The kitchen has a high ceiling and windows to allow the smoke to escape. A gallery runs around it, leading to rooms where the cooking staff slept. The clerk had his own quarters above his office, with a little window allowing him to look down into the kitchen. Nothing was allowed to escape his eye.

The efficiently
designed kitchen
at Gainsborough Old
Hall, with one of the
two open fireplaces
to the left and the
ovens to the right.

The serving of the food was a complex ritual. The entire household would be assembled in the hall. At the far end on a raised platform sat the Lord of the manor. Only when the Lord had eaten his fill would the rest of his household eat, with homage paid to hierarchy, those high in the pecking order being served first and offered the choicest dishes. The details of how the food was served were explained to me by Peter Brears, a food historian who has assiduously researched the procedure, basing his findings in part on an extraordinary manuscript printed in 1508 but dating back to the early fifteenth century: *The Book of Carving*. This details not just how to serve the food, but how to set out a table and even how to lay out the tablecloth and fold napkins.

I was served a meal in the approved way. My vision of imitating the Lord sitting at his high table chewing on chicken legs and throwing the bones to his dogs in the style of so many Hollywood films was quickly dispelled. Small slices of meat were carved for me one by one and carefully placed on a square of bread, which served as a plate. There was a profusion of roasts: a pig's head, a haunch of venison, chicken, rabbit, pigeon, and a cockatrice (the head of a cockerel fused into the back end of a pig). With them came a meat pie, a salmon, a pastry castle, sweetmeats, pease pottage, custard, and green sauce for the chicken. Beer or wine and a sweet dessert wine accompanied the food. 'The English delight in drink and make it their business to drain full goblets,' wrote an Italian friar surprised by this profligacy.

The servers bringing the food to the table would have been boys attached to the household to learn courtly manners, the children of aspiring families, who in return for their service would be trained in horsemanship, in fighting and in music, all the attributes of a gentleman or squire. These young students were instructed in etiquette. 'Do not rush in rudely but walk at an even pace with your head held high and kneel before your lord. Do not claw your head or your back as if you were a flea or stroke your hair as if you were a louse. Do not pick your nose or let it drop clear pearls or sniff. Do not pick your teeth or grind or gnash them, or with puffing cast foul breath upon your lord.'

In the early Middle Ages the hall served as the focal point of a household. It was the place where business was transacted, where meals were eaten, and where members of the Lord's court slept, huddled around an open fire. The Dutch scholar Erasmus, travelling in East Anglia in the 1520s, gave a vivid picture of the unhygienic state of these halls, whose floors were often only earth carpeted with rushes known as 'the marsh'. They were, he said 'usually of clay, strewed with rushes under which lie ... an ancient collection of beer, grease, fragments, bones, spittle, excrements of dogs and cats and everything that is nasty'.

As the Middle Ages drew on, habits started to change. It had once been thought essential that the Lord and his Lady should be on display. The Countess of Lincoln was advised in the thirteenth century that she should sit 'in the middle of the High Court ... so that her visage and cheek be showed to all men'. By the fourteenth century, however, the bonds between the Lord and his knights and tenants were loosening, partly as a result of the plague, or Black Death. It so reduced the population that it shifted the balance of power

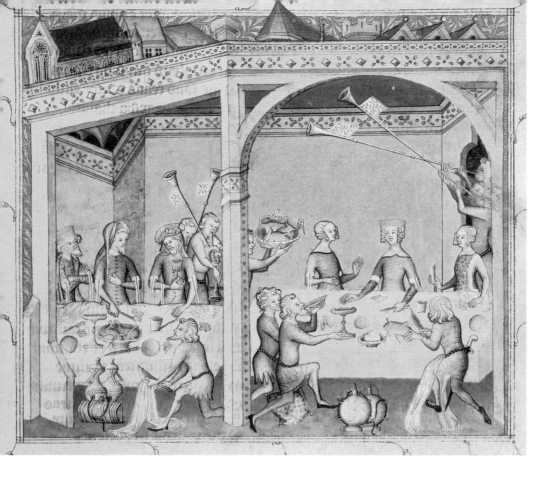

This fifteenth-century banquet scene shows rich food being served by a host of attendants to the accompaniment of trumpets.

perceptibly in favour of the poor, whose labour had become more scarce and who could therefore demand a better wage. But there also developed an instinct for greater privacy. Gainsborough has a separate living chamber for the Lord and his Lady high up beyond the hall, but still built with shuttered windows looking down to the hall itself. Here the Lord and his family could eat alone, only appearing in public on special occasions. Throughout the Middle Ages this trend towards privacy was a dominant feature of the great halls. With the increasing use of staircases and particularly of corridors, which allowed servants to go about their business without disturbing the family, a pattern of life closer to the houses of the Tudor era was emerging.

Not everyone approved. In *The Vision of Piers Plowman* (1362) William Langland complained:

> '*Wretched is the Hall ... each day in the week*
> *There the Lord and Lady liketh not to sit*
> *Now have the rich a rule to eat by themselves*
> *In a privy parlour ... and leave the chief hall*
> *That was made for men to eat in*'

The barns of the Knights Templar

The Lord and the Church were the two dominant influences on medieval man. For proof look at the extraordinary impact of the Crusades. In 1095 the Pope called on all Christians to come to the defence of the Byzantine emperor against the Turks. Anyone who joined was promised he would be granted a full penance for his sins. The Crusader army marched against the forces of Islam, captured Jerusalem and its Holy Places and massacred many of its inhabitants. Nine major crusades followed during the next two centuries, and a pilgrimage to the Holy Land became the ambition of many devout Christians. The journey was dangerous, and to protect the pilgrims a religious society, the Knights Templar, was founded with its own rules of poverty, chastity and religious obedience. The Knights had their own headquarters in Jerusalem on the site of Solomon's Temple (hence their name). Funding for the expensive task was provided by the granting of land by kings and nobles throughout Europe. At the height of their power the Templars held an astonishing 7,000 manors, fifty of them in England.

Near Braintree in Essex is a spectacular reminder of the power and wealth they wielded. Cressing Temple was the first manor granted to the Templars in England, and the two vast barns they built there to store their harvests are the finest Templar barns left anywhere in Europe. They are known as 'the cathedrals of the countryside', not only because of their majestic scale but because to support their high, wide roofs they use the layout of a cathedral with a nave and two side aisles. The older barn, known as the Barley Barn, was built in the early 1200s, the Wheat Barn about fifty years later.

From the outside they are all roof, thousands of red tiles sloping down from over thirty feet up towards the ground, where a modest wall of timber and brick appears to support them. But the magic is inside. It takes time to adjust to the complexity of the structure. Nearly 500 oak trees were used in the construction of each barn. Each length of wood has its own purpose and name: trusses, braces, collars, arcade posts, purlins, and so on. The language is confusing and the best way to understand the building is to stand inside and look at the work each piece of wood is doing, what it supports, and how it fits in with its neighbour. You only need to have tried to build a tree house or a bivouac, or even put up a shelf, to be full of admiration for the skill and discipline of these early builders.

While I was at Cressing a carpenter who has made a study of medieval techniques showed me how they went about their work. Rick Lewis was armed with axes modelled on those seen in the Bayeux Tapestry, with narrow blades that widen out at the end. This curious and rather delicate shape saved on metal while still giving a long cutting edge, kept sharp with a special stone imported from Bohemia. A carpenter had to buy his own tools, so limiting the amount of expensive cast iron and steel used in the making of the axe was important.

Rick deftly trimmed a newly felled oak and in moments it had changed from a round trunk to a square beam. All the rough edges and knots were trimmed back. The wood was hoisted on to a seven-foot-high trestle platform.

He perched above, holding one end of a double-handed saw, and I stood underneath. They say the expressions 'top dog' and 'under dog' came from these saw-pits. On a hot summer day, with sawdust cascading down on me and doing what seemed to be the hardest work, there was no question who was the underdog. Once the wood was in planks, Rick began cutting joints to lock two beams together in a V shape, and then, so that they could be identified, chiselled a number into each. These carpenter's marks allowed an entire barn to be prefabricated on the ground and reassembled on site, which is how Cressing Temple's barns were built. With hundreds of joints required for each barn, numbering was an art. If you look at the beams in any old building you can easily identify the various codes used, but what is harder to discern is that a further variation was provided by using different tools to scratch the identification on the wood, so that it could be a hard or a soft cut, narrow or broad.

Cressing had access to over 1,200 acres of land, including woodland and pasture. But most important was its arable land, planted with corn that had to be processed after it had been harvested in late summer. The barns, now so peaceful to contemplate, were the factories at the centre of the estate's life, full of noise and dust. The corn was brought through the higher of the two doors that face each other across the barn and unloaded. The empty wagon then passed out under a lower doorway. The corn was trampled down to save space, with horses sometimes used to tread it flat. Inside the barn the corn was threshed by beating it with flails, the grain falling to the floor and the husks being winnowed away by the draught blowing between one doorway and the other.

They say that one work-horse at Cressing disappeared while trampling the corn. It was thought at first that it had run away, but several days later it was discovered where it had slipped down inside the stack of corn. It had kept alive by eating the grain but was almost dying of thirst. Solicitous farm workers took it to a water trough and let it drink its fill – with disastrous results. Too much corn and too much water swelled its stomach and it died.

Cressing was a great estate served by a workforce largely made up of tenants of Cressing lands who provided at least part of their rent in the form of labour. Apart from a household staff to look after the warrior monks, there was a warden, three chaplains, a steward, a baker, a cellarer, a cook, a mason, a thatcher, and a smith to run the forge, and forty-six tenants and their families, a potential workforce of two or three hundred. Building on the wealth of this enterprise and thousands like it all over Europe, the Templars became too rich and powerful for their own good. They were offering banking services to the most powerful kings and princes in Europe and are credited with having invented the cheque.

In 1291 the city of Acre was recaptured by Muslim forces and the great era of the Crusades ended with Christian forces being driven out of the Middle East. There was no longer a role for the Templars, whose wealth and privilege allied with a notorious secretiveness about their affairs aroused resentment and hostility. On the pretext that they were corrupt and heretical they were forcibly disbanded by edict of the Pope, endorsed by Edward II in England,

A medieval barn at Cressing Temple. Nearly five hundred oaks were felled to make the beams of this 'cathedral of the countryside'.

and all their lands were given to another religious society, the Hospitallers, or Knights of the Order of St John the Baptist of Jerusalem. The Hospitallers survive to this day as a religious and charitable society.

Memories of the Crusaders' mission are kept alive by another organisation: the Equestrian Order of the Holy Sepulchre of Jerusalem, whose uniform is a white robe with a red cross and a floppy black cap. I came across a number of them, an exotic sight, processing along a quiet Norfolk lane. They were led by a cross-bearer and chanted prayers as they went. With several hundred other pilgrims they were on their way to Walsingham Priory, a less arduous journey than that to Jerusalem, but a destination for pilgrims since the twelfth century.

Today all that remains of the priory is the gaunt stone framework of the east window. Near it is an altar with flowers placed around it. This is the site of the original shrine of Walsingham. It is a strange story. In 1061 a recently widowed lady of the manor dreamed that she should build on her estate a reproduction of the house in Nazareth where Jesus lived with his parents. When she awoke she even remembered the precise dimensions of the building but could not decide where to build it. The Virgin Mary had sent down a heavenly dew that fell on the garden leaving two dry patches where dew had not fallen. It was interpreted as a sign that the replica house should be built on one of these places. The builders tried to erect it on one site but could not get the pieces to fit together. When they returned the following morning they found the house had been assembled overnight on the other site, by angels. Hence the shrine to the Virgin and to the miraculous construction of her family home.

Today Walsingham attracts both Anglican and Catholic pilgrims. On the afternoon I was there the Catholics were praying somewhat optimistically for the return of the Anglicans to the Catholic fold. 'O Blessed Virgin Mary, Mother of God ... Intercede for our separated brethren, that with us in the one true fold they may be united to the Chief Shepherd, the Vicar of thy Son.' What price the ecumenical movement?, a sceptic might ask. But despite the occasional lapse Walsingham is ecumenical and welcomes all comers. It also offers a glimpse of the fervour of religious belief of the Middle Ages, allowing us to leap back across the centuries. It is these insights that make looking at old buildings so exciting. What we are offered is not just beautiful buildings, satisfying though they are in themselves, but a chance to let our imaginations roam the centuries to picture the lives of the people who built them and used them. In the Middle Ages this means trying to enter a society with different attitudes and a wholly different culture. There are some events from that time that are particularly hard to comprehend. Chief among them is the Black Death, or Great Mortality, the plague that ravaged Britain and changed the way we lived.

Pernicious disease and its legacy

Britain in the Middle Ages was used to illness and early death. A man who lived into adulthood had a life expectancy of thirty, a woman of thirty-three. There was no treatment for disease. Norwich had an important hospital, founded by the Bishop of Norwich in 1249. You can still wander among what remains of the Great Hospital or St Giles, with its fine cloister and tower. It was not a hospital as we would understand it. Those with contagious infections such as leprosy were denied entry. Surgery was also forbidden because shedding blood was thought to be sacrilege in a consecrated place. St Giles opened its doors to elderly and infirm priests, scholars and paupers. It fed them properly and kept them warm and well clothed. The treatment, such as it was, was religious. Confession and prayer were offered as a way to prepare for death. But the effect of simply treating these infirm people properly was that many recovered. It reinforced the medieval conviction that ill health was a consequence of sin and that repentance could alleviate it.

These methods were no help to the people whose skeletons I examined in a crypt in the city. They were from a graveyard of the early fifteenth century and Jane Bowen, the archaeologist who had been working on the site, showed me her gruesome findings. We looked at a leg bone that curved from knee to ankle, a sign of rickets. A left forearm had been broken and, without treatment, had mended itself, but crookedly. There was a skull that showed symptoms of syphilis. Instead of being smooth it was roughened by lesions. It was a moving experience to look at these old bones and imagine the people they had once been. And it was chastening to hear that half the skeletons uncovered in this cemetery showed signs of chronic ill health or serious injury. But even such close acquaintance with disease and death could not have prepared Britain for what was to come.

Before the Black Death, England was enjoying a period of unparalleled prosperity. The country was settled and socially stable. The Normans had been absorbed, become English, and the worst of the upheaval they created was over. The country was at peace and prospering. But in July 1348 the Bishop of Bath and Wells warned that a catastrophic pestilence starting in the East had arrived in France and that the people must 'pray devoutly and incessantly' that it did not cross the Channel. Too late.

A month earlier, thought to have been carried on a boat from France, the plague had arrived in Weymouth. Its effects were devastating. That summer it had taken hold in Florence and the poet Boccaccio described in horrifying detail how it afflicted sufferers. 'Its first symptom ... was the appearance of certain swellings in the groin or armpit, some of which were egg shaped whilst others were roughly the size of the common apple.' It spread until 'many people began to find dark blotches and bruises on their arms, thighs and other parts ... Few of those who caught it ever recovered, and in most cases death occurred within three days from the appearance of the symptoms.'

Within weeks it spread throughout the kingdom, affecting all ages and all classes. Henry Knighton, a canon of Leicester Abbey, recounted how corpses lay in the streets for want of people to bury them. The effect was devastating: children orphaned, farms with no one to work them, villages and towns facing catastrophe. It is thought that almost half the population died, reducing it from over four million to two and a half million in a few years. The plague of 1348 was only the start of regular recurrences of the disease that continued

The cloisters of the Great Hospital at Norwich, a refuge for the sick and dying.

The Eagle Ward is
a Victorian creation
within the medieval
church of the hospital.

until the end of the seventeenth century, but the first onslaught had the greatest effect, changing the way we lived and worked.

Knighton, writing forty years later, gives this vivid account of the aftermath: 'Many buildings of all sizes in every city fell into total ruin for want of inhabitants. Likewise many villages and hamlets were deserted with no house remaining in them, because everyone who had lived there was dead, and indeed many of these villages were never inhabited again. In the following winter there was such a lack of workers in all areas of activity that it was thought that there had hardly ever been such a shortage before; for a man's farm animals and other livestock wandered about without a shepherd and all his possessions were left unguarded.'

There is, as with any event so far in the past, some disagreement about the precise consequences of the plague, but there seems to be consensus about some of the most wide-ranging effects. The first, and most obvious, was that there was now a shortage of labour on the land. The peasant who survived found for the first time that he had something of value to offer and, in spite of attempts to regulate wages, could increase his income. Others were able to buy land cheaply from their lords, who could no longer work it at a profit. Some lords simply rented out all their land and lived as landlords rather than manage their estates. For the first time a peasant unhappy with his lot could move elsewhere to seek work, knowing there was a demand for his labour. The ties of feudalism were weakened.

One of the most significant effects was a change in agriculture. Before the Black Death, England's farming was labour intensive. There were herds of cattle and flocks of sheep, but arable land, fields of corn, predominated. In the wake of the plague it became impossible to find enough workers to dig the soil, plant the seed, keep it free of weeds, cut it and thresh it. Sheep rearing, needing fewer hands, offered a solution, and the effects can still be seen in the towns and villages of East Anglia, the prime wool producing and cloth manufacturing region of Britain in the Middle Ages.

Flourishing cloth towns

Wool production had been a thriving industry in England since the Norman Conquest. We had more sheep than the rest of Europe and our wool was of high quality. When Richard the Lionheart was ransomed from imprisonment in Austria, having been taken prisoner while returning from a Crusade, the payment was made in English fleeces. Superb wool came from sheep carefully bred to suit the land where they were farmed. Among the best was a sheep farmed in north Lincolnshire, now known as the Lincoln Longwool.

The Lincoln is a rare breed, kept in existence by a few enthusiasts, but in the Middle Ages sheep like this were the best wool-producing factory on four legs. The Lincoln has advantages that set it apart from other sheep. It is huge. It does not easily suffer from foot rot, so it can do well on wet ground. It is docile. And then there is its wool, which is not wool as we know it. This is a

35

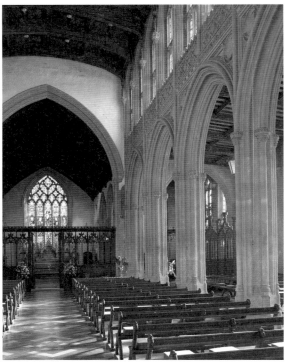

sheep that has grown rasta dreadlocks. Each ringlet, tightly curled, is six or more inches long, giving when straightened twelve inches of wool. And it has hair everywhere, covering its eyes and reaching along the vast expanse of its stomach. To shear the sheep's belly you sit on the ground and hold the sheep in your lap with its legs outstretched, making an ungainly coupling, reminiscent of a student paraglider firmly clipped into the lap of his instructor. It takes twenty minutes to shear by hand, five with electric clippers, and today the wool is worth only £4.50. In the Middle Ages, before cotton or artificial fibres came on the market, it would have been worth a great deal more.

At first England exported raw wool but not the cloth manufactured from it. It was left to expert weavers, dyers and fullers in the Low Countries to do that. But in the 1330s Edward III offered refuge to Flemish wool makers facing persecution. They settled in East Anglia, creating a new industry of cloth manufacturing. The signs of the prosperity it brought can still be seen in the churches and towns that flourished in its wake.

Lavenham, in Suffolk, must be the best preserved of all the cloth towns. It has a fine church boasting the tallest tower in the county, but what most visitors go to see is the centre of the town. To our modern eyes this is a perfect picture-postcard place. Thousands of visitors come each year to photograph the houses and cottages with their beam and plaster walls, a style of building that seems to appeal above all others, having the same 'olde-worlde' look as Anne Hathaway's cottage in Stratford-upon-Avon. Perhaps it is the apparent simplicity of construction, using natural materials, and the cosiness of it compared with brick or stone, that is so attractive.

Lavenham, Suffolk. The fine fifteenth-century church (left); and oak beam and plaster houses (right). The black-and-white look is less authentic than the grey timbers.

I doubt whether it would go down so well if it could be seen as it was in the fourteenth century. There was nothing neat or twee about it then. Wool arrived on wagons from further north, most often from Lincolnshire. In yards behind the great clothiers' houses were workshops where, in an early example of industrial production, groups of spinners and weavers worked in shifts. It would have been noisy, with carters yelling imprecations as they drove their wagons down the narrow streets. The stench from the roadway would have been overpowering, as waste from the dye vats would have been mixed with offal from the butcher's, dung from horses and cattle, and human excrement. All this effluent ran down the centre of the street. It was not until years later that the first drain was built to carry the sewage away underground. I wriggled through a manhole to look at this drain, luckily now carrying only rainwater, and admired the elegant brickwork that saved Lavenham from the worst excesses of prosperity.

Lavenham was eventually hit by a slump in the demand for cloth. In the wake of the collapse of the market many of the larger merchants' houses were pulled down. The smaller houses remained intact, and pictures of them now embellish the lids of a thousand chocolate boxes. Curiously one of the most admired features of the houses, the black-and-white look produced by black beams on white plaster, is a Victorian fashion. In the Middle Ages beams were left plain or covered in a protective lime wash. The National Trust have recently applied this original technique to the grand Guildhall in Lavenham. This building is now all off-white, the beams no longer picked out in black, but not a day passes without angry complaints from visitors that the Trust has got it wrong.

Before brick came into vogue (stone always being in short supply in East Anglia) the rich were forced to find ways of displaying their wealth using the ordinary materials then to hand. One technique was to build with more wood than was strictly necessary for the construction. Any building with beams very close together and narrow patches of plaster between was almost certainly once the house of a rich family. A later means of flamboyant display was the use of plaster decoration on the outside of the house. This technique is known as pargeting (from the Old French *par jeter*, meaning to throw over a surface). Pargeting is undergoing a revival. It involves mixing a plaster of lime, sand and goats' hair that is allowed to sit for a month before being used. This is sculpted on to the outside walls of a house, usually on the gable ends or the main façade. With a trowel the pargeter can make complex geometric patterns, or more often figures of people, or birds, rabbits and foxes. In the Middle Ages complex patterns of this kind displayed wealth and position. They are at their finest in East Anglia, where I met Bill Sargent, a pargeter who had been so busy restoring old designs or creating new that for thirty years he had never travelled further than twenty miles from his home to find work.

A fashion for brick

We are so used to brick buildings now that it is strange to think that in the Middle Ages brick was both a novelty and a luxury. The Romans had made and used brick, but the technique seems to have been forgotten. The poor built in wood and wattle, the rich in stone. In northern Europe brick making was a well-established industry. In Britain brick was only produced on a small scale and for particular needs such as floors or fireplaces. It is not as though brick is difficult to make. It simply involves finding a supply of clay and then kneading it thoroughly to give it an even consistency and to remove any air bubbles. It is moulded into shape and left to dry before being fired in an oven. Anyone who can make bread ought to be able to make brick (and some home-made bread would be better used as brick). But England was slow to catch on to its uses until the fifteenth century, when it appears to startling effect, a material with its own character and able to produce effects impossible to achieve in stone. Brick can be baked long or short to produce light or dark shades of red, thus allowing the builder to make geometric patterns in a wall, or it can be glazed to achieve the same effect. Brick can be moulded to make smooth banister rails for staircases and can be cut to shape arches or a vaulted ceiling.

The fashion for brick spread when it received royal patronage. Henry V built his palace at Sheen of brick, and Henry VI used it to build Eton College at Windsor. I went to a fortified manor house built perhaps forty years after Eton that uses brick to good effect. In 1482 Oxburgh Hall in Norfolk was issued with a 'Licence to Crenellate', which was the royal permission required before a house could be fortified against attack. By the end of the fifteenth century the fortifications were almost entirely spurious, but a gentleman of standing would still build his home in the fortified style as a symbol of wealth and status. Oxburgh is surrounded by a moat, and its entrance is through a fortified gateway flanked by two tall towers with battlements at the top. But between the two towers is a giveaway sign that none of this is meant to be taken seriously. There are two large glass windows, one above the other, that give on to the King and Queen's chambers. They would shatter if you threw a stone at them, let alone fired a cannon. There was never any question of Oxburgh being built to face attack. This brick has been used to make a home not a fortress. It is warm and glows red in the sun. At dusk and dawn all the detail of windows and chimneys, false battlements and crenellation can be seen highlit against shadows, displaying the ingenuity of its craftsmen to best effect.

The battle against poachers

South of Oxburgh but still in Norfolk is an area of sandy soil and scrub, punctuated by a few pine trees, which is known as the Brecklands. The soil is thin and worn and pockmarked with rabbit holes. This bleak countryside was another beneficiary of the Black Death. It is difficult soil that used to be worked for a few years and then abandoned. Great sandstorms swept across it. Sheep overgrazed it. When as a result of the deaths caused by the plague there were no longer sufficient workers to farm the land effectively, the

This fourteenth-century illustration from the Luttrell Psalter shows a warren mound. Holes were dug for rabbits to encourage them to stay in one place.

landowners turned much of it over to what had already become a truly thriving business: the breeding of rabbits.

Some people shun rabbit these days, but I have always thought of it as a delicacy when properly cooked. In medieval England it was a luxury. At the installation of the Archbishop of York in 1465, 4,000 rabbits were provided for the feast. It was not only the meat that was desirable. The fur was used to make coats and blankets, nightshirts even, and the finest was made into decorative trimmings on clothes and hats. The rabbit was valuable and had to be carefully farmed and protected against poaching. This job fell to the warrener, whose work was so risky that he and his family lived in a fortified house, both for their own protection from gangs of poachers and to guard the rabbit skins stored there.

Thetford Warren Lodge stands in a clearing in the woods. Five hundred years ago the land around would have been bare, and the lodge, built on a piece of slightly higher ground, would have been visible from miles around as a reminder that the warren was private. From the top floor the warrener would have been able, for his part, to watch over his rabbits and see any hostile gangs of poachers approaching. The lodge was strongly built and has survived well. Shaped like a keep or small fortress, it is constructed of flint with stone surrounds for the windows and corners of the building. The ground floor

A warrener's lodge at Thetford – built like a fortress to protect him and his rabbit skins from gangs of poachers.

was for the storage of rabbit pelts, and the floor above was the warrener's home. The floor itself collapsed long ago, but looking up you can still see the fireplace and chimney cut into the inside wall.

I met two present-day warreners at Thetford, Richard and Doug Frost, the fifth generation of their family to practise the art. They were catching rabbits in order to move them to a new warren rather than to kill them, though the techniques employed seem indistinguishable. Low netting had been placed around the warren and ferrets let in to drive the rabbits out, which is not as easy as it seems. As they worked they explained how the rabbit can defend itself by using its network of tunnels to hide from the ferret or by kicking at it with its powerful back legs. As they spoke a rabbit leapt into the air just in front of us kicking vigorously, the ferret narrowly escaping.

The warreners' job used to be to ensure there were rabbits for the lord of the manor to hunt, and this meant nurturing them as carefully as a modern gamekeeper nurtures pheasant. The rabbits would be fed in winter if there was a shortage, though in extremis a rabbit will eat its own droppings, recycling the food. When the land around them was too barren they would be taken to new warrens and even have holes bored for them in suitable ground to encourage them to settle there. My warreners with their traps and ferrets would not have been out of place in the fifteenth-century Brecklands. I would certainly not have liked to try poaching on their territory – unless I had protection like that used by a gang of poachers recorded in 1444 in Thetford. They marched to their work dressed in soldier's tunics with steel helmets, bows and arrows, cudgels and staffs.

A revelation of doom

'What would you be you wide East Anglian sky, without church towers to recognise you by?' wrote the poet John Betjeman. And it is true. For mile upon mile in Norfolk, Suffolk and parts of Essex nothing disturbs the horizon except the church spire. It is possible to walk from one end of a county to the other without map or compass simply by going from one spire to the next. There are churches of all kinds. Churches with thatched roofs. Churches with round towers built apart from the church itself. Churches flooded with light, ceilings embossed with flying angels, pews carved with the faces of the seven deadly sins. Many of these churches were indirect beneficiaries of the Black Death or rather of the prosperity that followed it. They were built on the profits of the cloth trade to give thanks to God, and maybe in the hope that he would look benignly on the benefactor at the hour of his death.

In the wake of the plague, death and what followed it loomed large in the imagination of medieval man, and the Church traded on his fears to encourage moral behaviour and worship. The evidence is best seen in the Doom paintings. Most churches had Dooms and most have vanished. But one survives in startling and frightening detail. It is the Doom at Wenhaston. For many years it had been invisible, covered with whitewash. In the course of one

The fine Doom painting from the church of St Peter's in Wenhaston, showing the Devil next to St Michael, who is weighing souls (left), heaven (above) and hell (right).

of their compulsive restorations Victorian workers removed a white wooden panel and by chance did not destroy it immediately but put it outside in the churchyard. That night there was a downpour of rain. When the workers came back the next day the whitewash had disappeared and in its place was a spectacular portrayal of the Day of Judgement. Christ is seated on a rainbow watching as the souls of the dead are weighed in a balance while the Devil and St Michael argue over whether they should go to heaven or hell.

Lacework of stone: a medieval triumph

No tour of East Anglia in search of the origins of the building of Britain would be complete without a visit to the university city of Cambridge and a building that must rank as one of the triumphs of the end of the Middle Ages. Universities have always had a difficult relationship with the townspeople whose lives they disrupt. It was 'town and gown' conflict that led to the foundation of Cambridge University in the first place. In 1209 most students fled from Oxford after two or three of them had been hanged in retribution for the death of a woman killed by a student. The university was temporarily suspended. Some students went to Paris, others to Cambridge. At first their life there was not organised in the way we know today. The young students, usually only fourteen or fifteen years old, lived and studied in lodgings in the town. Keen to bring some order, Henry III granted a charter to the university and tried to resolve differences between the students and the townsfolk.

Over the next hundred years a number of colleges were founded, often by the church, to house students and teachers. Henry VI, who had established Eton College near Windsor, proposed to build a new college in Cambridge. He planned to put it on the banks of the river Cam, with its buildings running up towards the centre of the town. Other colleges had already encroached on land used by the town, but Henry, ignoring the ill feeling his plans engendered, destroyed markets, shops, houses and wharves to fulfil his dream. The foundation stone of the chapel, King's College Chapel, was laid in 1446.

This building symbolises the yawning gulf between the attitudes of Norman times and the end of the medieval age. The minds of the people who built it had been set free, and what they built still sets us free. I sat on a bench, head back, staring up at the great fan-vaulted ceiling. It is so delicately spun that it seems impossible it can stand. I fell into a trance, as though I was listening to ethereal music. Four hundred years separate this building from the arrival of the Normans with their mighty fortresses. Henry VI was long dead by the time his chapel was complete; in later years it was enhanced by his successors. Henry VII's heraldic beasts, dragons and greyhounds hold your eyes as you look down the nave towards the high altar, and there, blocking the view, is the flamboyant oak organ loft given by Henry VIII. And always there is that ceiling.

I was led up a long winding stairway to the very top of the chapel. The floor was rough stone. The roof was held up by wooden beams set at just the right height to give the unwary a mighty blow to the forehead as they pick their way along in the gloom. This is the top of the fan-vaulted ceiling, the part the public never see. It was like standing on an eggshell. Only four inches thick, it weighs nearly 2,000 tonnes and stretches for the full length of the chapel. If you crawl on all fours you can find a number of holes cut through it, no more than half an inch across. I had been told improbably that they were put there by the BBC to hang microphones for broadcasting the Nine Lessons and Carols service on Christmas Eve, an unlikely desecration. Some say the holes were drilled so that the masons working above could speak to those working below as they completed the task of fitting the fine stones of the vaulting together. Another claim is that they were there to allow cords to be passed through to haul platforms up to the underside of the ceiling to clean the stone. I put my eye to one of these holes. It was like looking through a keyhole. I could just see the choir stalls far below and thought how tempting it would be to drop a stink bomb through the tiny gap in the middle of evensong.

My East Anglian tour ended here on a blazing hot summer's day, lying in the cool of the roof space of King's looking down at the hundreds of tourists wandering below. It had been a breathtaking journey from the severity of Hedingham Castle to the serenity of King's. But life in Britain was about to enter a new era, this one marked not by invasion but by our country's own deliberate separation from its links with the Church in Rome, and the turmoil that followed that decision. And once again the buildings would tell the story.

A symphony in stone: the fan-vaulted ceiling of King's College Chapel, Cambridge.

44

ELSEWHERE IN MEDIEVAL BRITAIN

1066–1485

I travelled mainly in East Anglia to see our medieval legacy. But throughout Britain that legacy is apparent just beneath the surface. It has shaped our cities, our landscape and our road system. The sheer scale of medieval achievement is most obviously displayed in the castles, cathedrals and churches that still dominate Britain. But much of the spirit and vigour of the medieval world must be recreated in our imaginations: so much has been lost and overlaid by the work of later generations.

A rare surviving example of a type of fortified bridge once common in England. It was probably built in the late thirteenth century. Rivers formed formidable barriers and it was only by building bridges that communications across them could be made reliable and safe. Maintaining and constructing bridges was regarded as an act of charity in the Middle Ages. It also helped secure trade. The scale of medieval bridge construction has only recently come to be appreciated: until 1750, most bridges in England stood on the site of predecessors dating at least as far back as 1250.

A late fifteenth-century illustration of Charles, Duke of Orleans as a captive in the Tower of London. The Duke is shown inside the White Tower, then as now an immediately recognisable symbol of royal authority. Once believed to have been built by Julius Caesar, the White Tower was in fact begun in the 1070s by William the Conqueror to overawe the hostile population of London. Henry III had the tower lime-washed white, and in 1240 had new gutters added to prevent the colour being spoilt by rainwater. London Bridge and the City can be seen in the distance.

ꝭg nouuelles Albion
Bome en plaist escouter

:OM:- HIC PORTATUR :

WESTMINSTER ABBEY
LONDON

A section from the late eleventh-century Bayeux Tapestry. The church was rebuilt by Edward the Confessor, whose funeral was held there in 1066. The cortège with bell-ringers is shown approaching as the building work is completed. A figure to the left sets the weathervane in place. Westminster Abbey was constructed in a new style that attempted to imitate Roman architecture and was inspired by architectural developments in Normandy, where Edward had spent some of his youth in exile. The 1066 Norman Conquest introduced the style across England.

This thirteenth-century view of Gloucester at the bottom of a manuscript page offers a vivid impression of a medieval cityscape. Dominating the town to the extreme left is St Peter's Abbey, today the cathedral. Its spires form a striking contrast to the rugged outline of the great square keep of the castle adjacent, probably begun by Henry I around 1105. The two buildings celebrate visually the powers of Church and State that presided over the development of the medieval city. Above the houses to the right are heraldic banners and the spires and towers of other churches.

One of several courts that regularly sat in Westminster Hall. The judges are shown dressed in red at the top, the clerks of the court in the middle and the clients and their lawyers at the bottom. For state occasions the courts and their furnishings were cleared out of Westminster Hall, which remained the largest covered space in the capital until the nineteenth century. The feasts held here were sometimes unruly enough to be policed by riders on horseback. It may even be possible that jousting took place inside the cavernous space of the hall.

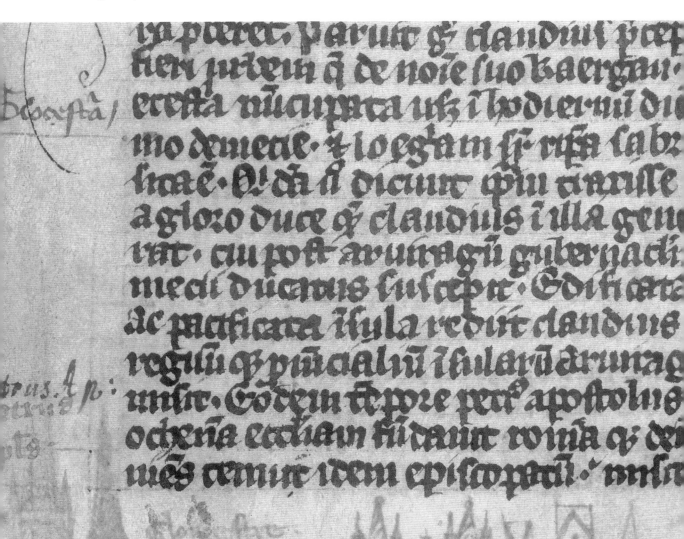

ST ALBANS ABBEY
ST ALBANS

A fourteenth-century
illustration of a king conferring
with his master mason over
the construction of a church.
The master mason stands
with a set-square and a pair
of dividers, the only tools
necessary for him to draw out
architectural designs using
complex practical geometry.
He is dressed in rich clothing
and gestures towards the
men at work on the building.
At ground level there are
masons hewing stone and two
workmen winching stones up
to the wall head. On the wall
itself, one mason lays a block
of stone while another uses a
plumb-level to check that the
structure is true.

Willegodum. ͨ intͤ ͤtaͭ ͧ volens bonū.
Gere ens vir bone fuit voluntatis· et dͤ

> **CONWAY CASTLE**
CONWAY

A bird's-eye view of Conway Castle and town in around 1600. Conway was begun by Edward I in 1283 as one in a chain of castles and towns intended to secure the newly conquered principality of Wales. The castle symbolically replaced the chief palace of the defeated Princes of Gwynedd, while their dynastic burial church (visible in the centre) was humiliatingly commandeered by the new town for parish use. Edward I's royal apartments in the castle occupied the court at the bottom of the drawing, overlooking a garden. Beyond the garden was the water gate, leading to the river estuary and the sea.

>> **ROUTE MAP OF A JOURNEY BETWEEN LONDON AND APULIA**

Part of a thirteenth-century route map drawn by Matthew Paris, a monk, who died in 1259. The left-hand strip shows England, with London at the bottom. The spire of Old St Paul's, shown in the centre, stood nearly 500 feet tall and was the icon of London for foreign visitors until it burnt down in 1561. In sequence above London are Rochester and Canterbury, 'chief of the churches of England'. At the top beside the sea is Dover, here described as 'the castle of Dover, the entrance and the key of this rich isle of England'.

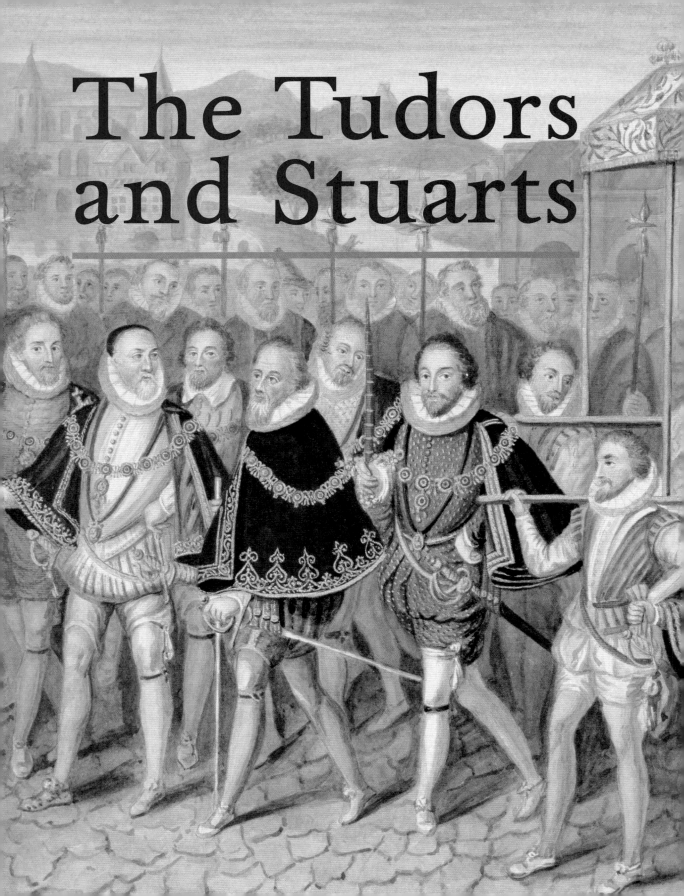

The Tudors
and Stuarts

The Heart of England
Living It Up

THE TUDOR AGE SAW A FLOWERING OF ART, OF MUSIC, OF IMAGINATIVE AND ORIGINAL POETRY AND DRAMA. The same spirit of adventure and ingenuity flourished in the buildings of the era. The key moment was the Dissolution of the Monasteries under Henry VIII. The bare facts are well known: how in a few years after his rift with the Pope over the annulment of his marriage to Catherine of Aragon, monasteries were closed down, the monks were pensioned off or fled, and their treasure was taken for the King. This upheaval saw the greatest change in English life since the Norman invasion 500 years earlier. It marked the decline of the power of the Church in favour of the power of the monarch, with all the consequences that flowed from that. As always the buildings tell the story best.

There are some buildings that can be called mouth-wateringly beautiful, that make you gasp with pleasure when you first set eyes on them. They do not have to be grand buildings, nor buildings with a distinctive style. Often they are of a mishmash of styles accrued through the centuries, but perfect in their confusion. Their setting is likely to be as important as the building itself, and the weather can help.

I approached Lacock Abbey in Wiltshire on a hot summer day. The drive curves gracefully through parkland with old trees and meadows defined by elegant Victorian cast-iron fencing. The front entrance of the house, with its delicate stonework and exotic decoration, would not look out of place as the entrance to a small palace in India. As you came round the side, however, you are transported firmly back to England. Two big bay windows look over a long terrace and beyond it to a river where the willows blow white in the wind and two boys lie on the bank fishing. A tall tower marks the next corner of the house. Beyond it the mood changes to religious, with the stone walls at ground-floor level punctuated by windows that would not look out of place in a church. This side could seem austere, were it not softened by a jungle of hydrangeas planted in a corner, ten feet high and fifteen yards round the base. You may not like hydrangeas, but I do. I even like the common purple rhododendrons that many gardeners hold in contempt.

The story of Lacock is the story, in microcosm, of England after the Reformation. It was founded as a nunnery in 1232. Nunneries were rarer than

PREVIOUS
Elizabeth I carried in procession. Courtiers built on a lavish scale to receive the Queen as she travelled around England on her summer progress.

monasteries and generally had smaller and poorer communities. The nuns at Lacock were recruited from daughters of the gentry, not from the lower classes, and their families paid for the privilege of placing them there. They observed the same religious obligations as their brother monks, saying seven services each day. When Henry's commissioners were investigating corruption in monasteries at the start of the Dissolution, they could find no fault with Lacock. They reported that the nuns were scrupulously following the rules of their order, that there were no complaints against them, and that they had adequate funds to remain solvent: stores worth £257. 10d. and jewels, plates and ornaments worth £104. 9s. 2d. They escaped with a fine. Despite this, three years later they were ordered to disband. The nuns were pensioned off, the abbey was closed and the lead stripped from its roof.

Four years later the abbey was sold by the King to William Sharington, who came from a family of minor gentry in Norfolk. Like many ambitious men in Tudor England he had acquired wealth and status by attaching himself to a grandee, Thomas Seymour, the brother of Henry VIII's third wife, Jane Seymour. Sharington planned to make Lacock his country seat. As a condition of his purchase he had first to demolish the church attached to the abbey, and he used the stone from the church to build a stable block. One of his descendants lives there today in the former hayloft, now converted to a comfortable flat. She says that Sharington was a rogue, but his reconstruction of the monastery was imaginative. He left the medieval cloisters at the centre of the house and their surrounding rooms, building his private quarters above them. Even on a

The tower William Sharington built at Lacock to house his treasure and to entertain guests.

warm summer day these cloisters are cold. The nuns would have needed their fur-lined cloaks as they processed from their quarters to attend service during the winter months, watched by the Abbess through a hidden window the size of a letter-box that allowed her to keep an eye on her charges.

The octagonal tower was Sharington's most original contribution to Lacock. It contains a strong-room to hold his treasure. The only access is through an iron-bound door. In the centre of the room is a finely carved octagonal table in stone, matching the octagonal shape of the tower. Above there is a similar room with a similar table, reached from the roof. Here Sharington's visitors, following the habits of the grandest families, could come to admire the view, eat sweetmeats and drink wine after dinner.

But Sharington was almost brought down by his greed. Not content with what he earned as a money-lender and a trader in Bristol, four years after he bought Lacock he secured an appointment as under-treasurer of the Bristol Mint. He was soon using his office to clip the coinage, reducing the official weight of the coins that were issued and keeping the surplus gold or silver for himself. When he was discovered, he confessed to embezzling £4,000 over three years. His estates were confiscated and he was sentenced to death. He only escaped execution by shopping his patron, Sir Thomas Seymour, who had fallen out of favour with the king and was executed. Sharington himself

The front of Lacock was charmingly remodelled in the eighteenth century in the Gothic style, and merges happily with the earlier building behind.

received a royal pardon and his estates were returned to him. It could be called an everyday story of county folk under the Tudors.

The appearance of Lacock reveals the glorious mixture of styles that predominated in the Tudor era. Apart from the medieval remains, the new building is partly modelled on the latest fashions taken from the Continent and partly on a purely English design. The entrance hall, a high room with strange terracotta statues set in alcoves, was built in the mid eighteenth century and just adds to the delight.

Lacock retains at least something of the pre-Dissolution appearance of Britain. But we paid a heavy price in the loss of so many great monasteries. The miserable remnants that remain, a ruined arch here, the foundations of the monks' dormitory there, all now preserved within neatly mown lawns, are a reminder of what was once a dazzling inheritance. Worse still, the churches were stripped of their decoration, paintings, statues and valuable ornaments. We have become used to the simplicity of English churches only because, at least until the Victorian revival of rich decoration, we have known no better. The money from this loot went first into Henry's coffers to strengthen the power of the king and the magnificence of his court. But ultimately, through the distribution of the former monastic lands, the wealth was spread, as at Lacock, among the aristocracy and the gentry. It was they who created a building boom and gave us some of the finest houses and palaces ever built in Britain.

The face of inspiration

'Her hearse ... seemed to be an island swimming in water, for round it there rained showers of tears.' I could have used these florid words when commentating on the funeral of Diana, Princess of Wales. They would have perfectly described the emotions of that day as the coffin, on a gun-carriage, was pulled along Kensington Gore to Westminster Abbey. I did not think there was something mawkish or over-emotional about the reaction to Diana's death. She had struck a chord with the British public and the outpouring of grief seemed natural to me. The 'hearse ... an island swimming in water' is not, however, a description of Diana's funeral but an account of the funeral of Elizabeth I from the pen of a contemporary of William Shakespeare, the playwright Thomas Dekker.

Now Elizabeth I and Diana do not stand comparison. One was a junior member of the royal family who showed a surprisingly human touch, the other a great monarch who presided over a period of unparalleled peace and prosperity and who was widely revered. But those who believe that the true British character is 'buttoned up' should look carefully at the response to Elizabeth's funeral. The tears came naturally, though perhaps Thomas Dekker went a little over the top in describing the reaction as her funeral barge was rowed on the Thames to Whitehall: 'Fish under water wept out their eyes of pearl and swum blind after.'

Elizabeth I never built anything notable for herself, but by her patronage of those who supported her, flattered her and wanted to bask in the glory of a royal visit, she inspired some of the most lavish buildings Britain has ever seen. Her royal visits were on an unprecedented scale. We know from royal tours today how everything has to be just right, the correct food provided, buildings that might be visited quickly repainted. Hospitals even do it for visits from politicians, giving them a distorted view of reality. A visit from Queen Elizabeth I was considerably more demanding. The mere possibility of being included in her itinerary would have ambitious noblemen building new houses, or extending those they already owned, in order to receive her. She would arrive with a baggage train of 200 horses to transport her court and her servants. She might stay just a few days, or a week or two. Entertainment had to be provided. Masques and music, fireworks and mock battles were arranged. The cost of running a house would rise from eighty pounds to two or three thousand pounds a week during her visit. No wonder her most faithful courtier, William Cecil, commented to a friend: 'God send us both long to enjoy her for whom we both mean to exceed our purses.'

There are many examples of the lengths to which her courtiers would go to win her favour. Robert Dudley, Earl of Leicester, spent £60,000 transforming his castle at Kenilworth to receive her. He built new rooms for her use four storeys high, with their own grand withdrawing chamber, constructed an impressive gatehouse, laid out pleasure gardens and bought deer for the park. Her arrival in 1575 to visit the man with whom she was said to be in love was marked, according to Dudley's usher, by 'a great peal of guns and such lighting by firework that the noise and flame were heard and seen twenty mile off'.

When Dudley fell out of favour, the Queen flirted at a masque with her future Lord Chancellor, Sir Christopher Hatton, and he became infatuated. Some of his correspondence survives. Once when he fell sick he wrote to her:

> 'Would God I were with you one hour. My wits are overwrought ...
> I love you ... I cannot lack you ... Passion overcometh me.
> I can write no more. Love me for I love you.'

Desperate to receive a royal visit, Hatton built what was at the time the largest private house in England to welcome her: Holdenby, in Northamptonshire. With its two great courts it was as large as the palace at Hampton Court, covering two acres. It was three storeys high with two series of staterooms, one for the Queen and one for Hatton. William Cecil, Lord Burghley, the Queen's most loyal adviser and himself no mean builder, congratulated Hatton on what he had achieved. He particularly praised the grand staircase leading from the hall to the staterooms above and proclaimed the whole so faultless that despite an exhausting tour he even forgot 'the infirmity of my legs'.

No expense was spared at Holdenby. A village was moved to improve the view from the house. No wonder Hatton was permanently short of money. In the spirit of the age he invested in some famous voyages of discovery, hoping for substantial profit. He helped fund Sir Francis Drake's circumnavigation of the globe, and when Drake reached the Straits of Magellan he duly renamed

Most of Holdenby House has vanished except for this entrance gateway (left) and the two fine arches (right) that led to an inner court. Queen Elizabeth, for whom it was built, never visited.

his ship *The Golden Hinde* in honour of Hatton, whose coat of arms contained a golden hind. Hatton made a profit of £2,300 on this expedition, but despite this enterprise and his own powerful position at court he died penniless. It is a sad story. Hatton refused to live at Holdenby until Elizabeth visited it. It was, he wrote, 'a shrine still unseen until that holy saint may sit in it, to whom it is dedicated'. But she never came, and all that remains of Holdenby today are drawings of the house as it once was, one room incorporated into an 1870 restoration, part of the original pillared doorway and two great arches, with the date 1583 inscribed on them, which once led into the lower court and now stand forlorn in a field, leading nowhere.

Flamboyance and splendour

Although Holdenby has vanished, other great houses of the period have survived to tell the story of England under Elizabeth, and they reveal the astonishing wealth of those who gained and kept power during her reign. Burghley, the house built by the same William Cecil who commented so favourably on Hatton's Holdenby, is among the most magnificent. Cecil was an extraordinary man. He had worked for Elizabeth I when she was princess, and on ascending the throne she appointed him Secretary of State. This meant that he in effect conducted all her business. 'No Prince of Europe,' she once said, 'hath such a counsellor as I have in mine.' Like the rich and powerful down the ages, his instinct was to display his wealth and power by building the largest house he could afford. It is a tradition still observed in England,

where everyone with a fortune, whether pop star, tycoon, Russian oligarch or minor royal must have a large country house to display their wealth and proclaim their social position. Today most of these houses are old. Only rarely does a newcomer to the ranks of the élite build to their own design. But Cecil, without using an architect, designed two great palaces: Theobalds, at Cheshunt, just north of London, which was pulled down at the end of the Civil War, and Burghley House, near Stamford in Lincolnshire, which stands intact in all its glory.

The best place from which to see Burghley (though it is not usually accessible) is the roof. The view is spectacular over the park that was laid out by Capability Brown long after Cecil's death. From here you look across to the distant hill from which spring water still runs to feed the house. Avenues of trees stretch into the distance. There is one garden laid out in the formal manner preferred by the Tudors. Below is the great circular gravel sweep, with wrought-iron gates at the end leading to the main entrance to the house.

But this is not what you come on to the roof to see. It is the roof itself that makes the long climb worthwhile. For this is no ordinary roof. This looks more like a small town. Clusters of tall columns even give the impression of a Roman forum. The columns themselves conceal chimneys. There are seventy-six chimneys in all, some hidden in the intricate balustrades that run round

Burghley House, the extravagant palace built by Elizabeth I's favourite adviser, William Cecil (above); and the Heaven Room (opposite), painted by Verrio in around 1696.

the roof. In Tudor times chimneys were an ostentatious display of wealth; count the chimneys and you can tell how many rooms a house contains.

There are other decorations here, with strange devices, flaming grenades or comets streaming twirls of copper ribbon behind them. The roof space is three-quarters of an acre. There are turrets at the corners and at the Prospect Room, where a banquet would be laid for Cecil's guests: a display of sweetmeats, fruit and wine, served as the last course of a great dinner. This roof was a place of privilege. To be invited to take the air up here was to be accepted as a member of the Cecil coterie. Here conversation was possible away from the prying ears of servants. Here political plots could be hatched in secret. Here erudite conversation could be had in the calm of a summer night under the stars. And all of it was conceived by Cecil himself.

How original these magnates of the Tudor age were. Under Henry VIII they had to watch their step, and avoid displaying their wealth too ostentatiously, for fear that their magnificence would be seen as a challenge to his. But under Elizabeth they let rip with a flamboyance and an energy that were not seen again in Britain until the Victorians had the confidence to flaunt their wealth as shamelessly and with equal panache. Not for Cecil a palace that aped the great classical buildings of the Continent, born out of an obsession with rules stipulating proper proportions inherited from ancient Rome. There were some classical touches, but Burghley is full of imaginative detail, unconcerned with any rules; a great, roistering romp of a house, as astonishing to our modern eyes as it must have been to those who saw it rise in the sixteenth century.

Humble dwellings

The impact of houses like Burghley or Holdenby must have been enormous. The peasants and small farmers would have been as much in awe of them as their ancestors in medieval times would have felt when they saw the great cathedrals and monasteries rise to dominate the landscape. Few working men's houses remain, but at Holdenby there is a convincing reconstruction of a yeoman farmer's cottage. It has been built a hundred yards from Hatton's great entrance arches to Holdenby and is as authentic as historical research allows.

At first sight it looks like a gingerbread house with a steep roof of wooden tiles, designed to allow the rain to fall off easily, and wattle walls, made of thin, interwoven branches daubed with plaster. It is properly known as a cruck cottage, the crucks being those naturally curved wooden beams that are cut from the branches of trees, usually oak. Fastened at the top by wooden pegs, pairs of crucks provided a strong framework to support the roof, so that the sides of the cottage did not carry the weight but were simply curtain walls to keep out the weather. The windows were just holes in the walls with wooden shutters. Glass windows were too expensive, except for the rich. At one end stands a stone chimney, down which the light floods on to the hearth. The floor is bare earth. There are wooden shelves suspended by string to keep food out of reach of mice and rats. A simple table and bench is the only furniture in the room, but a platform at one end, reached by ladder, provides a place to sleep. At the other end is a lean-to shed for livestock, typically a pig or two, perhaps a cow, and hens.

After the provision of food, making a proper shelter is a natural human instinct. Improving our homes is among our top priorities now, just as it was for our ancestors. Today it is central heating or double-glazing that we install, or a new porch or conservatory. In the Tudor era the equivalent improvements would usually have involved adding an extra room, perhaps to give greater privacy. Some parts of Britain saw the impact of better building materials too. In the Cotswolds timber was becoming harder to find as woodlands were cleared to provide fields to graze sheep. The wool industry in turn made the Cotswolds wealthy, so that even poorer families could afford to build in stone. Today these stone cottages are a symbol of Britain as potent as the Changing of the Guard or Windsor Castle. Visitors come from all over the world to take photographs of homes that would not have merited a second glance even a hundred years ago.

On a wet Sunday morning I watched a coach disgorge a tour group from Japan at Bibury, in Gloucestershire, a village set in a slightly claustrophobic valley. They had come to see the cottages known as Arlington Row. These tiny stone houses were for weavers, and were built on the edge of a stream so that cloth could be washed in the water, dyed and hung out on racks to dry. No longer seen as humble, they are now objects of fantasy, creating an image of an idyllic rural life that never existed. It is not just the Japanese who have fallen for Bibury. William Morris called it the most beautiful village in England, and Henry Ford tried to buy the whole of Arlington Row and ship it back stone by stone to Michigan for his history theme park.

New money, new directions

The increasing prosperity of the age can also be measured by the improvements in the homes of the new middle classes, the merchants and traders, the prosperous farmers and shipowners, the lawyers and doctors, bishops and men of learning. It has been calculated from probate documents that the average size of the middle-class house rose over 150 years from three rooms to six or seven. Larger houses were abandoning the use of the hall as the dominant feature, the place where everyone met and ate. Gradually new and smaller rooms were devoted to eating or to sitting. The hall's function became closer to its modern use as the main entry point to the house rather than a room to live in. The most luxurious addition of the age was the development of the long gallery. In a climate as wretched as ours a room on the upper floors, often running the full length of the house, provided a valuable place to walk and play games when the weather was poor. Its modern equivalent would be an indoor gym or swimming-pool.

In Cheshire there is a splendid example of a house built in this style. Little Moreton Hall had been expanding as the Moreton family became more prosperous. Its growth was halted when they supported the Royalist cause in the Civil War and were punished with sequestration of their land and heavy fines at the hands of Cromwell's men. Painful though this was for the Moretons,

The moated Little Moreton Hall. On the top floor is the Long Gallery, whose floor seems to buck and heave.

their poverty after the Restoration ensured that Moreton Hall has come down to us virtually unchanged from the seventeenth century.

At first glance it is a black-and-white timbered building of the most eccentric kind. Its arrangement is higgledy-piggledy, with walls and windows leaning at seemingly perilous angles. Every part is patterned with dark wooden beams running diagonally or criss-cross, or shaped to make four-leafed clovers. The exterior looks wildly over the top, with its jazzy patterns. If a trendy designer wanted to match the inside with the exterior, black-and-white zebra skins would probably hang on the walls, but the inside of Little Moreton sets a quite different tone, sober by comparison with the face shown to the world. It looks warm, almost cosy, though the National Trust manager who lives in the upper part of the house says it is the coldest place in Cheshire. This feeling of warmth is psychological, achieved by the use of comforting materials such as oak panelling and painted plaster.

The hall was changed by the Moretons in the early years as fashion changed. At first it was in the traditional medieval style, with a screen at one end to conceal the entrance to the kitchens and a dais or stage at the other to seat the lord and his family. In the middle of the sixteenth century the Moretons built a new floor with extra rooms for private use and added two high bay windows to provide light to the hall itself. At about the same time the walls of the parlour used as a sitting-room by the family were redecorated in the latest taste. The plaster walls were painted to look like wooden panelling, with a biblical frieze on paper set above it. This was a Protestant family and the choice of subjects reflected their beliefs. Instead of the Last Judgement or the Dance of Death, which were favoured before the Reformation, these paintings portrayed morality tales.

More injunctions decorate the Long Gallery. At each end is a plaster relief, one of Destiny the other of Fortune, with injunctions to self-improvement. The Elizabethans relished clever symbols or devices, plays on words or riddles to be deconstructed. They found an echo in the Victorian obsession with paintings or embroidered religious texts: 'God is Love' or 'Honour thy Neighbour'.

With its irregular, sloping walls, windows at crazy angles, and tilting floors, the gallery makes you feel you are in a ship at sea, and may at any moment lose your balance. Here the floor bucks and heaves as though the whole building could capsize, which, were it not for various attempts to strengthen it, it probably would. The latest device to rescue it for posterity is an ingenious steel cradle, hidden from sight, in which the Long Gallery now rests, firmly secured to the main beams of the house below.

The Elizabethan fascination with intricate design is reflected in a 'knot' garden, recently restored, beside the house. Low box hedges are planted in a complex pattern that reflects the design of the beams of the house itself. Between the trimmed hedges with their clover-leaf design is a grass lawn and raked gravel. These formal, almost austere gardens were seen as an extension of the house itself and are quite unlike the romantic, rambling, flower-filled

gardens that we create today. The box has to be neatly trimmed to keep the
shape precise and even-sided. The gardener, Alan Middling, told me that
one day he was on his knees carefully trimming the new growth under the
watchful eyes of a group of visitors when they suddenly burst into applause
in appreciation of his artistry.

Extravagance and hard times

Another fascinating house preserved by impecunious owners reveals how
the new rich lived at the beginning of the seventeenth century. Chastleton
in Oxfordshire was built just after the death of Elizabeth I. It remained in the
same family until the 1940s, when it was first opened to the public. Its then
owner would explain to visitors why the house looked a bit shabby: 'You see,
we lost all our money in the war.' They would commiserate, assuming that
disaster had struck during the Second World War, only to discover that her
complaint was about the poverty brought on by her ancestors' support for
the Royalist cause in the Civil War 300 years earlier. Like the Moreton family,
they had been punished with heavy fines by Cromwell and had never
recovered from it. The result is another house, like Little Moreton Hall,
which remains in a time warp.

Chastleton inverts the notion of display. Where Moreton is flamboyant on the outside, Chastleton reserves its extravagance for the interior. It was built by a member of a family grown rich on the wool trade. Walter Jones bought the Chastleton estate from Robert Catesby, one of the conspirators in the Gunpowder Plot, who was killed while resisting arrest. Jones pulled down the old house and built the Chastleton that we see today. The house looks as though the family has just left, taking most of their furniture with them. A few chairs remain, with prickly teasel heads placed on them to prevent visitors sitting down. (Occasionally you may see a tell-tale teasel stuck to a transgressor's skirt.) The rooms however are all intact. One, the Great Chamber, has an extravagant plaster ceiling, heavy with hanging bosses, like icing sugar dripping from the ceiling. The architectural historian, Nikolaus Pevsner, describes it as 'blatantly nouveau riche, even barbaric, uninhibited by any consideration of insipid good taste'. Right up my street.

Chastleton marks a turning-point in domestic design. It still has a great hall that retains at one end the usual screen with a passageway behind it. But this hall was no longer used as the main room of the house, for eating and talking. It was a place to gather before moving off to the smaller private rooms elsewhere. You would have expected the front door of the house to have been placed, as in later buildings, in the centre of the hall facing the fireplace. It would have been approached by steps leading up from the drive to a grand porch. However, the builder of Chastleton was keen to keep the medieval style at least in part, with the entrance leading visitors first behind the screen and then turning right into the hall proper. As a result Chastleton has a grand staircase in the centre of the main façade but no visible doorway. For a moment you think the builder is playing a trick and that there is no entrance on the

Chastleton –
the house of a rich seventeenth-century merchant (opposite); and Chastleton's stairway and dining-room (below). Families now dined in private.

main façade. But go up the steps and you will find, tucked away out of sight on the left, the porch and the front door, and a very grand front door too. Despite its hidden entrance the main front of Chastleton is a fine sight, a house that is imposing without being intimidating, the house of a man proud of what his family has achieved and fit to take his place among the higher ranks of the landed gentry.

Apart from the Great Chamber, Chastleton has a 72-foot Long Gallery with a barrel-vaulted ceiling, the shape of an underground railway tunnel, made of moulded plaster. We know its use, because shuttlecocks and tennis balls have been found under the floorboards. From its windows Walter Jones could show off his estate, with its gardens, its church and village, and his land stretching away over 14,000 acres. I looked down on the eternally English sight of white-cotton-clad ladies playing croquet and went outside to join them. It was at Chastleton that the rules of croquet were codified in the mid nineteenth century. Anyone who plays croquet knows that each house has its own rules, usually made up as the game goes along to ensure a home team win. Within minutes I was in dispute over their rules, which seemed unduly tame. In particular they did not allow the sadistic ploy of 'roqueting', which gives one full rein to destroy the opposing team by driving them off the field. It was only later that I discovered that their game was 'golf' croquet, which seems to be a rather genteel version of the game, though they insisted that the strategies for their version were just as complex. Under the benevolent gaze of Chastleton we whiled away an hour of a sunny afternoon. I think Walter Jones would have thought it a proper use of his house.

A monument to ambition

If Chastleton is an example of an elegant country house for a gentleman, Hardwick Hall in Derbyshire is quite the opposite: a stupendous house built towards the end of Elizabeth's reign and designed for show. I had passed it many times when driving north on the motorway, admiring it fleetingly on top of its hill, but I had never been there. The drive snakes its way through parkland and past the quarries that provided the stone to build the house. As you reach the top of the hill, the first glimpse of it through trees is of the initials of the name of its builder, cut in stone and silhouetted against the skyline: ES. Elizabeth Shrewsbury, Bess of Hardwick. Four times married, Bess rose from being a squire's daughter to become one of the richest and most powerful women in the country, second only to the Queen. Her progress through the intricate social and political structure of Elizabethan England was the result of her mostly canny ambition, determination and, not least, the premature deaths of the wives of three men, each of whom she married. She avoided an early death herself, outliving all her husbands and died aged 81, according to contemporary records with 'the blessing of sense and memory to the last'.

She made a conventional enough start on her upward trajectory. She worked as a gentlewoman in a grand house near her own home, rather as boys

Hardwick Hall on the left and the Old Hall on the right: landmarks for miles around, not least from the M1.

in the Middle Ages were sent to be brought up in the homes of grandees. She was first betrothed to her cousin, who was already sick and who died with the marriage unconsummated a few months later. He left her a modest annuity and free to marry again.

Her next husband was a shrewd choice. Sir William Cavendish was old, rich and in need of an heir, his two previous marriages having produced two daughters but no son. It was said, though it barely needs saying, that 'being somewhat advanced in years, he married her chiefly for her beauty'. In the ten years of their marriage she had eight children, of whom six survived. At his death Cavendish left her estates in Derbyshire and Nottinghamshire, making her a rich woman.

Marriage number three was to another widower, who was also a courtier and a favourite of Queen Elizabeth. This husband conveniently died after only five years, putting her back on the market with an enormous fortune. The modest squire's daughter was now in the upper ranks of English society and ready for her last marriage, to a forty-year-old widower with six children who just happened to be the head of one of the richest families in England, the Earl of Shrewsbury.

George Shrewsbury owned land, and had investments in coal-mines, iron- and glass-works and shipping. It was a bad marriage and ended miserably with rows between the two and the intervention of both the Privy

Council and the Queen herself, acting first as marriage guidance counsellors and then as arbitrators. When Shrewsbury died, having lived latterly with his mistress, he left Bess as one of England's richest women.

Now in her sixties, she could have retired content with the status and wealth she had acquired, but for Bess, it would be fair to say, life was for living. She embarked on her grandest scheme, to build a palace in which she would hold court while waiting for the day when the Queen would pay a visit, or better still her own granddaughter Arabella, whom she imagined succeeding Elizabeth and coming to Hardwick as Queen of England in her own right. No such visit was achieved, but her brilliant legacy, Hardwick Hall, leaves those ambitions in the shade.

Houses like Hardwick have become known as prodigy houses. Trophy houses might be a better description. They were built with scarcely a thought for the cost, the public display of wealth and power being their object. Here both aims are achieved but, more important, the result is a house of great beauty, a triumph of English building in the Elizabethan era. It combines different styles gleaned from the Continent, classical Roman, Gothic and Flemish, to make a uniquely English house, with its owndistinctiveappearance, and full of those little tricks of design, allegorical allusions and devices that were the signs of a cultured Elizabethan mind.

Hardwick Hall. 'More glass than wall': the main façade of Hardwick (below); and a painting of Queen Elizabeth I there (opposite). Though popularly seen as the Queen's rival, Bess was always careful to show loyalty.

Bess of Hardwick's initials, ES (Elizabeth Shrewsbury), built in stone on the rooftop – lest anyone forget who built Hardwick.

Hardwick is properly called Hardwick New Hall. It stands only a short stroll from Hardwick Old Hall. The Old Hall is where Bess was brought up and where she lived while the New Hall was being built. They are similar in one way: they both have vast rooms for entertaining with large glass windows. But where the Old Hall grew like Topsy over a number of years, the New Hall, Hardwick as we now know it, is all of a piece. This may have been because it had in charge a man who prided himself on being not just a builder but an architect. Robert Smythson called himself 'architect and surveyor'. This was something of a novelty. Previously buildings, whether monasteries, cathedrals or grand houses, were constructed by skilled craftsmen. Smythson had himself been trained as a stonemason. On becoming a master craftsman he had worked on the Thynnes' house at Longleat, near Bath. By assuming the title of 'architect' he claimed that he was more than a craftsman. At Hardwick his role was to pull together the ideas put forward by Bess, and no doubt other members of her family, and design a coherent building that met her needs.

The outside is famous chiefly for the huge size of the windows, which give a lightness and delicacy to the façade. As you look at it, you marvel at the cleverness of its design. Such expanses of glass hung within their stone framework look fragile enough to weaken the structure of the house. The glass itself was a display of wealth. Inside there is a wide staircase whose shallow steps lead from the ground floor, where children and servants were kept, to the first floor, where Bess herself lived, and finally to the grand second floor. Here there are two astonishing rooms, the High Great Chamber and the Long Gallery. The Long Gallery is today almost as it was when built. Over fifty yards long, with tall windows letting the sun stream in, it is hung with tapestries. Bess, no fool when it came to her business affairs, bought them from the son of the bankrupted Christopher Hatton, who had commissioned them for Holdenby. She even negotiated a discount for the cost of removing the Hatton coat of arms and replacing them with her own. You can see the rather clumsy needlework patches at various places in the design.

The best room, though, is the High Great Chamber, which is so grand it is almost comic. Round the walls are more tapestries and above them a painted relief plaster frieze. It shows the goddess Diana, the huntress, surrounded by animals, lions and elephants, camels and deer, in an exotic setting of a forest of palm and other trees. The mythical Diana was a virgin, and the frieze was intended as a tribute to the virgin queen Elizabeth herself. The Chamber is sparsely furnished, as were all houses of the time, but there was a throne chair on which Bess, never modest, would sit when holding court, beneath a lavishly embroidered gold canopy. The canopy on display today was made for a descendant, but it gives a good impression of the impact that a visit to Hardwick to pay homage to Bess would have made on a visitor. When I was there someone said, as people always say of grand houses, 'It's fantastic, but you wouldn't want to live here, would you?'

'*I* would,' I replied.

Secret passageways for the persecuted

When our own Queen Elizabeth II came to the throne in 1952, there was a deliberate attempt to suggest that Britain was on the verge of a new Elizabethan Age. The reign of Elizabeth I was recalled, with reminders of our exploration of the New World, of the defeat of the Armada, of the flowering of music and poetry, of Shakespeare and Marlowe. There was a popular song, which would not make the charts today, but which, in the days before the Beatles and the Rolling Stones changed musical tastes, was a great hit, played constantly on the radio. It had a catchy but rather irritating tune which is going through my head as I write. It was called 'Let's All Be Good Elizabethans'. The impression was given that the first Elizabethan Age was one of prosperity and creativity, which in many ways it was. But life was not tranquil for everyone in Britain, certainly not for those who still professed Roman Catholicism and who owed their spiritual allegiance to Rome. As always, these strains revealed themselves in our buildings, that sure guide to who we once were.

The persecution of Roman Catholics under Elizabeth and her successor James I took various forms, at times token, at times ferocious. All depended on the degree of threat that Catholics, with their loyalty to the Pope, seemed to pose to the security of the State. The threat was at a peak when with the Armada, Catholic Spain attempted an invasion of Britain, and once again after the discovery of the Gunpowder Plot, when conspirators nearly succeeded in destroying the entire élite of the Protestant aristocracy, including the King, during the State Opening of Parliament.

We celebrate Guy Fawkes Night now as a chance to make a bonfire and let off a few fireworks. I sometimes go to my local town, Lewes in Sussex, on Bonfire Night. Here the anti-Catholicism can seem harsh, as the town remembers seventeen Protestant martyrs burnt at the stake by Elizabeth's predecessor, her Catholic sister Mary. But although the event can prove a shock to the uninitiated, the participants see it as a jolly celebration rather than a serious attempt to revive memories of the most serious political conspiracy that we have ever faced. We tend to think of Guy Fawkes merely putting a few barrels of gunpowder in the cellars of Westminster. In reality there was enough high explosive to destroy the building, kill the King and all the nobility assembled for the ceremony. The intention was to incite a revolt in the Midlands and to install a Catholic on the throne. No wonder Catholics were viewed with extreme suspicion.

It is not easy at this distance to imagine life as a Catholic in the Britain of the sixteenth century. The great Catholic families often carried on life as normal, living on their estates, sometimes even being accepted in royal circles. As recusants, or refuseniks as we would say, they could be fined for not attending church, and were liable to have their lands sequestered or heavy levies demanded from them if there was any suspicion that they were conspiring against the Crown. They could expect arrest and imprisonment, though rarely execution. They were not, in other words, put to the sword so much as continually watched and punished for their faith.

Two Catholic threats to the State embroidered in around 1621 on a cushion: the Armada (1588) and the Gunpowder Plot (1605).

The full fury of the State was, however, unleashed on those who were believed to be deliberately fostering subversion. In 1570 Pope Pius V proclaimed Elizabeth I deposed and Catholics released from their allegiance to her. When Spain launched the Armada in 1588, the Pope urged English Catholics to assist the invasion. Throughout this period priests were being trained on the Continent as missionaries, to be smuggled into England to foster Catholicism and encourage rebellion. A network of safe houses was established to allow them to travel secretly from the channel ports to find refuge with Catholic families across England.

Just near Kidderminster, in Warwickshire, is a tall red-brick and sandstone house surrounded by a moat. It is not, I think, a particularly beautiful house, but the secrets of Harvington Hall reveal the strains of life as a Catholic in Elizabeth's England. A cross-section of the house reveals secret passages, hiding-places and escape routes that would not have disgraced Stalag Luft III, the German prisoner-of-war camp for Allied airmen who made ingenious attempts to escape by tunnelling. The priest holes at Harvington were built by the best professional in the business, Nicholas Owen, a servant of the senior Jesuit in Britain. He began designing and building these special hiding-places in 1588 and continued until he was captured shortly after the discovery of the Gunpowder Plot and was tortured to death in the Tower.

Owen's work at Harvington is among his most skilled. To disguise what he was up to he installed a new grand staircase in the house as cover for his work. Most of the hides and secret passages lead off this staircase. There is, for instance, a smaller staircase that has a lifting stair-tread. A search party discovering it would find a cavity with a few jewels or some money concealed in it. Owen meant the soldiers to steal what they wanted and close the tread. But behind it is another panel. This conceals not another safe box but a room big enough to hide one or two priests. Elsewhere, in a bedroom, there is a chimney-breast blackened with soot. No fire has ever been lit in the grate, for it has no chimney. Instead there are steps inside the fireplace, providing an escape route to the attics. The attics had a false wall at one end, on the other side of which was a large chamber where a dozen or more priests could hide. Most ingenious of all is a vertical wooden beam which appears to be one of a set of beams providing the framework for a brick wall. This beam, however, pivots outwards to reveal a narrow entrance to another secret chamber. I tried to get through the gap but could not quite squeeze myself in. Young Jesuit priests must have been kept on a meagre diet.

Harvington is now owned, appropriately, by the Roman Catholic archdiocese of Birmingham, who restored the house when it was in danger of collapse. It is visited by people of all faiths, but is a particular place of

Not beautiful but intriguing: Harvington Hall has more priest holes than any other house in Britain.

pilgrimage for Catholics. In the hallway hangs a wry reminder of the history of the house: a cartoon from *Punch* of 1982. Two torturers are standing before a hapless victim on the rack. They are playing a version of *Mastermind*. 'This is John Smyth. He is a Catholic and he is going to answer questions on his specialist subject: "Priest holes in the Midlands".'

Cryptic construction: riddles, codes and symbols

Building priest holes and celebrating the mass in private were one way of keeping the Catholic faith alive, but there were other ways of proclaiming the faith in a hostile society. If you travel on the London to Sheffield line, keep a sharp look out to the west as the train rumbles through Northamptonshire and you may catch a glimpse of a strange triangular building in the middle of a field. It looks like a folly built by some rich landowner with time and money to spare amusing himself with a pretty, if useless, addition to his property. It was officially built as a warrener's lodge, to house the guardian of the estate's valuable population of rabbits, thousands of which were sold in London for their meat and fur at three pounds a hundred for grey rabbits and five pounds a hundred for black. The best quality rabbits, the so-called rich rabbits, were black and white, plump and furry, and made ten pounds a hundred. Lucrative though the rabbit trade was, however, the warrener hardly needed so grand a lodging to hang his pelts and keep his traps. This Triangular Lodge was built to serve a different purpose, even if nominally intended for the warrener. It was designed as a statement of Catholic faith of the most complex kind, a building that held a secret code, some of it still not cracked today.

Triangular Lodge was the brainchild of Sir Thomas Tresham, a man of style and learning. He was converted to Catholicism by Jesuit missionaries but remained loyal to Elizabeth, who had knighted him during one of her royal progresses. Eventually, because of his religious beliefs, he fell foul of the authorities and spent twelve years in various states of imprisonment or house arrest, as well as being forced to pay heavy fines. Finally released, he retired to his estate at Rushton and built the lodge.

It is not clear how overtly Tresham intended Triangular Lodge to flaunt his religious defiance. The Elizabethans enjoyed their riddles and conundrums, but interpreting the lodge is almost impossibly difficult, so obscure are its messages. At first glance the building could be simply a game played with the name Tresham, or Tres (three) as his wife called him. It is three-sided, and there are several triangular devices incorporated in it as well as the trefoil, like a three-leafed clover, which was on the family coat of arms. But this is only the start.

I cannot here list all the clues to a deeper meaning that scholars have discovered in Triangular Lodge, but here are a few. The sides of the building are thirty-three feet long, Christ's age at his crucifixion. Among the many Latin inscriptions on the walls are exhortations to belief taken from the Bible and which would be acceptable to Christians of all persuasions. The veneration

of the Virgin Mary and the celebration of the mass however were not acceptable to Protestants. Here Tresham's message becomes more secretive. There are nine angels under the roof, each with one or two letters carved under them. The letters read SSSDDS and QEEQEEQVE, the first letters of two key phrases from the mass. 'Sanctus Sanctus Sanctus Dominus Deus Sabaoth', or Holy Holy Holy Lord God of Hosts, and 'Qui Erat et Qui Est et Qui Venturus Est', or Who was, and who is, and who is to come. On the three sides of the chimney are carved IHS (for Christ), ECCE (behold) and SALUS (Salvation). Again ECCE is the start of the phrase 'Behold the Lamb of God who takes away the sins of the world', which is spoken in the mass as the bread, the body of Christ, is held up for the congregation to see. SALUS is spoken as the wine, Christ's blood, is offered up.

I have only described a fraction of what the outside walls of the Triangular Lodge display. There are countless other symbols, dates, heraldic devices, birds, seven-branched candlesticks, seven eyes, a dove with her offspring, a pelican feeding her young, a serpent, a globe and a chalice. I should not give the impression that this is a building interesting only for its cryptic clues. It is also of great beauty, with fine delicate carving and, if you stand at one of its sharp corners, it offers a magical vista down two of the three sides, rather like standing at the sharp end of a giant piece of cake. Perhaps what is most surprising is the insouciance with which Tresham displayed his beliefs, albeit in code. It makes the age seem not just bold and fearless, but imbued with a light touch, almost a sense of humour about issues that were also deeply serious.

Puritanism and the dawn of restoration

This sense of fun, of life being lived to the full, is seen in many of the buildings of the Elizabethan age and that of James and Charles, the Stuarts who followed her. It came to an abrupt end with the Civil War and Cromwell's Commonwealth, a dour period in the history of building. The homes of many families on both sides of the battle were damaged or destroyed, and new building came virtually to a halt. Some idea of what the Puritans would have liked to see in Britain can be gleaned from an odd little chapel built at Littlecote, near Hungerford.

Littlecote is a crazy jumble of a house with both back and front looking as though they are meant to be the most important sides. It has a fine, unspoilt Elizabethan garden, formally laid out, with no trace of romantic softness. At one end of the house is the last Puritan chapel remaining in an English country house, and it is a sobering sight. The entrance is through a simple, heavy oak screen. There is no decoration of any kind. There is no altar. Instead, at the far end is a double pulpit. On its first floor, slightly raised, is a position for reading the Bible. A short flight of stairs ascends to a preaching pulpit with a wooden canopy overhead. The pews are narrow and slope slightly forwards, so that if any member of the congregation was lulled by the droning of the preacher's voice and nodded off, he would slide noisily to the floor.

This chapel is quite pleasing to look at, but you leave thinking that maybe one such chapel is enough and that Britain's buildings had a lucky escape when Cromwell's rule came to an end. His men had, after all, destroyed many beautiful churches, removing statues, smashing old stained glass, breaking up and burning wooden carving. Cromwell's Parliament, of which the owner of Littlecote was a member, fortunately voted against a proposal to pull down all our cathedrals, but they successfully vandalised them, turning St Paul's and Canterbury into military barracks, damaging Durham and Norwich and almost demolishing Carlisle.

Once Cromwell was dead and Charles II back on the throne, work started on restoring those buildings that could be saved. Theobalds, Cecil's other great palace apart from Burghley, had been demolished, as had Holdenby. Two hundred great houses and castles were lost. But the Restoration of the monarchy brought with it the restoration of the pleasures to which the landowning aristocracy had become accustomed.

At the start of the seventeenth century Sir Charles Cavendish, a son of Bess of Hardwick, had bought a castle at Bolsover in Derbyshire and began to rebuild it. His son William, infused with his grandmother Bess's energy, finished the work after his father's death. Cavendish planned to turn it into a pleasure ground, a place to forget the tribulations of the present by glimpsing the promise of paradise, both in heaven and, through a fine set of erotic

Roundhead reaction: the chapel at Littlecote was built during the Commonwealth by a supporter of Cromwell.

paintings, in the here and now. With its small windows and impressive battlements, the Little Castle, as it is known, looks like a fortified building. Inside, however, it has grand rooms for entertaining, decorated with paintings of the Labours of Hercules and the Five Senses. There are fireplaces set with coloured stones and, in two rooms off the main bedroom, ceilings painted with the gods of Olympus and the company of Heaven.

William was a fanatical horseman. He built a riding house and stables to pursue the art of High School horsemanship, putting horses through complex manoeuvres. He played host to Charles I, and a special new masque was commissioned from Ben Jonson for the king's visit: 'Love's Welcome to Bolsover'. William took the Royalist side in the Civil War and was commanding their forces when they were defeated at the Battle of Marston Moor. He went into exile and, on returning at the Restoration, found Bolsover badly damaged. Undeterred, he spent the next fifteen years adding a new hall and staterooms so that at his death, although widowed by a wife he loved and suffering from Parkinson's disease, he had at least the consolation that Bolsover had been brought back to life.

Erotic painting by an anonymous artist in the Elysium Room of the Little Castle at Bolsover.

The thrill of the chase

Another pleasure dome survived Cromwell's depredations because its owner judiciously made friends with the Protector. As a result John Dutton, of Sherborne Park in Gloucestershire, was allowed to keep undamaged one of the most curious buildings of the Stuart era. I saw it on one of those gloomy summer days that lower the spirits, but the sight that greeted me at Lodge Park was so odd and so quintessentially English that I cheered up. Members of the Deerhound Club were holding their annual meeting.

Deerhounds are themselves objects of curiosity. They are quite rare. They are huge, as big as a small pony, and they are immensely friendly. Never doubting that you too want to be friends, they put their long legs up on your shoulders and enthusiastically lick your face. More curious still were the owners of the hounds, who were dressed either as Roundheads or Cavaliers, in leather jerkins or silks and feathers. This was to give the feel of a Jacobean deer-coursing event.

In those days deer were set free at one end of a walled enclosure a mile long. The hounds galloped after them, hoping to bring them down before they reached the end of the course, which was marked by a ditch so wide that the hounds could not cross it but which the deer could leap over to regain their freedom. Bets were taken on which hound would get closest to the quarry.

Racing in style: Lodge Park was built as a glamorous grandstand from which to watch deer coursing.

If an extra large wager was placed, twenty pounds or more, the race would take place over a 'fleshing' course. This race ended in a kill. With no protective ditch at the end, the winning hound was the first to bring a deer down.

Modern deer coursing turned out to be a tamer affair. The hounds can no longer chase deer, nor hare, nor even rabbit. Instead they lollop along rather limply after a piece of old fur that is dragged the length of the course. It surely cannot be long before they conclude that this is a mug's game. One or two had already made that decision. They started down the course, lost heart, and ran back in the opposite direction. 'I knew it would be a bit boring,' I heard a child say to her mother, 'but I didn't know it would be *this* boring.'

The reason I had come to Lodge Park was to see the lodge itself. The deerhounds were a bonus. Lodge Park was built as a grandstand, a very grand grandstand, for watching the deer coursing. It is an imposing building with an entrance through three arches, making a loggia or porch, leading to a large hall with a big fireplace. On the right are stairs to the main reception room on the first floor, where a banquet would be laid on race days. On the floor above is a wide balustraded balcony stretching the full length of the lodge. From here the entire mile of the racecourse could be seen.

The building with its perfect symmetry is the finest viewing platform you can imagine, but it is notable for something else. It is said to have been inspired by the grand Banqueting House that was built for James I in 1622 by Inigo Jones and which still stands in Whitehall. Inigo Jones is the man, more than any other, who brought to Britain the classical style of building as seen in Rome. He had travelled abroad, studied Roman architecture and looked carefully at the work of the Italian architect Andrea Palladio.

Palladio had drawn up his own rules for designing successful and harmonious buildings after studying the proportions of classical temples and villas. He believed that there were ways of making a building look well balanced and easy on the eye by adopting particular proportions, the length, breadth and height all being in ratio to each other. Inigo Jones followed similar rules, such as making the principal room the size of two cubes placed side by side – the double cube. Jones did not build much, the Banqueting House, the Queen's House at Greenwich and the church and piazza in Covent Garden being his main memorials. Inigo Jones's powerful influence revived in British building half a century after his death.

It is a long journey from Henry VIII through the reign of Elizabeth I and the period of the Stuarts. Those years saw some of the finest and most original buildings Britain has ever seen. They spoke of enterprise and daring, of fearless exploration, of a lively and imaginative interpretations of the universe. This originality was to give way to the dominance of the rational mind, with its interest in science and order, and therefore to lead to a style of architecture that was similarly well ordered and which matched the mood of a new age: the Georgian.

ELSEWHERE IN TUDOR AND STUART BRITAIN

1485–1714

During the sixteenth century the foundations were laid for an architectural transformation of Britain. Henry VIII's assault on the wealth and power of the Church brought about the destruction of many great buildings and their contents. It also released the resources that funded an extraordinary construction boom that was to last into the reign of Elizabeth I. Hugely ambitious and often quirky, the architecture of the Tudor and Stuart ages reflects at many levels the influence of Continental design and the revival of classical forms. Over this period, architecture itself came to be seen in a new light, so much so that the Roman title of 'architect' was assumed by builders to dignify their profession.

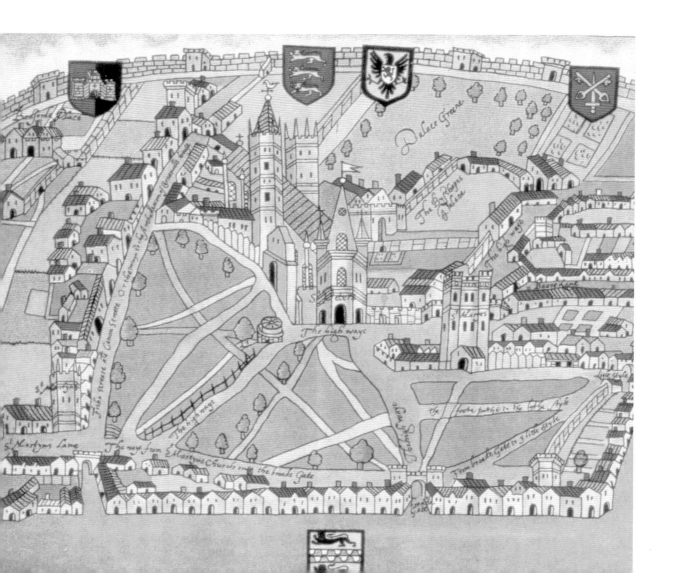

This map of the cathedral close at Exeter, drawn in the late sixteenth century, reflects the degree to which the medieval character of towns and cities was preserved throughout the Tudor period. The cathedral close is enclosed at the top by the walls of the city, and its internal boundaries are marked by gates. The church remains the dominant building in the close. Visible above and to the right of it is the bishop's palace and its gardens. The green in front of the church was used as a cemetery, but it was also a place for public recreation and games.

In 1539 Henry VIII initiated a massive programme of coastal fortification funded by the spoils of the Dissolution of the Monasteries. This is a design for an artillery fort intended to command the important anchorage off the Downs, in Kent. Three such forts, connected by earthwork fortifications, were built, and this drawing is probably a draft design for the largest, at Deal. It seems to have been designed by masons at Hampton Court. The baskets around the walls were filled with earth and were intended to protect the gunners.

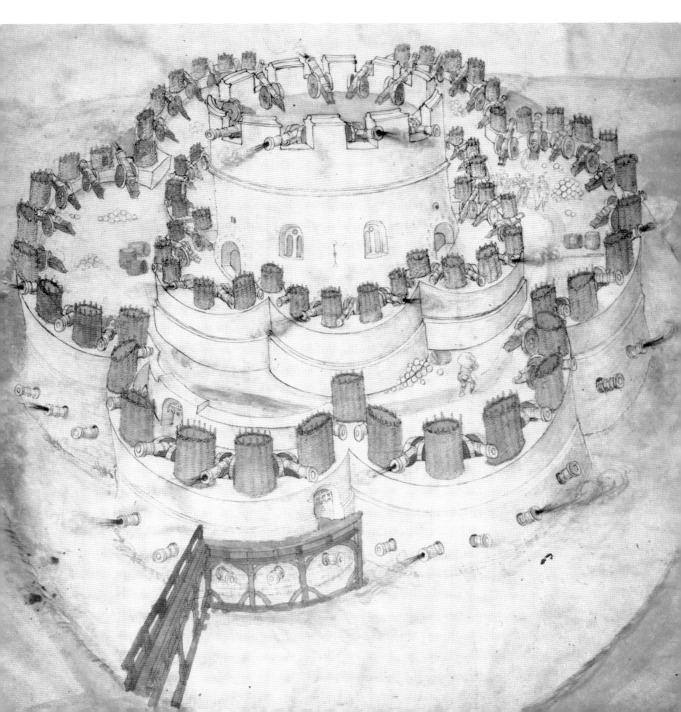

GLOBE. SOUTHWARKE.

" our theaters are raßd donne
and where they stode ßoare twentye
now ase ...
by ... of ...
... midwaye of ...

< GLOBE THEATRE
LONDON

This is a drawing of the
second Globe Theatre, built
in 1606 immediately after
the first Globe (built in
1598) burnt down during a
performance. The form of the
building as 'a wooden O' was
inspired by the theatres of
ancient Rome, with tiers of
seats arranged around the
principal stage. The open
court around the stage offered
cheap standing room and
was not protected from the
weather. The modern replica
of the Globe at Southwark,
completed in 1997, stands
several hundred yards from
its predecessor. It is the first
large timber-frame building
erected in London since the
Great Fire of 1666.

> NONSUCH PALACE
SURREY

Nonsuch Palace was begun
by Henry VIII in 1538. This
1560 drawing, which probably
shows the arrival of Elizabeth I
at the palace, perfectly
captures its fantastical,
castle-like architecture.
Nonsuch was a vast timber-
frame building, smothered
in ornament by a team of
craftsmen working under
the direction of an Italian
craftsman, Nicholas Bellin.
Etched and gilded slates
were hung over the structural
timbers, and the spaces
between them in-filled with
stucco, a type of plaster
mixed with marble. These
were modelled with scenes
from classical history and
mythology as well as images
of the King and the future
Edward VI. Nonsuch was
demolished for the value
of its materials by one of
Charles II's mistresses.

< QUEEN'S AND KING'S BATHS
BATH

This illustration of Bath in 1675 offers a surprising view of the city and its hot water springs before they were taken in hand by eighteenth-century planners and architects. Enclosed by a chaotic array of buildings, the scene at the Queen's and King's Baths – to the left and right respectively – is one of carnival. Men and women bathe together while boys dive-bomb naked into the water. Around the sides of the baths there stand fashionably dressed onlookers. The covered bathing space in the centre of the King's Bath is here entitled the 'kitchen' and that beneath the hut in the Queen's Bath the 'parlour'.

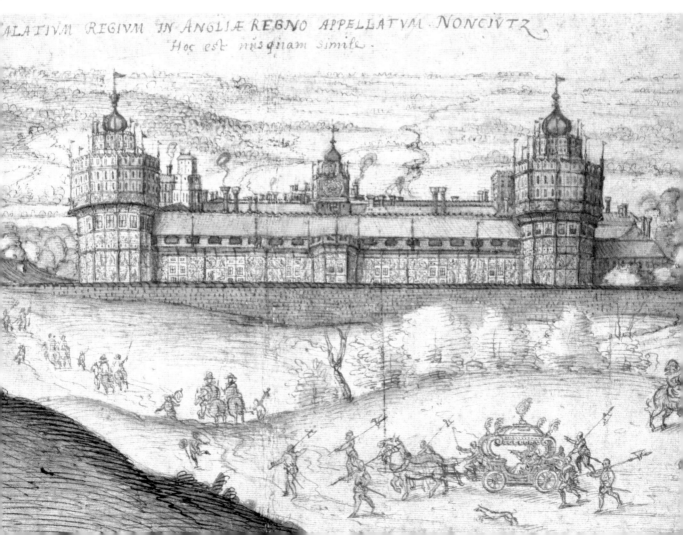

LONGLEAT HOUSE
WILTSHIRE

A 1675 view of Longleat House, built by Sir Thomas Thynne over a long period from the 1550s. A disastrous fire in 1567 caused the plans to be considerably changed, but the house was largely complete by Thynne's death in 1580. The house is symmetrically planned with projecting towers and regular grids of windows. Classical detailing reflects the influence of contemporary French architecture. From the flat roof with its banqueting houses and forest of chimneys, it was possible to enjoy splendid views over the countryside. The interest in formal planning extends to the gardens and the discreet placing of service buildings.

TICHBORNE HOUSE
HAMPSHIRE

This 1671 painting of Sir Henry Tichborne, with his family and household, preparing to give bread to the poor in the forecourt of his house, expresses ideas of social hierarchy and obligation that would have been familiar even in the Middle Ages. At this date, Tichborne House in Hampshire (since demolished), was a decidedly old-fashioned building, a reminder that the people of every age live with the architectural legacy of earlier generations. The hall, identified by its entrance porch, formed the centre of the house. To the right, the main court entrance is decorated with the Tichborne arms.

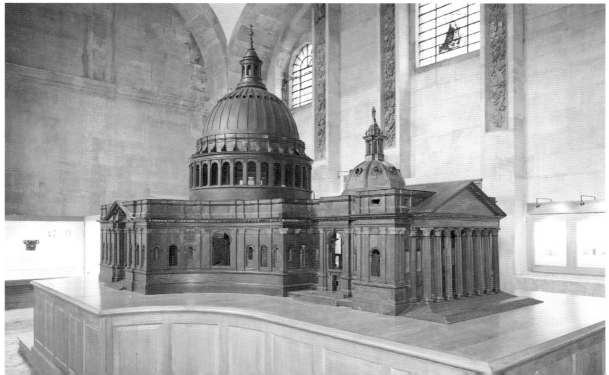

The Great Fire of London began in Pudding Lane on the morning of Sunday 2 September 1666 and burnt for five days. The fire is thought to have extended across 373 of the 450 acres enclosed by the city wall, and it destroyed 13,000 houses, eighty parish churches and the great cathedral of St Paul's. Even before the flames had been extinguished Charles II had been presented with several proposals for the complete redevelopment of the city. Although strong resistance to such proposals caused London to be rebuilt on its historic plan, the new city had a different character.

< MODEL OF ST PAUL'S
LONDON

Having approved Sir Christopher Wren's design for St Paul's, Charles II instructed in 1672 that a model be built 'soe large that a man might stand within it, the better to consider all the proportions of the same as well within as without'. This huge model in oak and pear wood was begun the following year by the joiner William Cleere. It stands thirteen feet high and in its finished form was painted and gilded. The chapter of St Paul's later rejected the design, asserting that it was not sufficiently cathedral-like, and Wren went on to design the present building.

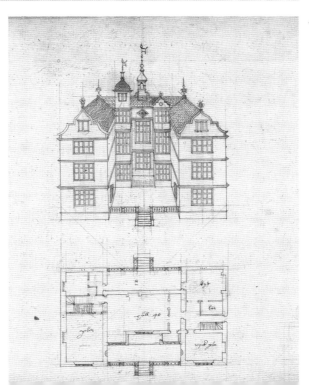

< JOHN THORPE'S DESIGN
FOR A HOUSE

This charming design for a house comes from a large collection of drawings created by the surveyor and architect John Thorpe, who died in 1655. It reflects the seventeenth-century interest in creating houses on compact and regular plans. Thorpe was based in London and had a wide clientele who used his designs to build houses across England. Although very few architectural designs exist from the Middle Ages, it is thought that similar architectural drawings could be obtained as early as the fourteenth century.

Scotland

Scotland
Towering Ambitions

AS AN ENGLISHMAN I CAN TRAVEL THROUGH MOST OF MY OWN COUNTRY AND FEEL AT HOME. Its history is my history. But take me north of the border and I am a stranger in a foreign land, more of a stranger in some ways than I am in Italy or France. Like most Englishmen I have constantly to relearn Scottish history, to try to see the country through Scottish eyes. The journey is made easier because the buildings themselves are like the pages of a history book – whether it's the great castles, many in ruins, dating from times of warfare and unrest, the fine classical public buildings of Glasgow and Edinburgh, the Scottish baronial houses, half castle, half palace, built by rich landowners, or the curiously ambiguous new Scottish parliament building, of which more later.

I began my Scottish journey in one of my favourite parts of Britain, the Outer Hebrides. My first visit was many years ago on impulse after a night of Highland dancing in Oban. The Scots take their dancing seriously. Before going to the Oban ball we had evening practices, where our hostess put us through our paces. I was soon absorbed in the intricacy of the steps. The sight of a hall full of burly men in kilts and girls in long ball dresses with lengths of tartan thrown over their shoulders was intimidating. Resisting the urge to take the night sleeper back to London, I danced the night away with the confidence, probably misplaced, that I was getting most of it right. My reward was to catch the ferry to Barra as an antidote to the sound and fury of Oban.

The same instinct to escape took me back there a few months later, to find some respite from general election fever in Westminster. I chose to film Barra as an example of a constituency far removed from the fray. We had a fine time of it too, drinking whisky until the early hours and rarely stirring before ten or eleven the next day. Now, forty years later, I was going back to the Hebrides, this time to Lewis and Harris, just to the north of Barra in the island chain of the Outer Hebrides.

PREVIOUS
A view of Edinburgh in 1825 from Princes Street by Alexander Nasmyth. To the right, work begins on the Royal Institution, later home of the Royal Scottish Academy.

The blackhouses of the Hebrides

These islands share with Barra a particular Hebridean style: deserted beaches of sparkling sand, low scudding grey cloud occasionally disrupted by brilliant sun, simple houses with their slate roofs and fenced gardens in which so little seems to grow. But there is one major difference. Unlike Barra, this part of the Hebrides is not Roman Catholic but strict Presbyterian. It was one of the Free Presbyterian churches that recently tried to prevent the Caledonian MacBrayne shipping company from opening a Sunday ferry service to the island. Travel on a Sunday is forbidden by this church. It is seen as a day to be kept holy, when nothing is done that could be done on a weekday instead. Even cleaning shoes and shaving are in theory outlawed. Feeding livestock is permitted, but humans should eat food prepared on Saturday. As for the ferry service, it did not matter whether a majority of the islanders wanted the ferry or not. In a majestic rebuke the Free Presbyterians said it was 'a false assumption that democratic principles carry greater authority than God'.

I had come to Lewis to see one of the oldest forms of habitation still standing in Britain. The blackhouse is a low, thick-walled thatched cottage, usually built on a slope, which housed a family and all their animals. At Gearrannan, a village on the edge of the sea looking out across the Atlantic, there is still a small cluster of blackhouses restored for letting as holiday homes. There is one cottage, at nearby Arnol, which was occupied until the middle of

Blackhouses huddling by the Atlantic Coast at Gearrannan in the Outer Hebrides.

A blackhouse: netting secured by ropes was used to hold the thatch in place against winter gales.

the last century and has been preserved intact. It is the perfect eco-house. The outer walls are built of huge slabs of rock. Between them and the inner walls there is a cavity, filled with earth and topped with clay. The clay allows the rain to run off, while the earth acts as a drain for any water that seeps through. The roof of thatch is laid over a wooden framework and held down against the gales by fishing nets tied with ropes and stones.

The key to the success of the house is the use of peat. Day and night throughout the year a peat fire was kept alight in the centre of the main room. There was no chimney. The smoke seeped up into the thatch (keeping it dry) and escaped through it. When the thatch deteriorated after two or three years, it was taken out to the fields and spread as fertiliser. It was believed that breathing in peat smoke was a protection against disease. When a law was introduced making chimneys mandatory, the crofters complained that they had become prey to illnesses. This, however, was probably the result of the dampness caused by the thatch no longer being kept dry by hot smoke rather than the absence of smoke inside the house.

The houses conformed to a simple pattern. At the top end was an area set aside for sleeping. Next came the main room for cooking, eating, spinning and weaving, and mending nets. Further down the blackhouse were storage places, with shelves and hooks for grain and flour, and finally the animals' quarters. During the dark days of winter, livestock would be kept inside. When spring came, the bottom wall of the blackhouse could be broken down and the cattle bedding that had accumulated over the winter swept out for use on the fields as fertiliser. And there was one last eco secret: the warmth given off by the cattle living at the lower end of the blackhouse rose to the higher end and so helped keep the family's living area warm.

Space was kept in many blackhouses for a pedal-driven loom used for weaving. Harris tweed has been made for centuries but only became fashionable in the middle of the nineteenth century, and as a result was astutely patented at the start of the twentieth. Only tweed bearing the Orb trademark and the number of the weaver can now be sold as Harris tweed, providing a livelihood for some islanders. When I first went to boarding school, a Harris tweed jacket was part of our school uniform. In the winter of 1947, when there was a coal shortage and the ground was frozen for weeks on end, I was grateful for this heavy woolen coat that made my chin itch but kept me warm.

The other staple of the Hebridean economy was kelp, which is collected from the beaches in summer. Kelp is a tree-like seaweed, which waves its slimy arms under water and clings to your legs when you swim through it. It is rich in iodine, potassium, magnesium, calcium and iron. Originally it was used to make glass and soap. It is still, mysteriously, an ingredient in tomato ketchup and the gum is used on postage stamps.

I asked islander Duncan Macleod, who is now ninety-one, about his childhood living in a blackhouse. Speaking to me in Gaelic through an interpreter, he recalled the harshness of life in his early years. The men were usually away from the village, either fishing or serving in the merchant navy. The women had a hard time looking after their families and the animals. As a child his job was to spend the day watching over the cattle. The staple diet was herring, either boiled or fried in oatmeal over the open fire. He said it was still his favourite dish today. He remembered the time before they had radio or television, when evenings were spent sitting round the fire while the elders told stories or retraced the history of the family.

This frugal life crammed together in the blackhouse led to members of the family growing up very close to each other, but he had no regrets when the time came to leave the blackhouse and move to a house built of stone. Sentiment was all very well, but was no substitute for a bed of his own in a room with a fireplace instead of sleeping three to a bed in a croft full of smoke.

Resettling the crofters

Crofting was a way of life for thousands of Scottish families in the Highlands. The croft was rented from the laird and with it a small patch of land. The mainstay of the crofter's life was whatever crops could be grown on the poor soil, and a few cattle, hens and sheep. If the croft was near the sea, his income would be supplemented by fishing. Every crofter was also entitled to dig up peat for fuel with an area of peat bog assigned for his use.

This centuries-old culture came to an abrupt end when the lairds were persuaded that they should make more profitable use of their land. The old ties of clan were already beginning to fade when, towards the end of the eighteenth century, there was a movement to improve the use of the Highlands and so enhance the economy. Learned tracts were written, and Improvement (always with the capital 'I') became the vogue word. It was generally agreed

that Improvements could be best achieved by moving the crofters off the land. It could then be fenced and farmers brought in to raise sheep. Alternatively, estates could be released to rent out for stalking or fishing. But first the crofters had to go.

The crofters believed they held moral if not legal title to the land they had lived on for centuries. Their removal was as painful for them as the enforced removal in the last century of thousands of black South Africans from their tribal lands to make way for efficient white farmers. Some landlords tried to persuade their tenants to move voluntarily to the coast and take up fishing as a trade. Fishing villages were built all round the Scottish shoreline. Many families lived there in shacks they made themselves and in severely overcrowded conditions. Other crofters took the brave step of emigrating, often to Canada, leaving behind their impoverished crofting life and the famines that regularly wracked their communities for the risky opportunities offered by the New World. The journey itself was dangerous, and separation from older members of the family left behind was heartbreaking. It says much for the determination of those early emigrants that many succeeded, as demonstrated by the sheer numbers of Canadians who roam Scotland in search of their roots today.

But moving people off land that they believed to be theirs of right, even with the offer of better conditions in their new homes, created a resentment that has lasted for generations. The most notorious of the clearances were those carried out in the far north of Scotland by the Duchess of Sutherland and her husband between 1808 and 1814. She and her advisers at first hoped that the crofters would move of their own accord. She thought they would understand the advantages of a new life and would choose to leave the land in favour of

108

The tension over clearances grew during the nineteenth century. Here the Illustrated London News depicts the riot of the crofters of Lewis in 1888.

resettlement by the sea. She preferred that outcome to the alternative of the wholesale emigration of the population, believing that resettling the crofters would benefit Scotland and increase its industry and wealth. But the resettlement of families on the north-east coast was not a success. The overcrowded conditions meant that many of them had to seek seasonal work elsewhere. For their part the Sutherlands still believed the clearances were desirable, even essential, and that they would relieve families of an intolerably primitive life on the land.

The tenants reacted with hostility and occasional outbursts of violence. Finally, impatient to proceed with their plan, the Sutherlands' agents began forcibly removing families by demolishing or burning the crofts and driving the people out. Some were said to have died in the process.

After one incident the Duchess's agent was charged with murder, though he was later acquitted. As a result of the evidence that was produced at the trial, however, the name Sutherland became reviled in Scotland. Others in Scotland had been ruthless, but the scale of the clearances in Sutherland, inspired incidentally by the Duchess's English husband, blackened their name both at the time and for posterity. A nineteenth-century historian took a slightly more charitable view. He wrote of the first Duke that 'like so many reformers [he] was willing to dedicate his life and fortune to making other folk do something they found desperately disagreeable for the sake of what he believed to be their future good'.

The present heir to the Sutherland title Lord Strathnaver told me that his ancestors' plans to force up to ten thousand people off the land had gone wrong because they had acted too ruthlessly. The shadow of those events, he said sadly, still hung over his family. Memories are long, and even recently there have been attempts to blow up the tall stone column with its statue of the first Duke which dominates the skyline near the Sutherland's ancestral home at Dunrobin.

Fearless Dunrobin and its walking gardens

The reputation of the Sutherlands may not have been enhanced by this extravagant castle built only twenty-five years after the worst of the clearances. Dunrobin was the largest home in the Highlands. Charles Barry, the English architect who had already rebuilt the Palace of Westminster after its great fire, was hired to redesign the old castle, parts of which dated back to the thirteenth century. The rebuilding was not paid for from the profits of the clearances. The money came from the Duke's investments in England, which included coal-mines. Nevertheless Dunrobin, in its splendid site by the sea, seems to epitomise the arrogance of that failed attempt to force improvement on the hapless Highlanders. 'Sans Peur' (without fear) is the Sutherland family motto. Dunrobin bears witness to it.

The model for the new house is a French chateau, though it would not look out of place in Hollywood or Disneyland. It is not entirely to my taste, rather bleak on the outside and soulless indoors. As an example of the scale on which one of the most powerful families in Scotland lived in the mid nineteenth century, however, it is without parallel. It gives a vivid picture of grand country house living in the Victorian era. There are for instance not one but two staircases at the entrance, one for people and the other for their luggage, which was taken to a special luggage room. There are coats of arms and family portraits on every wall. There are plenty of hunting trophies too, mainly heads, but including a fully grown and stuffed red stag who greets you at the entrance to the hall.

The main rooms are lavishly decorated, and each is assigned a purpose. There is the breakfast room, only used by the men of the party, the women always being served breakfast in their bedrooms. There is a huge drawing-room, but also a ladies' sitting-room, a music room and a library with 10,000 books. Linking all these rooms, out of sight under the floorboards, are miles of brass wire, still in perfect condition, which connect to a bell-board. Each wire is attached at one end to a bell-pull, at the other to the board where the bells rang. Each bell bore the name of a room. Servants hearing the bell ring would go to the bell-board, see which bell was still shaking and set off to do their master's bidding.

Dunrobin Castle: a dramatic sea coast setting for the home of the Sutherlands (below). Its towers look like Disneyland but were inspired by French chateaux (opposite).

Dunrobin has a grand Italianate garden, warmed by the Gulf Stream from Mexico, which hits the west coast of Scotland, travels round the north coast and is still warm when it reaches the north-east. This benign climate allows all kinds of plants and flowers to grow further north than you would think possible: giant rhubarb or gunnera, fuchsia and orange blossom. There are also low dividing walls of box hedges.

In the throes of a recent restoration the gardeners were having difficulty working out the alignment of these hedges. They did not seem to fit the formal layout of the Italianate garden. After taking careful measurements they realised that the hedges must have moved. They deduced that each year the hedges grew more strongly towards the sun than the shade, and each year when the gardeners trimmed them back they would instinctively favour the new strong growth on the sunny side and cut back the weak in the shade. This new growth would then put down roots, and so year by year more new growth would reach out towards the sun.

The gardeners estimated that by this means over the passage of 150 years the hedges had moved nearly five feet from their original position. The 'jewel in the crown of the Highlands' is how Dunrobin is described in the brochures. It can now boast a new attraction: 'the Walking Gardens of Dunrobin'.

A landscape of warring clans

I remember once reading a description of the state of Swat on India's old north-west frontier which called it 'nothing but scenery and warring tribes'. The same could be said of Scotland before it had castles. Castles were the defence against warring tribes and changed the landscape for ever. They are what makes the country distinctive. If you travel any distance you pass them, sometimes still in as fine condition as when they were built, but often just a pile of old grey stones, the roof gone, the windows gaping holes through which the rooks and bats fly. The warring of the tribes, or clans, meant that every man of power had to defend his land and people against his neighbour, and the castle was the best line of defence. There were about 150 major clans in the seventeenth century, though the shops on Royal Mile in Edinburgh sell so many different tartans that you could be forgiven for thinking there were several thousand. There is nothing exclusive about tartan nowadays. It is designed on a computer. You just list the colours and shades you would like and out it comes. I was offered a Dimbleby tartan, and if the Dimblebys can have a tartan, anyone can.

The two grandest castles in Scotland are at Edinburgh and Stirling. They were both royal castles, serving to display the power and wealth of the Stuart dynasty, whose James VI became King James I of England. His move south in 1603 brought to an end the predominance of Stirling, which until then had been used to flaunt the wealth and sophistication of the Scottish court. Stirling was built, like Edinburgh, on an outcrop of rock, naturally protected by steep slopes on three sides, while the fourth side was heavily fortified. The site had been used as a castle since at least as early as the twelfth century. It was at the centre of continuous disputes with England, notably in the thirteenth and fourteenth centuries. It was captured by Edward I of England in 1296, ceded by him a year later after his defeat at the hands of William Wallace at the battle of Stirling Bridge, lost again by the Scots the following year, regained by Robert the Bruce the year after that and then again surrendered to Edward five years later, and so on and so on.

But the grandeur of Stirling is due to the Stuart dynasty. In 1500 James IV began building the Great Hall. His successor James V brought in French masons to help create a palace within the battlements. Both these buildings could be seen from miles around, and even today they seem more impressive from the valley below the castle than from the rather confined courtyards on to which they look. James IV's contribution to Scottish life was immense. For a time he brought peace between England and Scotland. He was a man of the Renaissance who was enthralled by scientific discovery. His court attracted savants from across Europe, including an Italian alchemist called John Damian. Having failed to demonstrate his ability to turn base metal into gold, Damian tried to keep his place at court by assuring the King that he could fly from Stirling to France. Donning a pair of wings made from bird feathers, he jumped from the battlements and plummeted to the ground, landing, luckily for him, in a dung heap, from which he emerged heavily scented but alive.

A seventeenth-century view of Stirling Castle, seat of the Scottish kings, on its outcrop of rock.

The chapel in the castle was used for two spectacular christenings of future kings of Scotland. In 1566 Mary Queen of Scots had her son, the future James VI, christened there. As a Catholic in what was now a Protestant country, she nevertheless used the full Catholic rite, only refusing to allow the priest to spit into the child's mouth as the ritual prescribed. Two days later a magnificent dinner was prepared with King Arthur and the Round Table as its theme, King Arthur being supposed by the Scots to have held his court in the Lowlands rather than Cornwall. In the presence of ambassadors from England, France and Savoy a mock battle was staged, and the food was brought in on a stage pulled by servants dressed as satyrs with tails – to toast the English. It was an old Scottish joke that the English had tails.

The lavishness of his own christening may have influenced James VI when the time came to christen his son Henry. He had the chapel enlarged to its present impressive size. Dinner included fish brought in on an eighteen-foot boat floating on water and firing its thirty-six brass cannons. Serving food in this grand style has always been a symbol of wealth and power. I once went to a reception given by the US Democrats in the Rockefeller Plaza in New York. The centrepiece of their party was a lavish display of hundreds of oysters set on a bed of ice inside an eighteen-foot rowing-boat. James VI would have appreciated it. Some breaking news took all the guests away, except for me and a few others. I ate more oysters that evening than ever before, and not one of them bad.

From castles to tower houses

There are castles as grand as those of Scotland in Wales and in England, but what makes Scotland unique for castle lovers is what came next – the transformation of the castle into the tower house. In the rest of Britain, as life became safer, the preferred home was the fortified manor house, designed to offer protection against thieves and marauding gangs but not equipped to withstand a full-scale military assault. In time the fortified house morphed into a house displaying no need for security, with big windows and fortifications designed only for show. It is only in recent years that the rich have found it necessary to retreat once more behind protective walls and high metal gates, now with CCTV and guards round the clock. The so-called 'gated community' is a sign of how far we have slipped back into a climate of fear that would have been understood in the Middle Ages.

In Scotland, however, the castle's transition was different. The image of the castle proved more durable, and it emerged in the design of the tower house. Towards the end of the fifteenth century the wealthy, including the rising merchant class, built these as a badge of social rank, romantic reminders of Scotland's turbulent past and sometimes of a certain unease about the security of the present. By far the most dramatic example of this unique Scottish style is the tower house that lies west of Aberdeen: Craigievar.

Built in the early 1600s it is an astonishing and breathtaking sight. As at Dunrobin, you have to suppress the thought that you have come across another Disneyland fantasy. It is five storeys high, with a simple, solid base that bursts out in a profusion of circular turrets as it reaches the higher storeys. It has only one modest entrance door, protected with a metal grille on the inside. This leads not to an entrance hall but to the first of a series of winding staircases that

Craigievar: a tower house for a rich merchant (below); and the Great Hall there (opposite), with an elaborate plaster ceiling and stout furniture.

emerge in the Great Hall and go on to the eighteen rooms above. Lucky the generations of children of the Forbes family, who lived here from 1626 until 1962, and who had a playground perfectly designed for games of sardines.

It may have been fun, but it cannot have been an easy house to live in. Five storeys, with the kitchen in the basement and narrow circular staircases lit only by candles, is not what we would think of as luxury today. For the first Forbes, William Forbes, a timber merchant who traded wood from the Baltic through Aberdeen, it was the height of luxury.

Forbes was a younger son of a distinguished Scottish family. His elder brother was Bishop of Aberdeen and the family already owned an estate nearby. When William had made his own fortune he was keen to parade his success. The Great Hall, with its gallery, its fine plaster ceiling and its fireplace with a royal coat of arms above it, showed he had arrived. Interestingly, although the house was based on the medieval castle, Forbes was a modern man, influenced by the spirit of the Renaissance. Throughout the design of the house there are classical touches: extravagant gargoyles, heraldic beasts and, most surprising of all, busts in profile of Roman emperors set in the ceilings of the hall.

A new house of worship

The influences on Scottish building were not the same as those on building in the rest of Britain. The country was always open to new ideas from the Continent, particularly from France, England's traditional enemy. The Renaissance found an echo here and in the mid eighteenth century the period of intellectual fervour known as the Enlightenment left its mark. The Reformation too took a different shape from that south of the border. In England Henry VIII established the reformed church as the Church of England with the monarch as its supreme governor. The churches and cathedrals which had been Roman Catholic became the natural place of worship for the new church, stressing continuity.

In Scotland Protestantism, under the leadership of John Knox, took a more radical turn. The Presbyterians did not recognise the power of bishops and priests. Their form of worship eschewed the ceremonial of the old church and concentrated instead on reading the Bible and interpreting its message: an austere worship stripped of ceremony and which could be conducted as easily in a meeting hall as a church. So it was meeting halls that they built. One of the finest is by the sea at Burntisland, in Fife, built in 1592.

St Columba's, Burntisland, does not look like a church from the outside, rather a large manor house with a curious tower emerging from the middle. Inside there is no nave leading to the high altar. Instead the altar is set in the body of the church. No less important, seemingly, are the seats for the congregation and the pulpits for preaching. It was not egalitarian, however. There is a special box with plenty of red plush reserved for the local grandees, the Melville family. It is known as the Magistrates Pew and shouts: 'We paid for all this.' There is even a special pew reserved for the ladies of the laird's

The hybrid church of St Columba's, Burntisland, looking like a house with a tower on top.

household, with a reading table designed so that the ladies' maids could sit in front of them and turn the pages of the bible or prayer book in order to save them the trouble.

As befits a church by the sea, the building has a strong nautical flavour. There is a gallery reserved for seamen. It has its own exit door, so that if they had to leave early to catch the tide they could do so without disturbing the rest of the congregation. The front of their balcony is decorated with paintings of ships, one flying the saltire and another the red ensign, and there are sailors brandishing nautical instruments. Other trades from the town had their own places to sit, each marked by their guild's insignia.

In 1601 Burntisland was the setting for a momentous event. James VI was riding from Edinburgh to St Andrews to preside over an assembly of the Church of Scotland when he fell from his horse and hurt his shoulder. He decided to rest at Burntisland and summoned the assembly to meet him there. On 12 May 1601 this assembly agreed that a new version of the Bible (already much translated from Greek and Hebrew into English) should be prepared. Groups of scholars at Oxford, Cambridge and Westminster worked on different sections of the Bible to produce a version acceptable to the Church of England. Published in 1611 it became the King James Bible, or what we know as the Authorised Version, one of the great works of English literature.

Kinross House

Only fifteen or so miles north of Burntisland, but separated from it by a hundred years of history, is another iconic Scottish building. The seventeenth century saw the tower house eventually give way to a more sophisticated style of living. The scions of rich families from Scotland, as from England, were now going on grand tours of the Continent during their formative years and being exposed to a different kind of architecture. 'Who can delight to live in his house as in a prison?' complained the Earl of Strathmore, owner of the vast fortified castle of Glamis. 'Such houses truly are quite worn out of fashion, as feuds are, which is a great happiness, the country being generally more civilised than it was.' More civilised meant more at peace and no longer in need of even the semblance of fortifications on the private house.

Sir William Bruce, a Scottish architect who had travelled widely abroad, was the first to grasp this change of mood and to provide the houses it required. Bruce had a chequered career. After the execution of Charles I and with Cromwell in power, Bruce acted as a go-between to bring about the Restoration of the Monarchy. He encouraged Cromwell's General Monk to negotiate with the future Charles II in exile in Holland. When the Restoration was accomplished, he was duly showered with honours and positions of power in Scotland, including that of Surveyor-General of the Royal Works of Scotland. During Charles's reign his influence on Scottish building was inestimable. He introduced the new elegant architecture of the Renaissance, starting with a reconstruction of Holyrood House, the royal palace in Edinburgh.

But his most pleasing achievement was the house he designed for himself at Kinross. This was widely praised at the time, as much for its surroundings as for the house itself. The gardens and paths are set out in the formal baroque style with vistas stretching back down a long drive to the town of Kinross in one direction, and through the house and out across a formal garden to Loch Leven on the other. In the middle of the loch, and directly in the line of sight, is a small castle where Mary Queen of Scots was briefly imprisoned and from which she escaped. There could not be a more dramatic or romantic setting. Kinross House was described by Daniel Defoe on his travels as the 'finest seat I have yet seen in Scotland', and by another visitor as 'the first good house of regular architecture in North Britain'.

The house itself is like a breath of fresh air after all the castles and tower houses. It is built with perfect symmetry, the façade punctuated by grand Corinthian pillars but otherwise kept simple. The inside is simple too, but for a different reason. Poor old Sir William fell on hard times after William of Orange came to the throne. He was suspected of plotting to restore James II and spent months in prison. He ran out of money and fell out with his son. The result was that the interior of Kinross was never finished in the style Bruce had intended. It remains a family home, and although it was abandoned for many years in the nineteenth century it was carefully restored in the early twentieth.

I explored it from the bottom up. In the basement are huge rooms that were once wine cellars, dry storage larders, rooms for washing china and cleaning silver. From the basement, narrow staircases ran to the floor above, so that servants could move silently and unobserved from room to room, lighting fires, making beds, carrying pitchers of hot water. It was a house designed for the comfort of family and guests. The Grand Salon is on a scale rarely seen before, with high ceilings and light pouring in from big windows, giving a feeling of freedom and escape from Strathmore's 'prison' life.

The building of Kinross began in 1685. It was a radical departure from the buildings of the past and a sign of what was to come. It seems strange that Continental travel by wealthy young men should of itself have led to the overthrow of old styles of building in favour of a new style that imitated the temples and other public buildings of Greece and Rome. And, put like that, it *would* have been very odd – as though after summer holidays in Spain we all decided to build ourselves haciendas here in Britain.

But the grand tour was more than just a jolly jaunt around France, Italy and Greece. It could last up to three years, enough time to become absorbed in the buildings of the past and the art and philosophy of the present. In Scotland the period of the Enlightenment, after the Union with England in 1707, was a time of fervent intellectual activity, of new ideas in science and philosophy, of a belief in the power of reason to observe, measure and so explain the natural world. Not surprisingly, the buildings of such an age display a belief in man's ability to understand and control the forces of nature – a logical framework for buildings as much as for life.

The reinvention of romance

The New Town of Edinburgh, begun in 1765 and developed over the next eighty years, is a fine example of the impact of the Enlightenment. It is a Georgian city, connected by bridges to the old Edinburgh, with wide streets and pavements and generous squares. The houses are built on a stupendous scale to our modern eyes. In London they would be embassies or offices. In Edinburgh many remain in private hands. They have sitting-rooms as big as ballrooms, with windows almost reaching from ceiling to floor. The staircases are wide, the halls can take prams and bicycles and still leave room to walk two abreast through them. The New Town is beautiful but not uniquely Scottish in design. By the eighteenth century, in the wake of the Act of Union, London and Scotland were often building in the same style, and architects such as the Adam brothers were commuting between the two to execute their commissions. It took the romantic rediscovery of Scottish folklore, history and myth by Walter Scott to revive a passion for a peculiarly Scottish style of building.

Scott's influence is a mystery. How could one writer reinvent a country and give it back to its people with a new image? Yet that is what is claimed for Scott. His huge and ornate monument on Princes Street reinforces his standing. There is no similar memorial to any English or Welsh writer. So what exactly did Scott give back that changed Scotland? Pride in its history, I suppose, pride particularly in the story of the Highland clans. They had been looked on

The memorial to
Sir Walter Scott
on Princes Street,
Edinburgh. This
photograph was
taken before 1846,
when a statue of
the great writer
was placed inside.

hitherto as a rather rough and uncouth breed. Scott imbued them with romance. It was Scott who orchestrated the visit of George IV to Edinburgh and had the street lined with kilted Highlanders to greet him. It was Scott who so entranced Queen Victoria with his novels that she travelled from place to place to see the sites where the events described in them occurred. Victoria built Balmoral in the new Scottish baronial style, all towers and turrets and imitation fortifications. She could have chosen a classical design, but Scotland had returned to its roots, abandoned Greece and Rome, and false castles were once again in fashion.

Population explosion and tenement housing

In the nineteenth century, far away from the grand life of the Highlands with its developing leisure industries of stalking and fishing, another social revolution was taking place. Glasgow was growing, from a population of 80,000 at the start of the century to 800,000 by the end. The expansion had begun when the Act of Union in 1707 allowed Scotland free trade with the English colonies. From then on, tobacco, rum and raw cotton became staples of Glasgow's import trade, and cloth in all its forms a key export. With its trading port and shipbuilding it had become the sixth largest city in Europe, the 'engine room of the Empire'.

The big surprise of Glasgow to the first-time visitor is the sheer grandeur of its city centre, with its classical buildings and the noble terraces built to house the rich merchants who helped create the city's prosperity. It is a surprise because until recently, when a publicity drive planted the notion of 'Glasgow's miles better' and Glasgow was awarded the accolade of European City of Culture, Glasgow more often conjured up images of drunkenness on the streets, poverty, violence and of families living in squalid and overcrowded tenement slums.

The word tenement is misunderstood. Some of the first tenements in Glasgow were built not as housing for the poor but for the prosperous middle class. Glasgow, like Edinburgh, but unlike London, built upwards in the Continental style. These tenements were simply a block of flats, elegantly constructed, often in red sandstone, with a communal staircase and communal courtyard behind. Each flat had its own kitchen, a sitting-room, sometimes with a marble fireplace, and stained-glass windows in the doors. Bathrooms were a luxury but becoming more common by the turn of the century. The flat was carefully designed to maximise the use of space, with beds fitted in various unlikely places in cupboards or behind curtains in an alcove in the kitchen.

Great pride was taken in keeping the common parts of the flats clean: the staircases and the hallways. By-laws still exist which specify what the flat dweller was obliged to do to keep the tenement clean. The stairs had to be swept daily and scrubbed with water and a brush once a week, doormats shaken outside and all the brasswork polished. Anyone wanting to make a little money could be paid to do the work for a tenant. It was called 'taking in stairs'.

A middle-class tenement house in Glasgow: the parlour, showing a bed in a cupboard (left); and the kitchen, with its range (right).

The success of these tenements in fitting large numbers of people into a confined space also made them seem ideal as housing for the poor families who flocked to Glasgow from the countryside during the nineteenth century. Overcrowding in these tenements quickly became so severe that a law was introduced in an attempt to control it. The space in each flat was measured and a metal ticket posted to the front door saying how many people were entitled to live in the space. Inspectors called at night to count the number of residents. Such was the demand that they regularly reported people sleeping in cupboards, on the roof or in two layers on beds, one below and one on the mattress. It was these dirty, overcrowded and vermin-infested flats, in the Gorbals in particular, that gave the word tenement and Glasgow itself a bad name. They were pulled down in the 1960s, to be replaced by high-rise buildings, but the social problems of alcoholism, drug abuse and family break-up persist, as does the poverty that accompanies them.

Social reform and the schoolroom of New Lanark

One of Scotland's greatest social reformers was a Welshman, Robert Owen, born in 1771. He would have been saddened that such misery still exists. Twenty miles south-east of Glasgow, further up the Clyde, where the river is not the broad, shipbuilding estuary of the great city but a tumbling stream hurtling through narrow, tree-lined gorges, is the scene of his great experiment to make the world a better place. In a speech to the workers at the cotton mill he had bought at New Lanark he talked of his dream. 'I know that society may be formed so as to exist without crime, without poverty, with health greatly improved, with little if any misery, and with intelligence and happiness increased a hundred fold. And no obstacle whatsoever intervenes at this moment, except ignorance, to prevent such a state of society from becoming universal.'

Owen had married the daughter of the founder of the mill, David Dale. At the end of the eighteenth century Dale was employing 800 young children, mainly culled from the orphanages of Edinburgh and Glasgow. They made up the larger part of a work-force of nearly 1,200. Two hundred of them were under thirteen years old, and a few as young as six.

Child labour was considered normal at the time, and Dale's reputation for treating the youngsters well was generally admired. The hours were long. Work started at six in the morning and finished at seven at night, with breaks of half an hour for breakfast and an hour for lunch. After work children were expected to go to school for two hours, where they learnt writing, arithmetic and music. Dale recorded that at night the children slept three to a bed on straw mattresses which were changed once a month. The rooms were swept every day and the windows left open. Twice a year the walls were whitewashed with hot lime.

Within a few years Lanark was attracting a work-force from the Highlands, many of whom were victims of the clearances. The terraced houses and rows of cottages, which are well built, if very cramped, curve round the bank of the river whose rushing current drove the water-mill. Dale was an efficient businessman but was a philanthropist and educationist as well. For the education of his 500 child workers he employed sixteen teachers. When Robert Owen first visited Lanark he decided that it was the best place to 'try an experiment I have long contemplated'.

Robert Owen's cotton-mill, driven by the tumbling waters of the Clyde.

The classroom at New Lanark, where Owen tried out his enlightened theories of education (left); and a contemporary engraving of a dance class (right). Owen designed the girls' smocks himself.

Owen is usually described as a socialist, but it is hard to find traces of socialism in his early days at Lanark. When he bought the mill from Dale, his first act was to increase rather than to reduce the working hours. He devised a system for monitoring each worker's performance. Over their machines was a cube that could be turned to display one of its four sides. If the white side showed, it meant that person's work had been excellent, while yellow meant good, blue indifferent and black bad. The overseer would decide each day which colour to display, and Owen would walk down the lines of looms, look at the coloured side of the cube displayed and at the worker's face. 'I could at once see,' he wrote, 'by the expression of countenance what was the colour which was shown.' This emotional coercion of the work-force, almost amounting to blackmail, was pure Owen. He believed, like so many other liberal reformers, that if he imposed the right conditions on the ignorant and the poor they would respond and live happier, more fruitful lives. He was proud that his coloured cubes replaced the abusive language and beatings that were the more conventional means of controlling a work-force.

For a time Owen's methods were unpopular, but gradually his work-force were won round to the benefits that came from efficient production, particularly after Owen revealed a liberal streak. He kept them on full pay during a prolonged closure of the mill caused by an American embargo on the export of raw cotton to Britain. He introduced a sick scheme which gave his workers free treatment in return for a small weekly subscription. He opened a village shop, which sold at below market prices. He gradually reduced the use of unpaid child labour and campaigned throughout Britain for better child employment laws. But his great achievement at Lanark was his school for infants and young children. Here his reforming zeal and his benevolence could flourish.

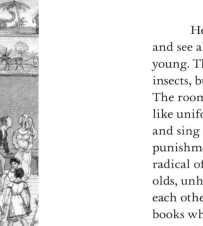

He opened the school in 1816. You can still visit the schoolroom today and see all its teaching aids, intended to stimulate the imagination of the young. There is a stuffed alligator. Wallcharts display different species of fish, insects, butterflies and moths, and offer classification of all living creatures. The room is large and airy. Each morning the children, wearing the smock-like uniform designed for them by Owen, would dance for an hour or more and sing in choirs 150 strong before lessons began. There was no corporal punishment, in fact no punishments at all; neither were there prizes. Most radical of all was his introduction of infant education for three- to five-year-olds, unheard of at the time. They were gently treated, urged to share with each other and, on Owen's instructions, they were not to be 'annoyed' with books while too young.

Owen left New Lanark in 1825 to set up a community in the United States: New Harmony. It was not a success, and he returned to Britain three years later to spend the rest of his life campaigning for radical reform and championing the working class. He was no longer as concerned with efficiency and profit as with education and conditions of employment. He argued for a reduction in the working day to eight hours. He preached that religion was a source of conflict and that marriage should be a civil contract, to be terminated by mutual agreement. In the schoolroom at New Lanark a phrenology head is displayed with a note saying it was bought in 1820 for 12s. 6d. It is New Lanark's tribute to Owen, and records that a phrenologist who had examined Owen's skull declared himself amazed by the size of his 'bump of benevolence'.

Charles Rennie Mackintosh

Where Edinburgh is thought of as restrained, even dour, Glasgow is generally recognised as a lively, vibrant city. Less pompous than Edinburgh, it boasts, in Charles Rennie Mackintosh, one of the most delightful architects of Scotland, the designer of friendly, amusing, easy-going buildings which still delight the eye. Mackintosh was the son of a clerk in the police force. He was not a healthy child and his doctor prescribed outdoor exercise and long holidays. Mackintosh used the time to draw trees, plants and buildings. The influence of both nature and Scottish buildings permeated all his work. He is a curious architect, hard to pin down, not part of any particular school. The influences on him were various, from the Japanese to the Pre-Raphaelites and the Arts and Crafts movement. In a lecture he gave when he was twenty-five years old he explained that he wanted to show 'joy in nature and grace of form and gladness in colour'. He was fortunate to be working at a time when young architects were no longer constrained by the rules of classical or Gothic building, but felt free to pick and choose their designs as they liked.

His lasting memorial is the Glasgow School of Art, perched awkwardly on a steeply sloping hill. He won a competition in 1896 to build this strange pile with its pink stone and its eccentric windows, some huge, some no larger

125

Mackintosh's
Glasgow School
of Art. From left, the
exterior; the library;
the entrance; and
the studio and
exhibition space.

than the arrow slits in a Scottish castle. It is a building that offers a different appearance depending on which side of it you are standing. There is nothing regular. It is as though Mackintosh is leading you around saying, 'Enjoy this. Look at what I have done here. Don't you think this is amusing?' The inside, which is devoted to huge studios, still occupied by painters, is simple and was built on the cheap. Dark pine and white walls predominate. Only in the library with its exotic lamps and art nouveau tables and chairs does he allow complexity. There are nice touches. The stairways, for instance, which make you feel as though you are inside a well-defended Scottish castle, are signposted with little coloured tiles, coded to guide the students around. One of them told me she 'always felt comfortable in this building, never intimidated by it. Mackintosh creates interesting spaces and that makes the building come alive.'

Mackintosh, like Gaudí in Barcelona or Frank Lloyd Wright in Chicago, is one of those architects who stands out as truly original, neither part of any movement nor becoming leader of one. Outside Glasgow there are very few Mackintosh buildings. He is more popularly remembered for his furniture and jewellery. I met Amy Kerr, a hairdresser from Ashby de la Zouch who was having tea in Mackintosh's Willow Tea Rooms in Glasgow. Today these rooms are a pastiche of the Mackintosh design. The chairs, as tall as thrones, are rickety copies – Mackintosh originals are far too valuable to be used. Amy came to Glasgow to see his buildings because she had always admired his jewellery and owned a reproduction bracelet of his design. She liked him because he was quite a 'girlie' designer, with flowers and soft colours. Joy, grace and gladness. It may be unfair, but I cannot easily imagine a Mackintosh coming out of Edinburgh.

Scotland's symbol of devolution

Edinburgh does, however, boast the building with the best claim to represent modern Scotland. If buildings tell us about the state of mind of the society that builds them, then the new parliament building should crack the code of the mood of Scotland today. Parliament buildings are designed to impress the electorate. Some are meant to uplift, like the Capitol building in Washington. Its great dome and classical pillars carry overtones of Greek democracy. Here we are patricians, it seems to say, giants among men engaged in our noble and disinterested calling on your behalf. Some, like the Palace of Westminster, are meant to embody the power structure of the country, although they invert it. The grandest rooms are reserved for the least powerful: namely the monarch, whose royal rooms and galleries are at the west end. Next comes the House of Lords, ornate and sparkling but influential rather than powerful. Finally there is the House of Commons at the east, more modest in design but holding all the power. The public is almost excluded.

So what does the devolved Scottish Parliament have to say for itself? None of the above. It is hugely expensive, but essentially modest. It crouches in a dip at the bottom end of the Royal Mile, facing the dark gloom of the royal palace of Holyrood. On the outside it does not seek to impose, nor to brag, nor to excite. It seems to apologise for being where it is. The main entrance, the opening statement of the building, with its glass swing doors and wooden trellis to shield you from the sun, could have been plucked from a design for an airport terminal in Tenerife. It was designed by Catalan architect Enric Miralles, and bears no relation to Scotland or Edinburgh, as even a passionate defender

of the building, the Presiding Officer George Reid, agrees. It would work, he says, in Seville when you are coming in from forty-two degrees of heat, but is less effective 'in a Scots February when it's dark and raining sideways'.

Inside, the building changes. It never stops changing. There are no straight lines, no impressive doorways, no long corridors lined with committee rooms, but beautiful wood, sloping floors, strange ceilings shaped like the hulls of fishing boats, and views over the city from quirkily placed windows which steal up on you unexpectedly. The debating chamber is the least impressive part of the building, laid out in the European manner: the semi-circle that is meant to encourage compromise instead of Westminster's conflict. When challenged about the message the parliament sends out, the Presiding Officer (the parliament's equivalent of the Speaker) told me it was not a building at all but 'a friendly village ... It says to the people of Scotland, "Hey, come on in, you're important".' The mystery deepened. 'It was never meant to exude power,' he went on, 'it was meant to exude legitimacy.' He had lost me.

I think the building is ambiguous about its role, because Scotland itself is politically ambiguous, divided about what it wants, full independence or simply a degree of freedom from Britain. I wondered as I walked away whether, if full independence were ever to return to Scotland, this parliament building could survive as the focal point of the nation's political life.

Scottish invention and MacAdam's road to success

It would be wrong to leave Scotland without mentioning one of the most important contributions the country made to building Britain. John MacAdam was born in Ayr in 1756. At fourteen he went to New York and worked in his uncle's business, making himself a fortune. He came home at twenty-seven and bought an estate in Ayrshire. Frustrated by roads that were frequently impassable because of rain and mud and snow, he devised a new method of road construction, the first since the Romans.

His method involved placing layers of evenly sized stones on top of each other which when bedded down would hold their position. There were large stones at the bottom, smaller on top. It was important that the dimensions should be uniform. The stones had to be cut to size. With insufficient gauges to measure the diameters, he told his stoneworkers to make them so they could fit easily in the mouth. If they did not fit they were too big. He was irate one day to find a pile of stones far bigger than his specification required. Rounding on the mason, he found himself looking at a man with a huge mouth and no teeth.

Notwithstanding these early difficulties, his road-building method was so successful that in his lifetime it was adopted throughout Britain, as well as in Europe and in the United States. Before the creation of the canals or the invention of the railways, MacAdam's roads revolutionised transport. The same method, improved by the use of hot tar to bond the stones (tarmacadam), is still the staple of road-building nearly 200 years later, and as powerful an influence on our lives as any building, however fine.

130

MOCK-ADAM-IZING — the Colossus of Roads.

This 1827 cartoon lampoons John MacAdam, who was nicknamed 'The Colossus of Roads'.

Scotland prides itself on the ingenuity and creativity of its inventors. It claims to have invented the steam engine, the bicycle, the telephone, the transistor, motion pictures, penicillin, electromagnetics, radar, insulin and calculus. I am quoting from the Scottish National Tourism Board, who attribute these successes to superior education, a prodigious work ethic, and even the weather (presumably because it kept the inventors indoors). The Board is too modest. They left off adhesive postage stamps, breech-loading rifles, pneumatic tyres, paraffin, the microwave oven, marmalade and the mackintosh.

And then of course there is television. Our next-door neighbour in the block of West London flats where I was born was that great Scotsman, John Logie Baird, the inventor of television. My mother asked him one evening to kiss me goodnight. He bent over my cot and planted a kiss on my forehead. I think of this as my fairy godfather moment – or was it my pact with the devil?

Baird lived in East Sheen as one of hundreds of Scots who have made their careers south of the border, just as thousands of English people now live in Scotland. But our two countries are not interchangeable, neither in their culture nor in their attitudes. The buildings tell all: we are two different countries. The mystery is how we have come to live together in relative harmony for so long.

ELSEWHERE IN SCOTLAND

Scotland has a rich and distinct architectural tradition of its own. Despite the country's relative poverty during the Middle Ages, the great churches and castles of the kingdom were ambitiously conceived. The Union of the Crowns under James VI and I in 1603 began a process of political integration between Scotland and England that was to be of enormous long-term importance. The conflicts and the benefits of this relationship have both left their mark on Scottish building. From the eighteenth century onwards Scottish expertise and mineral wealth contributed materially to the Industrial Revolution in Britain. The prosperity it brought made possible the redevelopment of several major Scottish cities, notably Glasgow and Edinburgh.

<　ROSLIN CHAPEL
MIDLOTHIAN

Roslin Chapel was intended to be the largest and most ambitious collegiate church in Scotland. Its foundation stone was laid by William Sinclair, Earl of Orkney and Caithness, in 1446 and work probably continued on the site until the 1460s. Only the choir, which is thought to have been modelled on that of Glasgow Cathedral, was ever completed. Every interior surface of the building is encrusted with carving. In the background of this 1897 photograph is the 'apprentice pillar', a spiral column particularly celebrated for its splendid decoration.

v VIEW FROM CALTON HILL
EDINBURGH

In this painting Princes Street stretches into the distance beneath the hill. To the right extends the New Town, which was developed on a regular grid-plan from the late eighteenth century. On the left is the Old Town, built on a spectacular outcrop of rock that rises to the castle. The contrast between these two settlements is what makes Edinburgh exciting. In the valley between the Old and New Towns is the city's central park. This is bridged by the Mound, visible here with its line of buildings in the Greek style, including the Royal Scottish Academy.

MELROSE ABBEY
THE BORDERS

Melrose Abbey was one of the most important monastic houses in Scotland. First established in the seventh century, it was re-founded as a Cistercian abbey in 1136. The buildings were badly damaged during the 1385 invasion by Richard II, who in the aftermath offered money and expertise to rebuild the church. Later the rebuilding work was undertaken by a French master mason, John Morow. His presence is a reminder of the strong architectural connection between France and Scotland that continued until the seventeenth century. Melrose was dissolved during the Scottish Reformation in 1560 and became a much admired Romantic ruin.

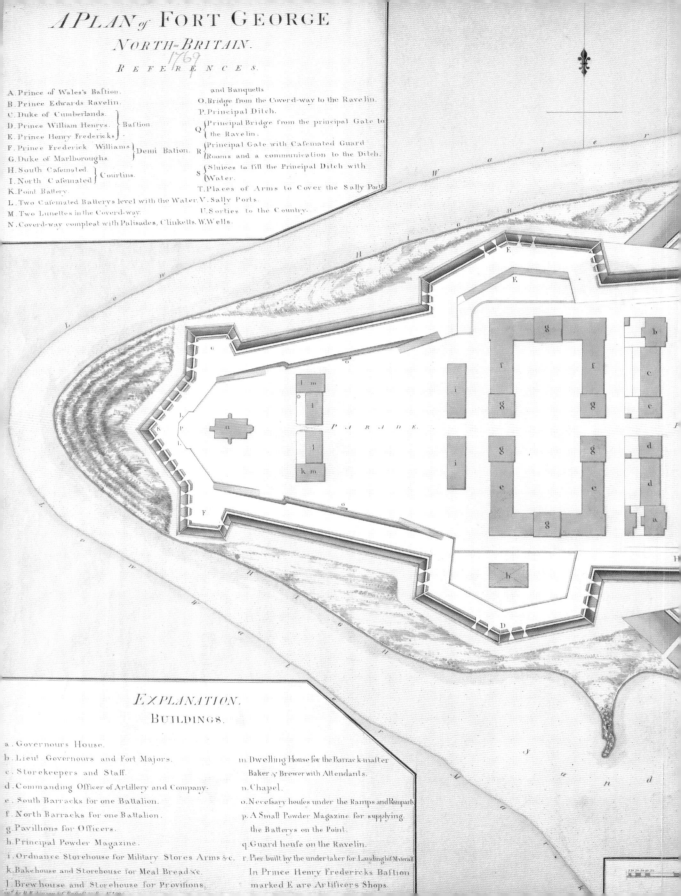

FORT GEORGE
HIGHLANDS

A plan of Fort George on the Moray Forth, designed by the engineer Colonel William Skinner. The fort was constructed between 1748 and 1769 just a few miles from Culloden in response to the Jacobite risings. It was laid out on an almost symmetrical plan with projecting bastions for cannons. The interior of the fort is shown with magazines for gunpowder, artificers' shops, a church and barracks. The latter, punctuated by 'pavillions for officers', are arranged around a central court. Similar forts, designed by military engineers, were built all over Britain's growing empire. The architectural achievement of these engineers was extraordinary.

Feet to an Inch.

The Church, Fort George.   Photo by D. Whyte, Inverness

"Cleanliness next to Godliness."

< FORT GEORGE
HIGHLANDS

'Cleanliness next to Godliness':
a neat pun for this postcard
of the church at Fort George
on wash day. Fort George
remains in military occupation
to the present day.

<GREAT WESTERN ROAD
GLASGOW

The Great Western Road, Glasgow, was a turnpike created by an Act of Parliament in 1836. It was intended to provide a major new approach to the city and to allow for the development of residential suburbs away from the centre. Although the new street was built up over a considerable period of time by various developers, it is an imposing creation. This 1905 photograph looks along the route towards the city centre. In the middle distance is a bridge that carries the road across the river. The late Victorian turreted building to the right evokes Scottish castle architecture.

∨ ROYAL EXCHANGE
GLASGOW

The Royal Exhange was enlarged and adapted from an eighteenth-century town house. The Glaswegian architect David Hamilton converted it to its present form in 1827. He added the portico to the front and the spectacular 'Newsroom' to the back. Hamilton was much influenced by Adam, but the austere grandeur of the building is typical of urban, institutional design in the nineteenth century. The Duke of Wellington's statue was erected in 1844. The absence of any figures in this 1899 photograph makes the view look like a stage set.

A photograph of the Forth Railway Bridge under construction in 1887. Stretching one and a half miles across the Firth of Forth, the new cantilever bridge took eight years to build and absorbed almost 54,000 tons of steel. The bridge supports two railway lines and had to be high enough not to obstruct boats. When opened in March 1890, it was the largest bridge in the world. Gustave Eiffel, whose contemporary tower in Paris is structurally related to the bridge, came to the ceremony. The bridge was designed to carry the main line from London to Aberdeen and remains in use.

The
Georgians

The West
Putting on the Style

IF YOU ASK A CHILD TO DRAW A HOUSE, THE CHANCES ARE YOU WILL BE OFFERED A SIMPLE SQUARE or oblong shape with four windows set in pairs one above the other and a front door between them: in other words, the kind of house we think of as Georgian. Ask a developer to show you his most sought-after design, and the chances are he will show you something similar, a Georgian-style house. Look at council housing that has been sold to its tenants and improved by them, and what do you see? The old front doors removed and replaced by Georgian-style doors. Georgian is everywhere. We use the word with abandon to describe what we think of as the buildings of the eighteenth century, but there is no single Georgian style. Instead, looking at the era, we find a host of different interpretations of a common theme: the influence of the architecture of the Greeks and Romans on the way we built Britain.

PREVIOUS
An early eighteenth-century view of Bifrons Park in Kent. The view celebrates the ideal of an English country seat, surrounded by a park and prosperous estate. A hunt is under way.

An echo of the ancient world

There is such a contrast between our life today and that of the eighteenth century that it is hard to imagine the mood of those times. I suspect we find it easier to identify with the uncertainties of the Middle Ages or the tumult of the changes ushered in by the Victorians than the period of apparent calm and order of the eighteenth century. It struck me forcibly as I rowed myself round a still lake in a quiet valley in Wiltshire. I feathered my oars across the glassy surface, leaving a ripple of movement behind me. A wintry sun rose over the high hills to disperse the morning fog, still dripping from the leaves of exotic trees. At one end of the lake was a bridge, perfectly replicated by its own reflection. I passed a small man-made island and paused below a grey stone temple set on a mound. This is the grandest building in the extraordinary gardens of Stourhead in Wiltshire: the Pantheon.

It is a copy in miniature of the Pantheon in Rome, with a pillared portico, domed roof, and niches for statues on either side. The interior is a circular hall with marble statues of gods and goddesses around the walls and, dominating them all, a statue of Hercules flexing his muscles. I felt transported back across the centuries, but it was an illusion. This temple was built in the

1750s, and the statue of Hercules was partly modelled on Jack Broughton, a famous prize-fighter of the day.

There are other temples around the lake at Stourhead dedicated to Flora and to Apollo. Beneath the Temple to Apollo the footpath that circles the lake divides, offering a choice of paths, one leading to Virtue, the other to Vice – the choice facing Hercules. I chose Virtue, and still do not know where Vice led. Virtue takes you through a dark tunnel and up a winding path to the Temple of Apollo and what the eighteenth-century writer Horace Walpole called 'one of the most picturesque scenes in the world'.

Nearby a gang of volunteers was working on a steep slope, trimming the laurels that provide ground-cover, an unrewarding task but essential if the gardens of Stourhead are to be preserved. Paul Alexander, the assistant head gardener, explained how the scenery was devised in what was once just a green valley. The temples and the islands were built first, together with the banks of what would become the lake. Only then was the spring that feeds the River Stour dammed to fill the valley with water. Several hundred people would

Stourhead: the artificial lake with the bridge designed after Palladio, and the Pantheon on the bank beyond.

have worked on the landscaping, with only the wheelbarrow and horse and cart for transport, and sixty gardeners were employed to plant trees and shrubs brought back from the Far East and the New World.

Stourhead was built on the profits of a bank that still stands at 37 Fleet Street, the last remaining private bank in Britain. C. Hoare & Co. was founded by Sir Richard Hoare in 1672. His grandson, Henry Hoare, was known as Henry the Magnificent. He was born in 1705 and travelled as a young man on the grand tour. Like so many of his generation he was enraptured by the remains of classical Rome and by the buildings of the Italian Renaissance. On his return he designed the gardens to keep alive the inspiration he had found on his travels. The Temple of Flora was the first building he erected. It was based on a temple at Spoleto, in Umbria. The design of the bridge came from a bridge in Vicenza built by the great Italian architect Palladio, one of the originators of the classical movement in Britain. The temple of Apollo takes its shape from the circular temple at Baalbek, in Syria.

Stourhead embodies much of what educated eighteenth-century taste celebrated. Henry Hoare wrote to his nephew attributing his achievements to 'the fruits of industry and application to business' which 'shows what great things may be done by it, the envy of the indolent who have no claim to temples, grottos, bridges, rocks ... Whether at pleasure or business let us be in earnest and ever active to be outdone or exceeded by none, that is the way to thrive.' The Hoares thrived by lending money, as their business archives show,

Stourhead. From left, the Temple of Apollo, reached by the path of Virtue; the classical dome of the temple; a statue in the Pantheon; and the underground grotto.

to other landowners keen to improve their estates in similar classical fashion. But Stourhead is not a flashy tribute to success of the kind the Elizabethans would have understood. Here everything is restrained, showing a reverence for antiquity founded in the belief that nature should be as ordered, as balanced and as rational in design as man himself. As Hoare put it: the most envied height of fortune could not be enjoyed 'without the pursuit of that knowledge which distinguishes only the Gentleman from the Vulgar'.

It is uncanny that Stourhead still has the calming effect on the mind that Hoare intended. Like me, I suspect most modern visitors do not immediately grasp the symbolism of many of the statues, not knowing the stories behind their appearance here or the allegories that a well-educated eighteenth-century man would have had at his fingertips. But the impression left is of a world more ordered, less hectic than it is today and in some ways the better for it.

Oxford: home of three classical styles

Changes in building styles that spring from the way Britain has developed over centuries do not happen in strict chronological order, with one style neatly following another. On the contrary, things happen in a jumble. Builders and architects are influenced by what they admire or what their patrons want to emulate. The start of the eighteenth century is a perfect example of this, and a handful of buildings at the centre of Oxford encapsulate the trends.

As an undergraduate I must have walked past these great places hundreds of times without making the connection. Like most students I was always in a hurry, rushing to the library to finish an essay, or to the Examination Schools for a lecture, or more often to meet people for lunch or tea or a drink in the constant social round that Oxford offered in the Sixties. Hurrying is a bad habit if you want to enjoy buildings. You are too busy looking down, so as to avoid tripping on paving stones, or looking out for friends, to have time to look up. Looking up is a habit I learned later, and going back to Oxford I realised how much I had missed, for within a few minutes' walk of each other is a group of buildings that tell the story of how Britain was changing from the seventeenth to the eighteenth century.

In a quadrangle is one of Britain's finest medieval interiors, the superbly vaulted medieval Divinity School, and leading from it the Convocation House. A great tower, known as the Tower of Five Orders, leads to the university's grandest library, the Bodleian. This tower, built in 1610, is already feeding off classical Rome and Greece with a series of columns one above the other in different styles, Doric, Ionic and Corinthian, each with their easily identifiable tops or capitals: one plain, one with what looks like a partly opened scroll of paper, and one decorated with acanthus leaves. The other two styles are Roman: the Tuscan and the Composite. The harmony of this courtyard, with its elegance, its lightness of touch and its pale golden stone, makes the spirits soar.

It was here that Charles I summoned his parliament to meet during the Civil War, when 150 MPs and eighty peers abandoned Westminster to the Roundheads and set up shop in Oxford, hoping to sue for peace. Cromwell soon put an end to that, and Oxford fell to the Commonwealth forces. During the twenty years of civil war and republican rule there was no new building of note, and instead an orgy of destruction of the old. When building started in earnest once more after the Restoration in 1660, the country was ready for an architectural renaissance, with subtly different interpretations of the classical theme predominating.

One of the first grand new building of Charles II's reign stands a hundred yards from the great quadrangle of the Divinity School. It was the work of the young Christopher Wren. At the time he was best known as a scientist and mathematician, having been appointed Professor of Astronomy at Oxford at the age of twenty-nine. But he was already fascinated by architecture and turned boldly to his new passion, his first design being a simple chapel in Cambridge for his uncle. Then, in 1664, only thirty-one years old and with no formal schooling in building, he took on the design of the Sheldonian Theatre.

He could have chosen from any number of styles, but his interest and instinct led him to design a building on classical lines. He was an admirer of the work of Inigo Jones, whose career had come to a halt at the outbreak of the Civil War in the mid seventeenth century, and who had died when Wren was twenty. Inigo Jones had stirred up controversy in conservative England when he brought classical architecture to London with his Banqueting House in Whitehall and his Queen's House at Greenwich. Wren, marshalling all he knew about this classical style from reading and examining drawings

Sir Christopher Wren's first major commission: the Sheldonian Theatre in Oxford.

of ancient Rome, decided to build the Sheldonian like a Roman theatre in the shape of a D. Some people say the building shows Wren's immaturity, and its main façade may seem unbalanced to the purist, but it is full of inventive touches, not least the daring decision to build the roof, seventy feet by eighty, without any visible internal support.

From the Sheldonian Wren went on, in his long and distinguished career, to build fifty-three churches in London and St Paul's Cathedral. His unmistakable churches in particular show how his style developed. From any high point in the city of London you can spot several of them standing tall among acres of dull office blocks. Their spires are always distinctive, and that of St Bride's is still copied for wedding cakes. Apart from St Paul's there is nothing pompous about Wren's designs, and nothing to intimidate either. He is an architect of friendly, welcoming places that do not make you feel unworthy to enter.

Just opposite the Sheldonian Theatre and built fifty years later, is an example of another interpretation of the classical approach. The Clarendon Building of 1711 is more strictly Palladian. It was designed to house the University Press, but looks better suited to act as a bank or a library. Its architect, Nicholas Hawksmoor, had worked with Wren as a young man and later with another fashionable architect, John Vanbrugh.

Like the young Wren, Hawksmoor chose a design for the Clarendon that stemmed not from any Continental travel but from the study of books about Roman architecture. With its great columns running from ground to roof, supporting a triangular pediment, it is strong, solid and, if a building can be such a thing, supremely self-confident.

The last of the three buildings that encapsulate the eighteenth-century approach to building is different. The Radcliffe Camera was built in the late 1730s. This was also originally designed by Hawksmoor, but on his death the job was taken on by James Gibbs, a Scottish architect. The Radcliffe is a great domed drum with columns in pairs all around the first floor. It was built and is still used as a library. Its style is what experts call English baroque, a rather loosely used term. It is said to come from the Spanish word *barrueco*, meaning an irregular shaped pearl. Whether true or not, it gives a good idea of what to expect from baroque, which is to expect the unexpected. Surprise, flamboyance and rich decoration are its hallmarks, but all reflecting classical design.

So, wandering around this small area in the middle of Oxford, you can see displayed all the trends of the new age: Wren's first flirtation with the classical, the baroque Radcliffe and, showing what would become the orthodoxy of the eighteenth century, the strictly Palladian Clarendon Building. These three buildings illustrate how different interpretations of classical style overlapped. The architects who came later and who favoured a simpler approach to the classical turned their backs on what had gone before, the inventiveness and free spirit of Wren, Vanbrugh and Hawksmoor, in favour of a plainer, more austere style. The Clarendon Building would probably have met with their grudging approval. Their *bête noire*, the kind of house that stood for everything they disapproved of, was Blenheim Palace.

Blenheim Palace: a magnificent rival to Versailles

Blenheim is only a few miles out of Oxford at the edge of the little town of Woodstock. It was built on land given to John Churchill, the first Duke of Marlborough, by Queen Anne to celebrate his victory over the French at Blenheim in 1704. His success prevented Louis XIV from dominating Continental Europe and, as his descendant Winston Churchill wrote, 'changed the political axis of the world'. Vanbrugh was commissioned to design a palace suitable for the hero, and £240,000 was voted for it by Parliament.

It was not easily accomplished. Marlborough fell out with the Queen, and his wife fell out with almost everyone, including Vanbrugh. The project ran short of money and Marlborough himself had to foot the final bill. These complications aside, however, Vanbrugh's design, much of it executed by Hawksmoor, achieved exactly the effect he wanted. It is not really a home, though the Marlboroughs still live there. It is rather a monument to England's triumph, intended to rival Versailles in splendour and rub the noses of the French in their defeat. It is not quite on the scale of Versailles, but is nevertheless a stupendous palace, far grander, both inside and out, than any royal palace. When George III came on a visit he conceded, 'We have nothing to equal this.'

The arrival at Blenheim is up a long drive through a park laid out by Capability Brown fifty years after the house itself was finished. It has his distinctive 'natural' landscape of gently rolling grass with lakes and carefully placed clumps of trees. The approach to the palace itself by contrast is theatrical, almost a stage set. On all sides are spires and columns, statues and golden balls, lions of England holding French cockerels in their paws, and battle honours carved in stone. A vast courtyard with colonnades on each side leads up steps under a tall, pillared loggia and through double doors with intricate brass locks into the Great Hall.

The Great Hall is the most majestic room in a house almost overburdened with the majestic. Facing the entrance doors is a pillared archway with a coat of arms in stone. More columns are to the left and right. A bust of the first Duke is set over a marble doorway. Then your eye is drawn upwards, past high windows, to the ceiling nearly seventy feet above. Here there is one huge oval painting that at first glance looks as though it depicts a classical scene with warriors and half-naked women, a snorting horse, and a triumphal gateway with a flight of steps leading to it. A soldier is kneeling, hands outstretched, pointing to a scroll of paper held by an angel. Opposite him a formidable woman, also helmeted, is holding a wreath and a spear. On the scroll of paper you can just discern the markings of a map with a few red lines drawn prominently across it. It is Marlborough presenting his battle plan for Blenheim to Britannia, the lines on the map showing his and the enemy's

Blenheim Palace, designed by John Vanbrugh to celebrate Marlborough's victory over the French.

troop dispositions. It is an image so pretentious as to be almost comic, but in keeping with the style of the house it succeeds as a superbly confident tribute to Marlborough.

From the Great Hall stretch rooms of incomparable grandeur, with gilded friezes, multicoloured marble fireplaces, tapestries showing, as you would expect, scenes of battle and surrender, more marble doorways, spectacular chandeliers and sparse but ornate furniture. Every item is exciting and exuberant, and none is discreet or delicate. No wonder this English baroque style did not win favour with the refined generation of Englishmen who dominated building during the rest of the century.

One of the many advantages of being an offshore island of Europe, unconquered by an enemy since 1066, is that it has allowed us to absorb influences from the rest of Europe without being dominated by them. Our buildings reflect this. Italian plaster work, Flemish gables, the flamboyant baroque, classical Greek and Roman designs, Gothic, and in more modern times the pure, almost abstract shapes first taken from Germany's Bauhaus school have all had an influence. We have absorbed and adapted but never slavishly followed these trends. The exception is Georgian building, which ultimately became almost besotted with one particular style: the pared-down, simplified form of classical architecture known as Palladian.

Palladio and his golden rules

Andrea Palladio worked as a stone-cutter in northern Italy and from these humble beginnings became perhaps the most powerful influence in Western architecture. When he was in his early thirties in 1541, a patron sent him to study ancient classical architecture in Rome. The result was a revival, first in Italy and then throughout Europe, of buildings designed along the same lines as those of ancient Rome, and their precursors in ancient Greece. Fascination with Palladio first reached Britain in the work of Inigo Jones, Wren and Vanbrugh. But it was not until the early eighteenth century that its full impact was felt in Britain, when Palladio's own *Four Books of Architecture* were published here for the first time in a lavish edition dedicated to George I. At the same time the Scottish architect Colen Campbell published another great tome containing engravings of the principal classical buildings recently erected in Britain. In his introduction he attacks the baroque as affected, licentious and wildly extravagant. Palladio's work, on the other hand, is extolled as better than any of his predecessors and even rivalling the work of the ancients.

These two books took the world of architecture by storm, changing the way the rich chose to build and in effect creating a dictatorship of style. Palladio had set down rules of proportion that successful builders slavishly followed. The ratio between the height and width of a window had to accord with one of seven set formulae. These in turn were similar to the harmonies produced by changing the length of the string on a musical instrument to the

The frontispiece of Palladio's Four Books of Architecture, a fundamental influence on Georgian building.

same ratios. A hundred and fifty years separate the grand villas that Palladio built near Venice from similar stately homes in Britain, but his work accorded with the mood of our eighteenth century. This was an era excited by the use of reason, in science, medicine and astronomy, to explain the world's mysteries. Alexander Pope encapsulated the faith in his *Essay on Man*, which catalogues man's failures but enjoins him:

> *'Know then thyself, presume not God to scan*
> *The proper study of mankind is man.'*

What better for the rational man than to build in a 'rational' style, according to rules in harmony with nature? We have never seen anything like this imposition of one agreed style before or since. We are still addicted to the Georgian today, which blights many of our new developments. Some architects try to follow the Palladian rules, only to discover that modern building regulations for the dimensions of homes or requirements for under-floor computer ducting and air-conditioning can make it impossible to keep to the proper proportions. The result could be called Disfigured Georgian, a sham that neither celebrates the past nor makes one particularly enamoured of the present.

Throughout the century the classical influence held sway, mainly through the study of books and drawings of the ancient world brought back by travellers. In 1753 Robert Wood published careful drawings with precise measurements of the Roman ruins of Palmyra, in Syria. Many architects wanting to emulate the classical style used it as their guide. The sharp-eyed can often spot a direct connection. During the Second World War British forces were fighting in and around Palmyra, where there was a German airfield. At night they would probe the enemy's defensive positions in the ruins of the Roman city. One patrol commander was astonished, on looking up into the roof of one of the grand buildings, to find himself, in his words, 'looking at the ceiling of our dining-room at home'. His home was Stratfield Saye, in Hampshire, bought for the Duke of Wellington by the nation after the Battle of Waterloo. The patrol commander was the his descendant, the eighth Duke of Wellington, and the dining-room at Stratfield Saye had indeed been remodelled in the early nineteenth century by James Wyatt, using the example of Wood's drawings.

The grand Saloon designed by Robert Adam for Saltram House, near Plymouth.

The hidden treasures of Saltram

There are many examples of houses either built or remodelled on classical lines during the eighteenth century. None of them is on the scale of Blenheim Palace, and none of them is intended to achieve that kind of flamboyant public display. If anything, the exteriors of big country houses became more austere as the years passed, though the interiors did indulge a display of wealth that remained within the bounds of classical taste. Some houses seem almost perversely plain. Saltram, near Plymouth, is one of the most striking examples left today, not least because the grandest rooms are unchanged since the eighteenth century.

The house was remodelled in classical style in the middle of the century. From the outside it is uninspiring. It looks more like a nursing home or council offices than a private house. The façades are of creamy white plaster almost unrelieved by decoration, an iced cake that only reveals its riches when you cut into it. And the inside of Saltram is full of riches.

Among the fascinating rooms is the Chinese Chippendale Bedroom with its Chinese-style chairs made by Thomas Chippendale and delicate wallpaper showing the production of tea. Tea was becoming a fashionable drink, displacing coffee and chocolate. It was a luxury, so expensive that it was kept in locked tea caddies. It was served in the finest porcelain. The hot water came from a silver urn and the tea was drunk with a little milk or cream and sugar. The tea ceremony was not as intricate as in China or Japan

but it was nonetheless an occasion, a far cry from our habit of putting a tea-bag in a thick mug. The fine silk wallpaper in the bedroom illustrates the exotic appeal of the new drink. It shows all the stages of tea production, from the planting and picking to the selecting and tasting of the tea, as well as making crates to transport it, packing them, and carrying them across the mountains to the sea. The journey from the tea plantations in China to the tea table in Saltram took over a year.

In the middle of the century Robert Adam the Scottish architect was asked to redesign the interior of Saltram and to add a new drawing-room, known as the Saloon. To walk into this room is to walk into the Georgian era at its most refined. For a start the colours are all pale, creams and pinks and greens, enhanced by gold leaf. Every detail, whether of furniture, mirrors or window hangings, was chosen by Adam. The ceiling is an intricate formal pattern of oval shapes interspersed with painted panels. The floor is covered with a specially woven carpet forty-six feet long and twenty-two feet wide that fills the room. Also designed by Adam, it mirrors the patterns and colours of the ceiling above.

The room was used for grand balls, when the carpet was rolled back and the floor was dusted with French chalk to allow dancers to slide gracefully across it. Even the chalk was patterned. The Countess of Morley described a ball that she gave at Saltram in 1810. 'The Saloon was prepared for dancing and looked quite brilliant and beautiful. We lighted it by hanging lamps over the windows and putting a quantity of candles over the doors, the places in which they were fixed being concealed by large wreaths and festoons of leaves and flowers beautiful to behold. The floor was chalked after an exquisite design of my own, by a celebrated artist from Plymouth. Out of the great window we had a temporary place erected for the North Devon Band which played the dances all night.'

These entertainments were a feature of all big country houses. Wealthy families usually left the heat and dust of London to retire to their country estates for the summer. But during the eighteenth century that habit was being challenged by a new leisure pursuit, with families retreating not to the country but to newly fashionable spa towns, among which Bath was pre-eminent.

The pleasures of Bath

Bath in its heyday was the Xanadu of England's aristocracy and new rich, a summer city devoted to leisure, much as Xanadu was for the Chinese emperors. It had been famous since before Roman times for its hot spring waters, the only springs in Britain where water emerges from the ground at up to forty-five degrees centigrade. Bathing in the water eased aches and pains. But until the eighteenth century Bath was a small town, and in 1700 it had a mere 3,000 residents. A hundred years later its population was 35,000. Its expansion during those years created the finest example of Georgian building and town planning of any city in Britain.

It began as a speculative venture whose success created a unique and highly organised summer retreat from London. The sense of order imposed on Bath's itinerant society is reflected in the appearance of order in its buildings. It was thought fashionable to stay in Bath for a maximum of six weeks. By coach from London the journey could take thirty-six hours, and a grand family would have their arrival announced by the ringing of the bells of the abbey. From the moment they took up residence, usually in rented houses or rooms, they were subject to strict rules of behaviour. This is the most extraordinary aspect of Bath life. It was as regimented as an old-fashioned holiday camp with its own Master of Ceremonies, whose every word had to be obeyed.

The grandest Master of Ceremonies, the man who put Bath firmly on the social map, was Richard Nash. Beau Nash, as he became known, had failed as both a lawyer and a soldier. He was, however, a skilled gambler and a famous dandy. Bath was just acquiring its reputation as a fashionable spa, and Nash came there to try his luck. Such was his charm and elegance (Lord Chesterfield said that dressed in all his finery he was mistaken for a 'gilt garland') that in 1704 he was chosen by the city elders to take over the job of organising the pleasures of the spa. This he did by a mixture of charm and autocratic regulation. He decided where receptions would be held, when dancing would start and finish, how everyone should dress, and even who should dance with whom. As long as they behaved with decorum and were

Thomas Rowlandson's wry cartoon of a ball in the Assembly Rooms at Bath.

well turned out, Nash enabled the middle classes to mix on an equal footing with the aristocracy, a radical step in an otherwise stratified society.

The growing popularity of Bath soon saw the city bursting at the seams. A young builder seized the opportunity to meet the demand for more housing suitable for Nash's grand clientele. John Wood, the son of a local builder, was a speculator on the grandest scale. Speculative building nowadays is often used as a term of abuse, but without it eighteenth-century Bath would not have been created. Wood, who had already tried his hand building 'on spec' in London, and who had nearly gone bankrupt in the process, came back to Bath when he was only twenty-three.

He had a vision of transforming the city, which at the time was still contained within its medieval walls, by renting land outside the walls and developing it. The grandeur of his ambition and the magnificence of his imagination were without parallel. He was supported by a curious and unshakeable faith that history was on his side. He believed in the local legend that long before Roman times Bath had been a great city comparable to Babylon. It had been ruled by King Bladud, King of the Britons and a

John Wood's great Circus. Each floor proclaims its importance with double columns of different styles.

patron of the Druids. After travelling in Greece, Bladud contracted leprosy and returned to Britain, working in disguise as a swineherd in Swainswick, a village just outside Bath. One day he watched his pigs wallowing in a swamp of warm mud. He noticed that they contracted none of the usual pig afflictions of scabs or scurf and so tried the mud-bath himself. It cured his leprosy. He returned to court and was able to succeed to the throne, but his reign was brought to a premature end when, having learned to fly, he unfortunately crashed and was killed.

If a modern speculative builder were to embark on a new scheme by publicising such a vision, he would be politely shown the door by potential investors. It is a measure of the tolerance of eighteenth-century Bath that Wood's plans for developing the city, though controversial, were allowed to proceed. His first project was Queen Square. Wood took out a 99-year lease on the land. He intended from the start to build on a scale that would befit the city of Bladud, and looked to Palladio as his model.

Everything was designed to make life agreeable for its residents. It would be protected from passing traffic (alas no longer true: it is now used as a one-way roundabout). Wide pavements would keep pedestrians clear of the mud flying up from the wheels of passing carriages. Three sides were built with individual houses making up terraces. But the real sensation, a novelty in Britain, was the building of the north side. It looks like a palace. It is one long building with a central triangular pediment supported by Corinthian columns. This palace is divided into separate houses, each with its own entrance and set of windows above. Imagine the front of Buckingham Palace looking just as it does but with a series of front doors instead of one main entrance gateway and you will get the picture. The beauty of the scheme was that everyone living there could feel that they were living above their station.

Wood introduced another clever innovation that became the norm for this type of housing in Georgian Britain. He only insisted on the façade being to his design. He left the construction of the home behind the front door and the windows to other speculative builders who would lease one or more bays and develop them as they saw fit. So, although the fronts of all the grand crescents and terraces in Bath have a pleasing uniformity of design, they are really no more than a curtain for what lies behind. Go round the back and you will see houses of all different shapes and sizes. As long as the front was not altered, anything within reason was allowed to be built behind it.

Just north of Queen Square is John Wood's other great triumph: the Circus. Sadly he died just after laying its foundation stone, but it remains his monument, remarkably unspoilt and now jealously guarded both by its inhabitants and by its listing as a Grade One site. The Circus is made up of three curved terraces, forming a circle. Wood imagined that the space in the centre would be used for games, as in the Roman circus. Today it contains a grove of five huge plane trees.

Wood's terraces were designed with the great Colosseum in Rome in mind. A façade in honey-coloured Bath stone is arranged in tiers. The ground

floor is faced with pairs of simple Doric columns, while above them the mood changes to the livelier Ionic and at the top the dashing Corinthian. Punctuating the narrow ledge that separates the ground from the first floor are curious designs that are said to spring from Wood's interest in freemasonry. There are birds, an owl in a tree, an anchor, a helmet, a scythe and a snake, a face and a harp; an odd departure from Palladio's simplicity.

Fortunately for Bath, Wood's work at the Circus was carried on by his son, John Wood the younger, whose achievements were as spectacular as his father's. After completing the Circus, with its slightly claustrophobic feel of houses keeping an eye on each other, he built the magnificent Royal Crescent. Perched on a hill, the Crescent is a wide curve that seems to embrace the countryside below it. It is not as exciting or as delicate as the Circus, but here the appeal lies in the sheer audacity of building on such a scale, unprecedented in Britain. Thirty grand houses all joined together, and as with the Circus, only the façade designed by Wood himself, the rest of the houses being left to individual builders to finish as they chose.

As a result of the pioneering work taken on by the Woods, father and son, Bath had attracted other speculative builders prepared to take on the commercial risks. By the end of the century there was a cornucopia of streets, terraces and crescents, all in the Palladian style, and mostly from designs taken from pattern books. These books were guides for the builder, rather like a good recipe book for the kitchen. They explained how to build staircases, how to

The great sweep of Bath's Royal Crescent, designed by John Wood the younger (above); and the wrought-iron railings leading to the classical doorway of Number 1, Royal Crescent (opposite).

position fireplaces and what their proportions should be, and the correct placing and size of windows. They included drawings of the proper internal decorations, columns, panelling and plaster work, allowing the builder to satisfy his client's requests without having recourse to an expensive architect.

One feature common to all the grander houses was an entry hall and staircase wide enough to allow a sedan chair, and later a Bath chair, to carry visitors discreetly to and from the spa. The Bath chair was a cloth contraption hung between poles and carried by porters. It allowed a bather to be taken home still swathed in towels. It did not stop in the hall but took the client upstairs to his own rooms, many of these houses being let floor by floor to visiting families.

The grander sedan chair with glass windows was the taxi-cab of eighteenth-century Bath, waiting in ranks outside the Baths or the Assembly Rooms. It was meant to be carried by two bearers of the same size, who shuffled along in a cross between a walk and a run. If they fell out of step the chair would bounce and sway. There are still one or two on display in Bath, and I tried a ride. It was comfortable and fast, though the passenger who took it after me was tipped out on to the pavement when the chair became unbalanced and fell on its side. I assume that when George II's daughter Amelia travelled by sedan chair from London to Bath she chose her chairmen more carefully. Ours were volunteers from Bath Rugby Football Club: burly, but somewhat lacking in finesse.

The Assembly Rooms at Bath, restored after bomb damage in the Second World War, with the original chandeliers.

John Wood the younger has one other grand building to his name: the new Assembly Rooms. They were built to provide an elegant setting for the twice-weekly balls held during the season, with other rooms for taking tea, playing cards and gambling. The ballroom is the largest eighteenth-century room in Bath, able to hold over a thousand dancers. It must have been a dazzling sight, with families dressed in their finery, observing each other, noting the latest fashions, and discreetly pairing off daughters with suitable suitors.

The room had no windows at ground-floor level, to ensure privacy from the prying eyes of the less privileged out on the street. It was lit by immense chandeliers, over eight feet high and burning forty candles each. They are among the oldest and finest in the world, each an intricate construction of crystal arms splaying out from the centre with pendants hanging from them. Fortunately, at the start of the Second World War they were dismantled and stored in safety, for the Assembly Rooms were bombed by the Luftwaffe in the so-called Baedeker raids in 1942, when Bath was attacked in retaliation for the bombing of the medieval city of Lübeck. The Assembly Rooms were restored and the chandeliers are now back in their rightful place. I watched them being cleaned. The whole chandelier was lowered from the ceiling to floor level by pulleys hidden in the roof, and each pendant was unhooked, washed and dried, and laid out on the floor so that it could be hung back in the right place.

There were other spa towns that offered similar entertainments to those at Bath, among them Tunbridge Wells, Buxton, Brighton and Cheltenham. All have traces of their Georgian past, but there was, and there still is, nothing to match Bath for its beauty, just as nothing matched it for its indulgence in luxury. Its attractions were castigated by the Methodist Charles Wesley who said that preaching in Bath was 'attacking the Devil in his own headquarters'. But then he had come over from Bristol, which is just down the road but a very different kind of city.

Bristol and the slave trade

Where Bath was dedicated to pleasure, Bristol was dedicated to trade, and particularly to the trade in slaves. Until 1698 all trade in slaves with the West Indies was the legal monopoly of the Royal Africa Company, but in that year, under pressure from ports such as Bristol, which wanted a share of the lucrative business, the monopoly was broken and a century of prosperity for Bristol began. The first ship to trade legally from Bristol was suitably named *Beginning*. Between her voyage and Britain's abolition of the slave trade in 1807, half a million slaves had been shipped from Africa to the Caribbean in Bristol ships, a fifth of the entire British trade in slaves.

The rationale for the trade was very simple. For some time European settlers had been working sugar and tobacco plantations to meet the growing demand for these commodities across the Atlantic. At first they used native workers until, wasted by disease and maltreatment, this source of labour died out. There were some European workers, mainly convicted criminals or the

very poor who crossed the ocean to work as indentured labourers, but not enough of them. Africans were in any case deemed better suited to the heat of the Caribbean. The outlines of the trade are well known. Ships from Britain would sail carrying all manner of goods ranging from guns and brass to cotton, beads, glass and pottery. The slave traders in West Africa took these goods in exchange for slaves, as many as 600 per boat. They could be prisoners captured in war, or convicted criminals, or people simply abducted from their homes. The ships set sail for the Caribbean, where they sold their human cargo and reloaded with sugar and tobacco for the journey home.

Bristol profited at every stage of this triangular trade. The city made or imported from other parts of Europe the goods they intended to trade in Africa. The cotton came from India or from Manchester, the guns from Birmingham. But local industries grew up to provide glass, pottery, iron and brass pans and all manner of knives: pocket-knives, penknives, scissors, razors, fleams (for leeching blood from humans or animals), and lancets – all, as one Bristol shop advertised, 'Articles suitable to the African Trade'. When the ships returned from the West Indies, Bristolians again set to work, processing the tobacco leaves, and turning the raw sugar into refined sugar-loaves for cooking, or for distilling into rum.

During the eighteenth century Bristol prospered from this boom in trade. The city's population of 20,000 grew to 60,000, every one of them needing housing. Many of the rich merchants invested their profits in big town houses, and as at Bath these were provided by speculative builders,

The crowded port of Bristol in its heyday, painted by Nicholas Pocock. There were so many vessels that they had to be moored side by side, 'ship-shape and Bristol fashion'.

offering individual mansions or houses in terraces and crescents. There is one particular house in Bristol that survives almost as it was in the eighteenth century. It was built by a plantation owner who had made his fortune on the island of Nevis and returned to settle in Bristol.

In 1764 John Pinney set out for the West Indies when he was only twenty-four to manage a sugar estate that he had inherited. On his arrival he discovered that the plantations were run down and many of the 140 slaves too old or sick to work. He set about buying replacements, pointing out in letters home that slaves were the 'sinews' of the plantation, and that 'it is as impossible for a man to make sugar without the assistance of negroes as it is to make bricks without straw'. Nevertheless, for all his justification, he had qualms about his first purchase of slaves. He wrote: 'I have purchased nine negroe slaves ... and can assure you I was shocked at the first appearance of human flesh exposed for sale. But surely God ordained them for the use and benefit of us; otherwise his divine will would have been made manifest by some particular sign or token.'

After nearly twenty years in Nevis, Pinney sold the plantations, came home, set up in business in Bristol as a sugar trader and commissioned his family house to be built at Great George Street. Number 7, Great George Street is a fine example of a middle-class home towards the end of the century. Apart from one eccentricity in the basement it follows a pattern that would have been seen in hundreds of houses built in Britain at the time. The exterior is not quite of classical proportions, the windows being a little on the small side for the walls around them. The ground floor is of simulated stone blocks, or rustication, the upper two floors being smooth plaster over brick. There are steps up to the front door, which has a fanlight over it and a pillared portico.

The engine-room of this house is the basement, with its kitchen range and spits for roasting joints over the fire. A large kettle provided hot water where it was needed for the whole house. There is a separate bread oven to the side of the main range. There are metal cooking pots and pewter plates for the servants to eat from, china being deemed too valuable. Beyond is a laundry and drying room, and the housekeeper's room with places to store food and keep the best porcelain and linen. The basement is connected to the upper floors by speaking-tubes, an efficient means of communication often used between the bridge and the engine-room on ships. The eccentricity in the basement is a small indoor swimming pool lined with bath stone. Pinney made a habit of taking a cold bath every morning, 'which I finds to be of great service to me'.

Upstairs on the ground floor there is a study with built-in bookcases and a mahogany writing desk. There must have been a fuss about the fireplace in this room, which is made of the rare Derbyshire Blue John (from the French *bleu et jaune*), a fluorspar, like a cross between crystal and marble, coloured deep blue with traces of yellow. Pinney had an estimate for the fireplace of twelve guineas. He noted that the bill came to twenty, but added tersely, 'paid twelve guineas'. He was equally cautious over the banisters for the staircase, which being in the fashion were made of cast iron. To keep costs down he employed one craftsman to make the simple uprights in Bristol and had the more complex decorative work done in London.

The ground floor also holds the breakfast room and the dining-room. Both look out over the garden and down to the city below. A butler's lift connects these two rooms with the kitchen. Pinney's best china adorned with his coat of arms was kept here. Upstairs is the drawing-room, the library and a further small drawing-room. Here Pinney kept a reminder of his time in Nevis, a painting of the island from St Kitts, done by a fellow Bristolian, Nicholas Pocock, a sea captain turned marine artist, who had made twelve voyages to the West Indies. On the floor above were bedrooms and dressing-rooms for the family, and in the attic five servant's rooms. Here no doubt the black slave Pero, whom Pinney had bought when he was only twelve, would have slept. Pero came with Pinney from Nevis to serve in Pinney's household, a phenomenon quite common at the time. A black servant was thought to give a household an air of glamour and sophistication.

Number 7, Great George Street is the epitome of Georgian building towards the end of the century, but for all its carefully balanced shapes and its properly proportioned rooms there is a flaw. It is a bit dull. Apart from the swimming pool there is nothing original here, no twists and turns of corridors, no surprises of the kind the Elizabethans and the Victorians relished in the planning of their homes. Everything is neat and orderly and predictable. It is the same with the many terraces and crescents that the later Georgians built, offering house after house of such similar layout that you could walk into your neighbour's house and find your way around it even in the dark because it would be just the same as yours.

Abolition and Wesley's New Room

It takes time for buildings to respond to changes in social habits or the mood of the times. You might deduce from the quiet Georgian terraces built in Bristol towards the end of the eighteenth century that this was a period of calm in the life of the city. But in Bristol as in the rest of Britain it was a time of change: the start of the Industrial Revolution, which was to upset the old order over the next hundred years.

Bristol had its own particular turmoil in the movement to abolish slavery. A city so dependent on slavery was inevitably divided on the issue. Many, including Pinney and his new partner in the sugar business, James Tobin, were strongly against abolition, and Tobin wrote pamphlets urging the retention of slavery. It was a practical as well as a moral issue for the city.

Looking back on it now, it seems so obvious an evil that you might think all people of good sense would be in favour of abolition. But it seems not to have been self-evident at the time. In 1805, two years before abolition, the poet William Wordsworth wrote of 'the contention which had been raised up against the traffickers in Negro blood' while admitting that 'that strife had ne'er fastened on my affections, nor did now its unsuccessful issue much excite my sorrow'. Wordsworth, fascinatingly, was a friend of Pinney. When he was twenty-five he had stayed at Number 7, Great George Street and went on to live for two years in Pinney's house in Dorset. He would have known of Pinney's views, and yet his sister Dorothy wrote: 'William is very much delighted with the whole family, particularly Mr John Pinney.'

Less welcome in the Pinney household, I suspect, would have been two of Bristol's famous firebrands, the founder of Methodism, John Wesley, and his brother Charles. John Wesley came to Bristol in 1739, when he was thirty-six. He had already established a reputation as a firebrand, travelling the country to speak out against the social ills of his time. He decided to make Bristol the headquarters of Methodism, building the first chapel of the movement there. The New Room, as it was called, still stands. Having narrowly escaped enemy bombs in the war, it is now encroached on by Mammon. It hides behind its wrought-iron gates in the middle of the Broadmead shopping centre, surrounded by Next and Boots, Marks and Spencer and Debenhams. A £200 million development is its nearest neighbour.

Wesley's New Room with its two pulpits – the scene of a riot when he preached against slavery.

The chapel itself is very simple, but not inelegant in its own way. To one side is the stable where Wesley and his band of travelling preachers kept their horses. The chapel itself is one large room with pale brown stone pillars supporting the roof. At the far end is a double pulpit, the lower part used for readings from the Bible and prayers, the upper part, with a window allowing

light to flood down on it from behind, reserved for preaching. The rest of the light comes from an octagonal lantern window high above. Just below the lantern are small windows that give on to a series of rooms on the first floor where Wesley and his fellow preachers could eat and sleep.

Sensible precautions were taken to protect the preacher. There is no access to the pulpit from the floor of the chapel, so that dissenting members of the congregation could not reach the preacher directly. To reach it you have to climb up to the gallery and then back down to the pulpit itself. There are also no external windows at ground-floor level. Crowds gathering outside to protest at the message Wesley was proclaiming could not see in, nor riot by stoning the windows. This was a building designed to ensure as far as possible the safety of those inside.

They were wise precautions. Wesley had been campaigning for some time against slavery. In 1774 he published a pamphlet attacking the trade. 'Where is the justice of inflicting the severest evils on those that have done us no wrong?' he wrote, '... of taking away the lives of innocent inoffensive men; murdering thousands of them ... year after year, on shipboard, and then casting them like dung into the sea?' Fourteen years later he was preaching in the chapel against 'that execrable villainy' when in his words, fighting broke out among the congregation and 'The terror and confusion were inexpressible. The people rushed upon each other with the utmost violence, the benches were broken in pieces ... Satan fought lest his kingdom should be delivered up.' Wesley was no stranger to violence. His sermons (he gave 40,000 in his lifetime) were often given before huge crowds in the open. Seen as a threat to the established order ('utterly incompatible with social or civil society', Dr Johnson said), he was attacked by mobs, stoned, and on one occasion seized and had his hair cut off.

The groundbreaking turnpike road

Methodism was able to spread its message because of a revolutionary change in the infrastructure of Britain. Improved communications in the eighteenth century made travel between one part of the country and another faster than had been dreamt possible. The revolution was no less dramatic than the creation of the railways in the nineteenth century and changed life in fundamental ways. Mobility, after all, is freedom. Freedom for Wesley to travel 25,000 miles on his mission. Freedom for smart Londoners to reach Bath in only ten hours by the end of the century, whereas it had taken sixty hours at the start. The revolution was the simple concept of the turnpike road.

Before the turnpike, British roads were slow and dangerous, often no more than muddy tracks in which coaches and carts would sink up to their axles. In theory they were maintained by the parishes they passed through. In practice they were too expensive to keep up and were largely neglected. In 1706 Parliament passed an act that allowed local businessmen, who had a vested interest in better communications, to build roads and charge for their use. The turnpike was a gate across the road, often with a house for the gatekeeper to live in, so that tolls could be extracted from road users day and night. Some of these toll-houses still stand, like little pepper-pots, with their windows on all three sides nearest to the road so that even from his bed the keeper could see who was approaching. They are now rather too close to the traffic thundering past, but are still prized by people who like the security of living in a doll's house with its octagonal sitting-room, heated by a blazing fire, and an octagonal bedroom above.

From the middle of the eighteenth century turnpikes spread out from London until the whole country was connected by a spider's web of roads, over 50,000 miles by the end of the Georgian era. The methods of road construction improved as the demand grew. Two Scottish engineers played a key role: John MacAdam, who invented a way of grading stones so that they held firmly together under the impact of coach wheels, and Thomas Telford, his contemporary. Telford adapted MacAdam's methods with a road surface of large cobble stones laid as a foundation and overlaid with finer stone, the precursor of modern concrete and asphalt roads. His greatest road was planned to run from London to Holyhead on the Isle of Anglesey, or Ynys Mon. This scheme involved spanning the Menai Straits, for at the time Anglesey could only be reached by ferries sailing the dangerous, fast-flowing waters of this narrow, rocky gap between it and the Welsh mainland.

The London to Holyhead route was needed for political reasons. Until 1801 Ireland had its own parliament in Dublin, with a House of Commons and House of Lords, but with the British monarch as its sovereign. It was therefore not quite independent nor yet wholly dependent. Relations were strained by uprisings against England fostered by Irish nationalists with the backing of France, with whom Britain was at war. There had even been an attempted invasion by France, with a small force landing on the Pembrokeshire coast. In 1800, after the suppression of the Irish liberation movement, it was decided to abolish the Dublin parliament, merge it with Westminster and run the country from London. This engendered a continuous flow of Irish parliamentarians, civil servants and troops between Ireland and Britain, with Holyhead in constant use, as the most convenient port for Dublin.

Telford's road crossing was intended to carry this traffic. The Admiralty insisted that it should not impede the passage of ships and demanded a bridge one hundred feet above the water. Telford controversially insisted that this was possible. He designed a suspension bridge, longer than any previously built, to stretch across the strait between two huge stone towers. The daring of pioneering bridge builders such as Telford and Brunel after him was recognised by a fascinated public, who celebrated every stage of the construction.

In April 1825, when the first of sixteen massive chains to hold the roadway was winched up into place, Telford was there to watch, accompanied by local vicars and gentry. Pleasure boats decked with flags sailed backwards and forwards below, and three Welsh workmen employed on the site daringly crossed the straits on the chain. Ten weeks later, when the final chain was raised, a band played 'God Save the King' from a platform slung between the

Thomas Telford's spectacular bridge across the Menai Straits to carry the turnpike road from London to Holyhead, and so to Dublin.

two piers. In September, when the decking was in place, there was a twenty-one-gun royal salute. Finally a crowd of 5,000 watched the official opening in January 1826, when for the first time the Royal London and Holyhead Mail coach was able to cross by road instead of ferry, followed by a cavalcade of 130 coaches.

We have become blasé about new bridges these days. The bridge over the Humber and over the Thames at Dartford each broke records in bridge design at the end of the last century and merited a mention on the television news – but were then forgotten. We seem quite wrongly to take these thrilling engineering feats for granted.

Georgian Dublin

The Dublin that Telford's road was designed to make more accessible was a city that, in its heyday during the Georgian era, deliberately challenged London by the sumptuousness of its building and the grandeur of its conception. Dublin in the eighteenth century was under the control of the Anglo-Irish or the Protestant Ascendancy. These families had come to Ireland over the centuries and, with their own parliament to govern them, prided themselves on being apart from England. The Ascendancy excluded Roman Catholics, who had lost much of their land, were not allowed to hold public office, were not allowed to stand for parliament and could not serve in the armed forces. The ruling élite, though sharing the same monarch as Britain, considered themselves in most respects to be a different, independent country and sought to demonstrate this in the development of their capital.

The River Liffey, flowing through the city, featured at the start of this development when it was decided in the seventeenth century that instead of turning its back on the river, the city should make the Liffey its focal point, with houses and public buildings facing on to it. Where London so often fails to make use of the Thames as a setting for its most important buildings, the centre of Dublin is enlivened by the river flowing through it.

In the eighteenth century a city sprang up with grand public buildings and spacious houses. There was even a 'Wide Streets Commission', controlling the width of pavements and the setting of avenues and terraces, to allow the city to breathe. Typical of the independent spirit of Dublin was the Parliament Building, begun in 1729, whose grand classical entrance with six huge columns supporting a pediment was used a hundred years later as the model for the British Museum. It was the first purpose-built parliament building in the world. Another grand building from the Georgian era is the Royal Exchange, now the City Hall, again with a classical portico. There are the buildings of Trinity College. There are the Four Courts, built to administer the four arms of justice, with a shallow dome supported by a central drum with columns around. And then there is the magnificent Custom House, built on the banks of the Liffey in 1781, with its fine façade complete with arcades, columns, statues and a dome.

Both the Custom House and the Four Courts were badly damaged at the hands of the IRA during the Civil War of 1921–2 that followed the partition of Ireland. The grand homes of Dublin, on the other hand, were nearly lost to decay following the Act of Union with Britain, which saw many of the Anglo-Irish élite abandon Dublin for the new centre of power in London. More recently much of what was left was savagely destroyed by the redevelopment of the city in the 1960s. It took a long and sustained campaign by the Irish Georgian Society to open Dubliners' eyes to what they were losing. Thanks to their efforts we can still see something of what Georgian Dublin was like, and very fine it is.

These were houses built for a particular way of life. On the outside they are plain, apart from their doorways, whose pillared porticoes and fanlights are now used to advertise the city's attractions in tourist publicity. On the inside they are lavish, with wide staircases leading to huge rooms for entertaining, decorated with unique Dublin plaster work. This had a style of its own, not restrained as in London houses of the era, but lively with images of faces, musical instruments, garlands of flowers and birds. The birds are everywhere, birds feeding and fighting and flying.

Number 12, Merrion Square, now offices, was built in 1764 by William Brownlow, a landowner and linen manufacturer. It was the second grand house he had built, and he kept records of every stage of its construction. When he leased the land it came with only one proviso, that it should be 'good and substantial ... three storeys and a half above the cellar, with a front area of eight feet and a flagged pavement of ten'. He built in brick, although he could have used stone for the ground floor, which his landlord offered from his own quarries at a discount.

Inside, the plasterer was given a free hand and was rewarded with a bonus for doing the work well. There were Wilton carpets, and damask curtains. The chandeliers and candelabra were imported from London. Brownlow's accounts show purchases of a silver writing stand, silver cutlery, a toothpick case, and even, giving an insight into the Georgian life-style, green tea and chocolate. It seems that he looked to France for his clothes. He returned from a tour there with embroidered silk waistcoats, silk stockings and gloves, silver buckles, and quantities of velvet, silk and lace.

Some of these houses are still in the process of being restored after the ravages of time. Number 13, Henrietta Street, for example, is one of the grandest houses in a grand street that fell on hard times after the Act of Union. The family who live there today bought it just over thirty years ago. Like many of the houses in the street it had fallen into disrepair, with multiple occupation. Its grand rooms had been subdivided and even cut in half horizontally to make an extra floor. You can still see where the plaster has been cut back and doors and staircases have been altered. There were eleven separate lettings in this house, with thirty-six people occupying them.

Michael Casey, who is slowly restoring Number 13, explained that after the Act of Union the rich no longer wanted to stay where there was no political

Dublin: the Custom House on the banks of the River Liffey (left); and Mount Street (right). The doorways have elegant fanlights.

power, and they became absentee landlords both of their Irish estates and of their houses in Dublin. Those who remained had spent lavishly on building them but were too impoverished to maintain them. Ireland's problem was that with no natural resources of coal and iron it had no Industrial Revolution, and it was not until the last half of the twentieth century that Dublin once again began to thrive.

What a difference between Ireland and Britain. In Britain, the Georgian era, with its belief in the power of reason and its enthusiasm for scientific research, was now reaping the reward in advances in technology that marked the start of the Industrial Revolution. Harnessing our natural resources of coal and iron, discovering the use of steam to drive pumps and engines and so mechanise work that for centuries had been done by hand, the Georgian age was underpinned by rising prosperity. Roads and canals provided a new, efficient infrastructure. We stood on the verge of a new era that would change the nature of Britain and of course the buildings of Britain, out of all recognition: the Victorian century.

ELSEWHERE IN GEORGIAN BRITAIN

1714–1837

I went to Oxford, Bath, Bristol and Dublin in pursuit of the Georgian, but its influence is to be found throughout Britain. It is impossible to imagine our cities and towns without their elegant Georgian houses, terraces and churches. Yet these buildings were once novel and daring works of architecture, created in response to radical social and economic change. During the eighteenth century Britain was involved in the first stages of the Industrial Revolution. Its cities were growing fast and the landscape was subject to new types of farming and industrial exploitation. At the same time roads and canals across the country were being constructed to improve communication. Beyond the shores of the kingdom, the expanding empire was creating a huge market for British goods and introducing novelties from abroad to the pleasure-hungry rich. Trade was also involving Britain in the first truly global conflicts in history.

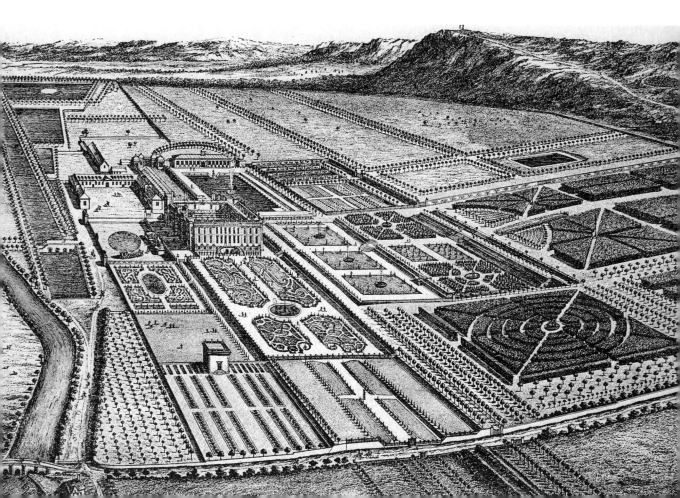

< CHATSWORTH HOUSE
DERBYSHIRE

From 1685 William Cavendish, first Duke of Devonshire, began to alter his inherited seat at Chatsworth. This view, dating from around 1700, shows the new classical façade he added, overlooking the vast formal gardens in the foreground. The new design was much influenced by contemporary French architecture. The castle-like façade of the original 1550s building with its twin-towered gatehouse is just visible to the left. At the same time the interior of the house was remodelled. This illustration is from a collection of aerial views by Kip and Knyff.

v ST MARTIN-IN-THE-FIELDS
LONDON

The medieval church of St Martin-in-the-Fields, Westminster, was rebuilt by James Gibbs in 1721–6. Gibbs's creation now overlooks Trafalgar Square, which was created in the 1820s, and has become one of the symbols of London. The spire is a particularly ingenious adaptation of a medieval architectural form in the classical style. St Martin's has inspired many copies, particularly in parts of the former British Empire. The interior is spaciously arranged with box pews and galleries. This view by David Laing was painted around 1825.

RANELAGH GARDENS
LONDON

The interior of the rotunda at Ranelagh Gardens in Chelsea, painted by Antonio Canaletto. Opened in 1742, the rotunda formed the centrepiece of the pleasure gardens. The interior was 150 feet across and heated by a central fireplace. Around the sides of the building were booths where small parties could drink wine and tea. There was also an orchestra stand. The gardens were described as 'crowded with the great, the rich, the gay, the happy and the fair; glittering with cloth of gold, and silver lace, and precious stones'. Ranelagh Gardens closed in 1803 and the rotunda, tragically, was demolished.

< COASTAL FORTIFICATION
PORTSMOUTH

By 1800 Britain had clearly emerged as the foremost imperial and maritime power in the world. But the sea, which carried British ships to every corner of the world, also offered enemies direct access to her shores. The Napoleonic Wars in particular encouraged a burst of coastal fortification focused on ports and potential landing places. Semaphores with swinging arms and flags permitted the rapid transmission of important information along the coast and to London. The investment in coastal defences continued in stops and starts until as recently as the mid twentieth century.

< FOXTON LOCKS
HARBOROUGH

Before the arrival of railways, canals played a crucial role in the industrial development of Britain. Their creation was a huge undertaking in both financial and engineering terms. This stair of ten locks on the Grand Union Canal was designed to raise the canal up the side of a 75-foot hill. Opened in 1814, they connected the Grand Union with the Leicester and Northampton Union Canal, begun in 1793 and one of the main links between the Midlands and London. It took about forty-five minutes and around 30,000 gallons of water to get each boat through the Foxton locks.

< WHITEHAVEN
CUMBRIA

Whitehaven was a prosperous colliery and port town from the late seventeenth century. It developed on a regular plan under the direction of local landowner and industrialist Sir John Lowther, who died in 1706, and his younger son James, who died in 1755. Prior to the growth of Liverpool and Bristol in the nineteenth century, Whitehaven dominated trade with Ireland and the United States. It was in Lowther's lifetime that the mines on which the town's prosperity depended were driven under the sea, an astonishing technical achievement. James also developed the system of turnpike roads around the town.

∧ ROYAL PAVILION
BRIGHTON

The great kitchen of the Royal Pavilion at dinner-time. The Prince Regent, whose visits in the late eighteenth century helped make Brighton fashionable, extended a farmhouse to create the Royal Pavilion. The finished building is a spectacular piece of fantasy architecture in a predominantly Indian style. The great kitchen of 1816 by John Nash is largely functional, with whitewashed walls, large windows (or lanterns for work at night), and a high ceiling to dissipate the heat. The fantastical treatment of the columns as palm trees is a reminder that this building was a pleasure palace.

TURNPIKE ON TOTTENHAM COURT ROAD
LONDON

A lively cartoon from the pen of Thomas Rowlandson (1757–1872). In his youth Rowlandson had led a somewhat dissipated life in London, which gave him an insight into the ways of the city. His drawings are humorous and affectionate. Note, for instance, the fat man on the right trying to squeeze between the bollards, the elderly man ogling the milkmaids and the chaos as the bucking horse is urged to drive past a boy on a donkey and a lady unable to control her mount. A reminder that, while the buildings might be elegant, life was still often rough and dangerous.

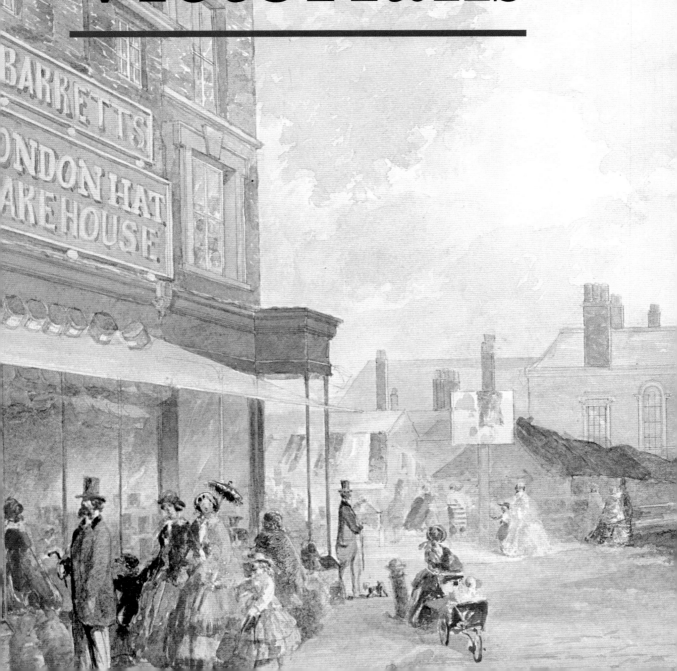

The
Victorians

The North
Full Steam Ahead

IN THE LONG SWEEP OF DAYS SOME MOMENTS SECURE FOR THEMSELVES A PERMANENT PLACE IN THE MEMORY. One of my unshakeable memories is of an idyllic day on the Berkshire Downs many years ago. It was like a scene from a Thirties film. Girls with their thin cotton skirts blowing in the breeze, giving glimpses of warm sunburnt calves, young men, awkward but excited, laughing as they strode ahead, and an old horse-drawn cart creaking up the hill carrying rugs and hampers for a picnic.

At some point in the afternoon I found myself standing next to a shabbily dressed man in a battered hat who asked me what I was going to do with my life. Flattered by the attention, but unable to define my confused ambitions, I muttered something about not knowing which way to turn. His advice was as unexpected as it was typical. 'Why don't you go into a monastery for a week or two and think it out?' Perhaps I should have taken the advice, but I never did, plunging instead into the first and most obvious opportunity that presented itself. But John Betjeman's suggestion, delivered in his slightly melancholy way, opened up the prospect of new possibilities, of a path through life that I had never thought of. He had this ability, given to few, to open our eyes to the world around us and make us look at it afresh. It is apparent in his poetry, and also in his powerful writing and broadcasting about buildings.

Of all the commentators on the Victorian era Sir John Betjeman must take first prize. He should have been presented with a trophy: a model of some public monument in silver gilt, crowned with pinnacles, and with statues of soft-bosomed women curled round its base. Its flowery inscription in Gothic script would record his contribution to our understanding of Victorian architecture, and it would of course have been paid for by public subscription.

Betjeman's passion for Victorian buildings changed the way a generation looked at them. Some buildings are easy to admire. It would be eccentric to find a carefully proportioned Georgian house ugly, or any Georgian building for that matter, let alone a Tudor or Elizabethan one. Perhaps the patina of time rescues buildings from obloquy. Victorian buildings are a different matter. Until recently many of them were written off as unworthy of preservation and demolished. It was thought ludicrous to want to preserve them. This may be partly because there is no single Victorian style to use as a standard by which to judge the buildings. They are by turns exuberant, flamboyant, quirky, turbulent, pompous, and sometimes unbearably gloomy. Betjeman and his fellow proselytisers taught us how to look at them.

Life in the slums

It helps to imagine yourself back at the start of the Victorian era, as one of the millions of poor who made up the majority of the population, living in the vilest of conditions, working long hours in a dangerous and unhealthy factory, your life made bearable only by recourse to cheap gin. This way of life has been well recorded, though few traces of it remain.

There is a jeweller's shop in Manchester that has a trapdoor into the cellar. It has no windows, but in one corner there are the remains of an open fire and a bread oven. The records show that, early in the nineteenth century, sixteen families lived down there in the half dark. They were by no means unique. In 1830, 50,000 workers lived in cellars in the city. There was no other accommodation for them. An earnest enquirer into the condition of the poor once visited a similar cellar in London and asked an old lady how she could live in such crowded conditions. Her stoical reply was that it was all right 'until the gentleman in the middle took a lodger'.

Life in a Manchester slum in the 1890s. During this period the city's cellars housed 50,000 workers.

The most vivid account of conditions in Manchester is to be found in *The Condition of the Working Class in England* by Friedrich Engels, which was published in 1844. Engels, who later supported Karl Marx financially and with him wrote *The Communist Manifesto*, was the son of a German industrialist who owned a cotton factory in Manchester. Sent to the city by his father, he was shocked at what he found. He was particularly incensed that the city was built in such a way that it was possible for the middle classes to go about their daily work and seek their pleasures without ever noticing – let alone coming into contact with – the poor on whose labour they depended. All the main thoroughfares were lined with clean and tidy shops. The poor lived out of sight in the streets behind them.

Engels wrote that it was hard to convey a true impression of the filth he saw: privies overflowing with urine and excrement, no cleanliness, no convenience, so that no proper family life was possible. In such dwellings 'only a physically degenerate race, robbed of all humanity, degraded, reduced morally and physically to bestiality, could feel comfortable and at home'. He described how he had tried to explain to a fellow businessman how dire living conditions were. 'The man listened quietly to the end and said at the corner where we parted: "And yet there is a great deal of money made here; good morning, sir."'

Engels was not alone in his outrage. The pictures of Victorian worthies, posed stiffly in their frock-coats, which reprimand our frivolity from the walls of a hundred town halls, may suggest a society that was uncaring and complacent. But among these men were visionary reformers who were determined to use the wealth of the age to eradicate the worst of the poverty and to offer the prospect of improvement both physical and spiritual. The best illustration of their intent is to be found underneath Manchester, or any other great Victorian city, in the sewers.

Underground ingenuity: the sewers of the north

In forty years from 1800 the population of Manchester had grown from 95,000 to 310,000. The cotton trade, expanding with steam-driven machines, lured workers from the countryside to seek a better life in the city. The same happened in Sheffield on the back of iron and steel production, in Bradford and Leeds through the woollen industry, and in Liverpool from the trade created by Britain's burgeoning economy.

The cities were unprepared for this influx of labour. The consequence of a tripling in size of the population was a tripling of waste. In Manchester 70,000 tons of human faeces a year had somehow to be disposed of. Some of it was just thrown into the street, to mix with the urine and washing water that ran into the gutters as a stinking grey sludge. Filthy children played in filth. Disease was rife.

No wonder life expectancy in these cities was lower than it had been at any time since the Black Death, 500 years earlier. Conditions were so bad that the government had to act. A General Register Office was established in 1837 to collect statistics on health. They revealed thousands of deaths a year from typhus and cholera. The report from Manchester spoke of unpaved streets acting as open sewers, obstructed drains, ditches full of stagnant water, dunghills and pigsties 'from which the most abominable odours are emitted'. I have myself seen living conditions like this in the slums of Bombay and Calcutta, and the sight of those cities today is a reminder of the scale of the problem that the Victorians faced.

The city fathers' determination to eradicate the worst effects of the prosperity that industry had created took a number of forms. Arguably the most important step was not the grand buildings, the town and city halls, nor the institutions for education, nor the care of the poor and the sick. It was the sewers. Without these none of the rest would have been possible.

It is difficult to visit a sewer these days. Health and Safety regulations with their often absurd injunctions have put paid to that. An official visit to Manchester's sewers would have required a two-day induction course, so I took the informal route. Chris Denson and James Westbrook call themselves 'drainers'. Their original hobby is to track the course of drains under cities by walking the length of them. Their favourite drains are those of London and Manchester, and they hope one day to walk a drain believed by them to run from the Bank of England to Buckingham Palace. MI5 might fear the worst but their intentions are wholly innocent. They love the excitement of underground exploration and the whiff of danger – to stay nothing of the whiff of the sewers.

They are infinitely ingenious. On one occasion, trying to gain access to a particularly difficult drain, they donned yellow plastic jackets and posed as workmen. It is astonishing, they told me, what you can get away with if you wear a yellow jacket. They had invented a company called ENVIROMEN and, using signs bearing its name, they closed the road, lifted a manhole cover and disappeared into the depths. They have never yet been caught, though they admit to one or two narrow escapes.

I met them on the outskirts of Manchester on a grey, drizzling morning. They were in shorts and T-shirts. I, expecting to be cold and wet, wore boots and an oilskin. I need not have bothered. We clambered down muddy a bank and through a pool into which the drain flowed. From there we stepped up into the mouth of the drain.

I was prepared for rats and a dripping roof, but apart from a steady stream of water underfoot it was dry and clean. By torchlight Chris and James showed up the workmanship of the Victorian builders, the close-fitting bricks all neatly pointed with cement. The quality of Victorian workmanship is always surprising. As much care was taken over the appearance of brickwork that, once completed, would never be seen as was taken over that subjected to public scrutiny. To find such attention to detail several feet underground and a hundred yards from daylight was to see a pride in workmanship far beyond anything the drain demanded.

Taking responsibility for public health

The requirements of public health brought to a head one of the most curious debates of the Victorian era. Some towns and cities had their own local government, but their nature and efficacy varied greatly. Many were inefficient, corrupt and, despite the Great Reform Act of 1832, still not elected by universal franchise. In 1835 a Municipal Corporation Bill was introduced with the intention of reforming local government and giving municipalities the power to take responsibility for sewage and street cleaning. In the political and philosophical societies that proliferated in Victorian England this aroused strong passions.

The debate centred on whether central or local government was the better way to achieve social improvements. This argument sometimes turned fancifully on whether Britain was culturally better attuned to its Saxon or its Norman past. The Saxons were seen as having ruled regionally, independent of any central power. The Normans by contrast had insisted on central control. The debate was fuelled by the popularity of Sir Walter Scott's novel *Ivanhoe*, with its romantic description of pre-Norman England as an idyll destroyed by William the Conqueror and his followers.

So what had this to do with public health? Only that the big issue in the northern cities was whether they should be individually responsible for the state of their infrastructure or whether Westminster should have the power to insist on improvements. This is an old battle. Saxons against Normans. Provinces against London. And nowadays local government against centralised power. Centralised power always seems to win in the end. There were many disputes on councils between those who wanted improvements and those, often backed by the ratepayers, who argued, believe it or not, that it was cheaper to let the poor die than to spend hard-earned money on drainage. In 1848 a Public Health Act was proposed which would have been able to force municipalities to act to ensure proper drainage and a sewage system. *The Economist* called the proposal 'little better than a plan for despotism'. Shopkeepers and ratepayers called it 'unsaxon'.

Cramped conditions: back-to-back housing

In Leeds there are still vestiges of one of the great conundrums that faced Victorian reformers: back-to-back houses. Back-to-backs are not terrace houses that simply back on to each other, with a yard or perhaps an alleyway between them. The true back-to-back was built for cheapness, with neither back-yard nor back-door. The only windows were at the front. The back walls of the terrace houses in one street formed the back walls of the terrace houses in the next.

Today these houses seem cosy enough. They have had inside toilets and bathrooms installed. When they were built they had no such luxuries. You either used a portable toilet inside the house, which had to be carried out of the front door to be emptied, or you walked down the street to the shared public toilets. The disadvantage of the toilet block was that you might have to queue and everyone in the street would know when you needed to go.

In 1840 the House of Commons passed a law prohibiting on health grounds the construction of any further back-to-backs.

There was one neighbourly benefit of the back-to-back that still survives in Leeds. Since the householders have no back-yards in which to hang their washing, they rig up a system of pulleys across the street from one house to another. The traffic waits while shirts and pants are pegged to the line and then hoisted up out of the way.

The age of Mrs Beeton

As the nineteenth century went on, the Victorians developed the terrace houses and small villas that still predominate in most of our towns and cities. They are well built of brick and have dividing walls that are often just thick enough to stop one family overhearing clearly what their neighbours are saying but, tantalisingly, not quite thick enough to cut the sound out altogether. The house was designed to be a refuge from the world outside, a self-contained shrine to family life.

Great care was taken over presenting a good face to the outside world, chiefly in the form of the front room overlooking the street. Even though this room was rarely used, the family usually congregating in the parlour or the kitchen, it was kept spick and span as a place to receive visitors. It would be decorated with displays of ornaments, clocks, stuffed birds, holiday souvenirs,

Supper table with decorations from Mrs Beeton's Book of Household Management, a guide for the upwardly mobile middle class.

religious texts, paintings or prints and needlework, and there would be hard upholstered chairs on either side of the fireplace and perhaps a piano against one wall. These were homes for a new middle class, the clerks and overseers, the shopkeepers and tradesmen who flourished as the economy grew. They were acquiring a new life-style with its own rituals, its own precisely defined social boundaries. This was the age of Mrs Beeton, whose 1861 *Book of Household Management* came to the rescue of many an upwardly mobile family. Beeton was their bible, leading them, for example, through all the hazards of employing, as most did, a servant: how to set them a good example by rising early and organising the day, and how to achieve a relationship that was cordial but not over-familiar.

The hum of industry

Moving up the social scale, it is impossible to overstate the pride that the Victorian businessman, industrialist or local politician (often one man fulfilling all three roles) took in his achievements. Britain had become the richest and most powerful nation on earth. The factories of the north of England imported raw cotton from abroad, processed it and re-exported it as woven material. All day and night the mills hummed and clattered.

The canals brought coal to drive the steam-engines that had replaced the earlier, water-driven looms and spinning and weaving machines. These men ranked their achievements with those of ancient Greece or Rome, or with the merchants of fifteenth-century Italy. They deliberately built in a style that recalled those past glories. If you travel through the centre of Manchester today and look up above the modern shop fronts to the grand buildings above, you can easily imagine yourself to be walking the streets of medieval Florence. You would need, of course, to ignore the constant drizzle, which was itself an essential part of Manchester's recipe for success, providing the damp climate that working with cotton requires.

The grandest buildings are often not the mills themselves but the warehouses in which traders displayed their wares. One is now a hotel: the Britannia on Portland Street. It was once the warehouse of S. and J. Watts and was in its time the largest building in Manchester. From the outside it is like a palace. If you look carefully you can see a mixture of styles: one storey Italian, the next French and the one above with a touch of English Elizabethan. The exterior is original and imposing. The interior is dominated by a magnificent set of staircases that runs from the ground to the seventh floor. Each staircase is joined to the next via a delicate wrought-iron bridge that looks remarkably and probably intentionally like a bridge over a Venetian canal.

The landings reached from one end of the building to the other, each floor selling different goods. Linens and carpets on the ground floor, dresses and woollens on the first, followed by fancy haberdashery, bags and portmanteaus, then ribbons, silks and underclothes and lace and millinery and furs. In short, S. and J. Watts was like a department store, though it was

The Britannia Hotel, Manchester, formerly the S. and J. Watts warehouse, built in contrasting styles (left); and the intricate metal work of its glorious interior staircase, which rises seven floors (right).

designed to sell mainly to retailers who came to order in bulk for their own shops. Bridget Graham, who cleans the hotel, took me as high as it was possible to go and held my hand to protect me from vertigo as we gazed down seven floors on to the vast chandelier below. 'Oh dear,' she said, 'there's a bulb gone. I'll have to tell maintenance.'

Shopping and the new arcades

I think it would be fair to say that the Victorians invented the idea of shopping as a leisure pastime. You will need to go to Leeds if you want proof. The four Leeds shopping arcades are unmatched anywhere. Harrogate has arcades but not on the same scale, as does London. But in Leeds you can smell trade. It was here that in 1884 a 25-year-old Russian émigré called Michael Marks had the brilliant idea of setting up a stall with a sign that read: 'Don't ask the price – it's a penny'. He later joined up with a Tom Spencer, and together as Marks and Spencer they did so well that City Markets has a modest clock on a green pillar commemorating Leeds's contribution to the retail trade.

It was technology that made it possible. Arcades with glass roofs to protect shoppers from the rain were the product of new materials and building techniques, as were the plate-glass shop-fronts that replaced the windows formed from little panes of glass in the traditional Georgian shop. Plate glass revolutionised luxury shopping. It was no longer a pastime reserved for the rich, because it was no longer necessary to go into a shop to enjoy shopping. Window shopping had become a diversion for people of all classes and incomes, who were also treated to further entertainments. Thornton's

arcade is distinguished by a clock with figures from Scott's *Ivanhoe* ringing the hours at one end and the Duchess of Devonshire at the other (a model based, it is said, on a portrait by Gainsborough).

Leeds's civic pride is reflected in these arcades. City Markets, or Kirkgate as it was originally called, was built at the very end of the Victorian era. It has a glass roof held up by a tracery of cast iron. In the roof are the coats of arms of this wool city inevitably bearing the image of a sheep. The markets were opened with great pomp in 1904. The ribbon was cut by G.W. Balfour, President of the Board of Trade, with Leeds's aldermen and councillors in attendance, as well as mayors from neighbouring towns. Today the markets are home to a mixture of shops selling everything from olive oil and nuts to shoes and pork pies. Moore's Confectionery is a sweet-shop from the Thirties. It sells sarsaparilla, white mice, jelly worms, and sweets in the shape of baby dolphins; fried eggs, cola cubes, and rhubarb and custard. There are fizzy giants, sweet tobacco, friendship rings and liquorice pipes. 'People come down here to stock up before they go down to London,' says the assistant. On cue an elderly lady, on her way south, asks for a bag of gobstoppers for the journey – here was one Yorkshirewoman determined not to be accused of talking too much.

The County Arcade, Leeds, showing the use of wrought iron and glass to make a seductive covered market where workers could window shop in comfort.

The magic of the music hall

Charles Thornton, who built the Leeds arcades, also gave the city the 'New Music Hall and Fashionable Lounge', to which I made my way. Music hall is a tradition that has almost died out, despite energetic efforts to revive it. I remember as a child watching *The Good Old Days* on television in some embarrassment. It was one of the longest running programmes in television's brief history – from 1953 to 1983. An audience in fancy dress, stiff white shirts for the men and ostrich-feathered hats for the women, kept up a barrage of insults against performers and against the host, the master of ceremonies, who sat in a box at the corner of the stage dominating the event with a series of unspeakable puns. I could never work out whether these were real lovers of traditional music hall or whether they just liked being on television and showing off.

On a wet Monday morning I came in search of the magic the Victorians found in this theatre. The auditorium is true late-nineteenth-century, with red and gold everywhere: red metal pillars and red plush seats, with two galleries hung with gold swags. According to careful exploration by restorers, the ceiling was once duck-egg blue but, as in so many theatres of this age, gas lighting and cigarette smoke have taken their toll and the plaster is now a rich brown, no doubt matching the lungs of the smokers. Waiting on stage was a music hall revivalist, Jan Hunt. She sang for me 'The Boy that I Love is Up in the Gallery' and Marie Lloyd's 'I'm a Bit of a Ruin that Cromwell Knocked About a Bit', followed of course by 'My Old Man Said Follow the Van and Don't Dilly-Dally on the Way'. I am ashamed to say that it took little prompting for me to join her on stage and belt out the chorus.

Jan's knowledge of the history of music hall is prodigious. She likes Leeds, because the theatre is designed to create an intimate atmosphere, with audience and performers close to each other. Audiences were encouraged to cheer or barrack or boo as they chose. It was from music hall, she told me, that the old theatrical term 'to bring the house down' originated. At Leeds and many other theatres the proprietor was also the landlord of the neighbouring public house, and if the show was going well he would 'bring the house down' to the theatre to watch.

Temperance lodges

The pleasures of the working class and the new lower middle class emerging in the cities were looked upon with suspicion by Victorian employers and those with high moral scruples. In our dressing-up box at home there used to be a small white and pale blue silk apron. As children we could never work out why it was there. It was useless for dressing up – not a patch on the real leather cowboy chaps my father had brought me back from Calgary. One day my grandmother explained all. The purse was part of the insignia her father had worn at meetings of the temperance lodge.

If you have ever thought that belonging to a Freemasons' lodge might not be the most exciting way of spending your evenings, imagine belonging to a temperance lodge. My grandmother had solemnly taken the pledge as a child and sworn to do her utmost to extirpate the demon drink. In later years she broke the pledge with brio, unlike my great-grandmother, who died believing that alcohol had never touched her lips. No one dared tell her that on her ninetieth birthday the orange juice she had been inadvertently handed and which she said was the best she had ever tasted was laced with vodka.

My family were Methodists, a movement that was in the van of the temperance movement. Methodists were rightly appalled by the drunkenness of city life, where work was hard and gin was cheap. There were pubs selling alcohol on every corner, some beautifully tiled, with mahogany counters and fine cut-glass mirrors to tempt the drinkers in, others far less salubrious. But among them in the Victorian era sprang up temperance pubs, like pubs in every respect except that they sold no liquor. Only one of several thousand now survives: Fitzpatrick's in Rawtenstall, Lancashire.

Fitzpatrick's is a tiny corner pub rented appropriately from the Methodist church next door. It was founded by Malachi Fitzpatrick, who had a chain of similar pubs across Lancashire. It sells dandelion and burdock, sarsaparilla, black beer and raisins, blood tonic and of course ginger beer, most of them quite sweet and none of them alcoholic. It is not exactly the place you would go with your mates to watch football on the big screen. There is in any case barely room to stand at the bar, and only a couple of small tables to sit at. But Fitzpatrick's is a striking reminder of the culture of self-improvement that the Victorians embraced with such ardour.

Fitzpatrick's temperance lodge – the last of thousands of alcohol-free pubs that were built by the Victorians to counter the demon drink.

Designing the 'ideal' village

A place that had no need of a temperance pub as an antidote to the lure
of the demon drink was Saltaire, near Bradford. Its creator, Sir Titus Salt,
simply refused to allow pubs into his model village. Salt was a fascinating
man, adventurous, innovative and paternalistic. In his early years he worked
in the wool trade in Bradford. With his father he imported fine wool from
Turkey and Peru to improve the quality of the cloth. He won prizes both
at the Great Exhibition of 1851 and four years later at the Paris Exhibition.
Instead of resting on these laurels he embarked in his late forties on an
astonishing experiment. He built a new mill and an entire village, as large
as a small town, in the countryside outside Bradford. He hoped that his
work-force would live a healthier and more fruitful life here, for both
their benefit and his.

  I first came to Saltaire while on a canal holiday and was quite unprepared
for the sight that met us as we nudged the narrow boat round the final bend
before the mill itself. Its scale is huge. Its upper floor, which housed the looms,
is over 500 feet long; when it was built it had the largest unsupported roof in
the world. It towers over the landscape and overwhelms the village. It has the
canal and the River Aire running alongside it to provide power, together with
the new railway line, that brought the canny Salt to this particular site. When
he opened the mill he pledged to do all that was in his power to avoid 'evils
so great as those resulting from polluted air and water' and said that he hoped
to 'draw around him a population that would enjoy the beauties of the
neighbourhood' and who would be a well-fed, happy body of operatives.

The village of
Saltaire. From left,
Salt's Mill, on the
bank of the Leeds
and Liverpool canal;
Saltaire's typical
cobbled streets;
and the memorial to
Sir Titus Salt in the
church that he built.

His architects had been instructed to spare nothing in the attempt to provide housing that would be a model for the whole country. The evidence that they succeeded is that modern Saltaire is now a des-res for executives from Bradford, as the purring of BMWs and Mercedes morning and night testifies.

Salt had clear ideas about how the perfect town should be built. Every house in the rows of terraces that run down to the canal and the railway had its own back-yard leading on to a lane that ran between the streets. The view down these lanes is to open countryside. At the corners of the streets, perhaps to keep an eye on the work-force, are larger houses for senior operatives. The top managers had houses with front gardens. So hierarchy is preserved, but in a layout that delights the eye. In addition to over 800 houses, there was a hospital and forty-five almshouses for the retired.

Salt was keen on keeping up appearances. He forbade residents to hang out their washing, instead offering them a central wash-house and drying area, though it seems that the no-washing rule was hard to enforce. He built a fine institute, protected by statues of lions (rejects from the competition for the lions of London's Trafalgar Square). The institute offered reading rooms, a lecture hall, which could seat 800, a gymnasium, a smoking room, art rooms, billiard rooms and a separate quiet space for chess and draughts. There was even a drill hall for the 39th West Riding Rifle Volunteers, who were based in the village. This institute was intended to 'supply the advantages of a public house without its evils'. Salt himself had not taken the pledge; indeed he kept a cellar of fine wines, but he saw no point in offering his workers similar pleasures that would be to his commercial disadvantage.

Titus Salt did not live in his own village, but he is buried there. He was a Congregationalist, and today his church is a United Reformed Church. Now listed Grade I, it was opened in 1859. It is the grandest building in the village, set back from the houses, with a pillared portico and a tall tower that feels just a little out of proportion, as though it might have been designed for somewhere else. The interior is dominated by an organ standing where you would find the altar in an Anglican church. The walls are pale blue, with mottled columns looking like marble separating the windows. In the entrance is a statue of Sir Titus Salt, made of the finest Carrara marble. At its base stand an alpaca and an angora goat, the beasts whose silky fleeces helped make Salt's fortune. There are fruits and olives to suggest peace and plenty. Did ever a man feel more assured of his fame and glory than this? And how he must have relished the inscription: 'Presented to Titus Salt Esq. by the work people in his employment as a token of their respect and esteem'. Perhaps he wrote it himself.

The Congregationalist church at Saltaire, with imitation marble pillars, heavy chandeliers, and an organ at the east end.

Self-help and the Victorian ideal

We tend to mock the Victorian concept of self-help these days, or to see in it merely a cynical attempt to create a docile and industrious work-force. But self-improvement was at the heart of the Victorian ideal and led to the building of the era's greatest monuments. Its noble, anti-aristocratic objective was the political and social elevation of both middle and working classes. Samuel Smiles, whose life spanned the nineteenth century, was its best exemplar. He spawned a host of irritating nostrums, some attributed wrongly to him, such as 'A place for everything and everything in its place' and 'The shortest way to do many things is to do only one thing at once'.

Smiles was a radical reformer. After studying medicine at Edinburgh he became a doctor, but he took a close interest in politics and in parliamentary reform. At twenty-five he gave up medicine to become editor of the *Leeds Times*, where he championed votes for everyone, not just the property owners granted the franchise by the Reform Act of 1832. He supported the Chartist movement and anguished about the high unemployment in Leeds, where in 1839, 10,000 were without a job. Later in life he was a supporter of Robert Owen and his socialist prescription for a better society. *Self Help* is the book for which he is best remembered. There and in his other writings can be found the essence of the Victorians' admirable belief that man's best hope for a better life springs from within himself. Smiles was not ashamed to urge his readers to strive always to do better: 'He who never made a mistake, never made a discovery'; 'Man cannot aspire if he look down; if he rise he must look up'; 'The work of many of the greatest men, inspired by duty, has been done amidst suffering and trial and difficulty. They have struggled against the tide, and reached the shore exhausted'; 'Observation, attention, perseverance and industry', taught Smiles, are the road to wisdom and understanding.

Some unfortunates, of course, fell by the wayside, and for them a different fate was in store. The Victorian workhouse seems to have been a place deliberately designed to force men back to work: poor relief legislation in 1832 had replaced the old system of individual parishes taking responsibility for the relief of their own poor. The philosophy of the new approach was that the poor should be coerced into working, and conditions in the workhouse should be so dismal that they would strive to leave at the first opportunity. The old workhouse in Ripon is a vivid reminder of this harsh regime. The notices on the walls tell much of the story. No male could be accepted unless his entire family came to suffer with him. Once inside, men and women were separated. Women with bastard children or suffering from venereal disease were forced to wear a special uniform with a distinctive yellow jacket and put on a diet of bread and water.

The buildings emphasise the grim conditions. One corridor, reserved for tramps, has small prison cells leading off it. But the rooms for permanent residents were no better. The first annual report of the Poor Law Commissioners in 1835 urged that the rooms should be no bigger than those found in a labourer's cottage, since substantial rooms 'were a luxury as attractive to the pauper as food and raiment'. The approach to poverty could be summarised by the words of the historian Thomas Carlyle: 'If paupers are made miserable, paupers will decline in multitude. It is a secret known to all rat catchers.' But Carlyle, as Henry James memorably described him, was 'an old sausage fizzing and spitting in his own grease'.

Lunatic asylums

If miserable conditions were thought to be the right treatment for the poor, what is one to make of the lunatic asylums that sprang up under the Victorians to house those who were suffering from all kinds of mental disorders? It is as though they felt it justified to be ruthless when they thought they could influence social behaviour, but when faced with intractable problems they decided just to act as decently as they could. Lunatic asylums may have been partly obscured from public view, approached by drives that curve away from the main highway (hence, it is said, the expression 'going round the bend'), but their grandeur suggests institutions proud of their place in the world. High Royds in West Yorkshire opened in 1888 as the West Riding Pauper Lunatic Asylum. It could just as easily be a university college, public school, town hall, library or museum.

 High Royds is a building that makes clear it has nothing to apologise for. Dominating its imposing Gothic façade is a high, square clock tower that can be seen from the moors. The entrance hall has stained-glass windows,

High Royds, founded as the West Riding Pauper Lunatic Asylum in 1888. Its impressive front (left); the ballroom and stage (centre); and the prison-like corridors for the more dangerous inmates (right).

202

amber tiles on the walls, and a black-and-red mosaic floor decorated with black daisies and the white rose of York. The hall leads to a vast ballroom with a properly sprung floor, lit by chandeliers. Dances were given weekly. With its own library, shops, bakery, butchery, dairy, cobblers, upholsterers, fire station and mortuary it was a self-contained community.

The wards and living quarters were high ceilinged, light and airy. To modern eyes it may seem callous to have locked up over 2,000 patients here, just a small share of 100,000 inmates across Britain. But in the nineteenth century there was no known treatment for depression, nor any way of alleviating it. The use of drugs for treating depression and schizophrenia did not develop until 1945. The only drug to which the doctors at High Royds had access was opium. If the language they used to identify different categories of inmates – imbeciles, idiots, dangerous lunatics and the mentally convalescent – sounds coarse, it is because so little was known about mental illness. A hundred years from now historians may well look back on our treatment of the mentally disturbed with equal astonishment.

Incidentally, High Royds closed in 2003. It is now being developed as a village with flats, housing for the retired, and every kind of luxury facility. Probably the mortuary, with its marble slab and semicircular viewing seat to watch the dissection of the dead, will not be retained. But the clock tower and main buildings will continue to dominate the parkland in which they are set, imposing and confident, just as their builders intended.

The Victorian debate: classical or Gothic?

When the Victorians built their great public buildings for music and the arts, of which St George's Hall, Bradford, was one of the first, they believed that they could encourage working people to discover that there was more to life than the drudgery of their work and solace in the pub. They felt that they were the inheritors of the great civilisations of the past, hence the grandeur of the great St George's Hall in Liverpool, which looks back to ancient Greece as its model. St George's Hall must rank as one of the most beautiful classical buildings in Britain. Its setting is superb, on rising ground, with the slightly less exciting Walker Art Gallery facing it across the cobbled square, and its columned façade is in perfect balance.

One of my favourite classical buildings: St George's Hall, Liverpool.

I came to Liverpool across the perilous waters of the River Mersey on the *Royal Daffodil*, a ferry ride that used to be provided by monks from Birkenhead Priory. It is only a short distance across, but the tides and currents run so fast that the brothers' journey could take up to two hours. That was in the twelfth century. Today it is a mere twenty minutes, just enough time to take in the spectacular approach to Liverpool by water. In its heyday it was one of the greatest seaports in the world and it has the buildings to show for it, not just the impeccably restored docks, but a host of trading houses in the centre of the city.

Among them is one building in particular which caught my attention. Although Victorian, it is so radical that its architect became the victim of his own far-sightedness and barely worked again. Peter Ellis used the strength of cast iron and plate glass to create an office block of which Norman Foster or Richard Rogers would be proud. Oriel Chambers is not a large building, but it is effectively all glass. 'Greenhouse architecture run mad' was the cruel comment of *Building News*, whose back numbers provide a contemporary commentary on the architecture of the period. Another critic called it 'a cellular habitation for the human insect'. Odd how something so pleasing to the modern eye could be so upsetting when it was built, but what you like and what you hate in building are always subjective. There are no rules to taste.

The fashion for classical buildings or Italianate palazzi was fostered by *The Builder*, which in 1849 published an article called 'Hints for street architecture', providing illustrations of Italian palaces. But there was a counter-culture at work that turned its back on such powerful images of commercial wealth. It was fostered by those who thought that the ethos of modern industry was wrong, and that man should return to the working practices and aesthetics of the Middle Ages for inspiration. Foremost among them was the writer and critic John Ruskin.

Like William Morris, who was influenced by him, Ruskin believed that the curse of mechanisation was that it reduced men to automata. 'Men were not intended to work with the accuracy of tools,' he insisted. Ruskin urged builders to return to the romantic Gothic style of architecture. He was scathing about the pretensions of the new northern cities. Manchester could 'produce no good art and no good culture'. Bradford, which had been rash enough to ask him

to judge the competition for their new Wool Exchange, received a broadside. 'You cannot have good architecture merely by asking people's advice on occasion,' he told them. Architecture was produced by a desire for beauty, and for a city such as Bradford 'no architecture is possible'. Quite properly undeterred by this harangue, the burghers of Bradford continued their lively debate on the best style: Renaissance or Gothic? They plumped, incidentally, for the kind of delicate Venetian Gothic that Ruskin thought they did not deserve.

When Manchester came to build a new town hall in the 1860s, it too chose Gothic. Of the 136 entries in an open competition Alfred Waterhouse's ingenious and practical design was deemed the best. Waterhouse had been based in Manchester for over a decade before moving to London. His list of successful commissions reads like a list of the most striking Victorian architecture. Apart from the Manchester Town Hall he designed the Assize Court, Salford Jail, the Royal Infirmary in Liverpool, the Natural History Museum, the Prudential Assurance Building, St Paul's School and the National Liberal Club in London, and the Union Debating Buildings in both Oxford and Cambridge.

One test of a building is to ask what is it trying to say and whether it has succeeded. After a morning in the gloomy interior of Manchester's town hall I had no doubt what Waterhouse wanted it to say. It is a paean of self-congratulation, a recognition of the power of the great cottonopolis. From the mosaic bees set into the floor and the cotton plants embossed on the panelling to the organ in the Great Hall, this building celebrates success.

Today the town hall is still the centre of the city's administration, conducted in the language of modern bureaucracy: a notice on one door announced a meeting of 'the Community Regeneration Overview and Scrutiny Committee'. Upstairs in a deserted corridor are trophies from an earlier age. The extension of the gasworks in Bradford Road is commemorated by a sculpture of light, power and heat – presented to the Chairman of the Gas Committee. In another glass case is a table centrepiece in silver gilt given to Malcolm Ross for raising £35,000 by public subscription for three parks for the use of the people of Manchester and Salford 'to enjoy healthful recreation'. Nearby sits the gift to the Town Council of a huge punch bowl and two loving cups presented by 'the overseers of the poor'. A trifle lavish, perhaps, for those with such responsibilities? Outside the town hall is another curious sign, erected on 5 November 1980 to commemorate the 'world's first city to be declared a nuclear free zone'. Perhaps they should now declare themselves drug and terrorist free.

As for the design of the town hall, it is infinitely curious. As you climb the circular staircases, whose banister rails house gas pipes for lighting, you feel you could be in a Gothic church, probably in France. The internal courtyards are dismal. The daylight everywhere feels as though it has to fight its way through. The Great Hall with its murals by the Pre-Raphaelite painter Ford Madox Brown is undoubtedly grand, even if its ceiling offers a comic touch by giving the coats of arms of Bradford and Salford an equal place alongside those of the United States and Japan. But I felt there was something gloomy about the building, grand as it is. A visit to the bell tower cheered me up. I found the carillon and, no doubt to the surprise of neighbouring cafés and shops far below, played 'While Shepherds Watched their Flocks by Night'. Christmas had come to Manchester in May.

Recapturing religious fervour

On another May day, again cold and wet, I shared one Victorian's vision of heaven. I was standing in a church that its architect himself described, with no qualms, as 'perfect', and I was listening to a choir singing Gregorian plainchant. I think Augustus Pugin, for he was the architect, would have been pleased at the sight of this small choir, robed in white, singing the only music he considered appropriate for worship.

Pugin had converted to Roman Catholicism at the age of twenty-three. His passion for what he considered to be the only true religion, abandoned by England to its loss at the Reformation, has to be set in the context of the era. The influx of so many working families from the countryside to the new cities of the north had created a religious crisis. In their country villages, under the watchful eye of the local squire, many families still attended church as a hangover from their feudal obligations. But once in the cities and free to act as they chose, many abandoned religion altogether.

The huge Victorian churches built in so many cities suggest to the modern eye that they were put there to meet a need. Even if today they attract

congregations numbered in tens and twenties, in those days surely they were packed out each Sunday? But not so. They were usually half empty. Religious observance was stronger in the host of other places of worship used by the Methodists, the Unitarians, the Congregationalists, the Baptists and the Quakers. These groups spoke more forcefully to men and women who had to some extent been freed from the class-ridden obligations of village life and the Established Church of England.

Pugin believed that Roman Catholicism stood the best chance of coaxing lapsed worshippers back to church, and he had firm views on how it should be done. He was scathing of the many Roman Catholic churches that had been built in Britain in an Italianate style. He believed that they reinforced a prejudice against Catholicism by implying that it was a foreign religion, unsuited to Britain, almost unpatriotic. He thought the contrary was the case.

Pugin was convinced that the Gothic style of the Middle Ages, or pointed architecture as he called it, was the only appropriate style for Christian buildings. He looked for perfection to the parish churches built in the reign of Edward I. St Giles Church in Cheadle embodies his most profound beliefs. The spire is a striking 200 feet high, a 'heaven pointing spire' in Pugin's words, 'forming a beautiful and instructive emblem of a Christian's brightest hopes'. As you go inside, the church seems at first to be relatively – and with Pugin it is only relatively – plain. The windows at the west end are clear glass, but as you advance up the aisle the building takes on a greater intensity until at the east end, where the altar stands, Pugin offers a vision of heaven with two saints on either side, angels playing musical instruments and the Virgin being crowned.

High above the arch that frames the altar is the Doom – a painting of the Last Judgement – which appeared in many medieval churches as a reminder of what would befall those who did not make it to Heaven. The whole church is full of colour, the walls and ceiling painted or tiled. It is like an open jewel box with precious stones tumbling out: a dazzling display.

Pugin was very particular about churchyards. He disliked the Victorian habit of adorning graves with half-draped urns or broken columns, pagan symbols that for him had no place in a churchyard. He hated the new municipal cemeteries filled with flamboyant graves and tombstones. Some people find the Victorian approach to death over-sentimental. Personally I rather warm to it. We tend to forget that they led much harsher lives than we do today, with disease rife, treatment of illnesses often rudimentary, and many children dying very young. The instinct not to allow such deaths to go unmarked seems understandable and admirable.

Sadly, monuments on the scale of the Victorians' are no longer permitted in most cemeteries. The baleful hand of the Health and Safety Executive forbids monuments to be erected more than four feet high. Those monuments still left standing, with their angels praying, their children weeping, their temples and their broken pillars, can now be subjected to a pressure test to see if they can be made to fall over. If they do topple, as some inevitably do, they are demolished or re-laid ignominiously flat on their backs.

Dynamism and innovation

I began this account with the Victorians' ingenious response to the problems posed by the unprecedented growth of Britain's new towns and cities. I cannot end it without celebrating their originality and confidence, evident everywhere they built. Factories and warehouses, bridges and viaducts, railway stations and churches, schools and lunatic asylums: their verve is astonishing.

Steam was a driving force of change throughout most of the century, as more and more sophisticated methods of harnessing its power were invented. Mills had once been driven by water power, with great paddle-wheels turning relentlessly under the pressure of the flow from streams and rivers. With a complex array of great leather belts, they drove all the machines on all the floors of the mill. During the nineteenth century water power gave way to the more reliable and more powerful delivery of energy from steam-engines, with their huge, coal-fed boilers working day and night. Steam-engines have a magic of their own. Steam is elegant, sophisticated and almost silent, except for a faint hiss and the melodious clicking and clunking of the pistons it drives and the great array of cogs and levers and arms that move in time to its beat.

I have seen steam driving the huge beam engines with their tall, cast-iron columns surmounted with classical capitals that lifted water from the Thames at Brentford to Notting Hill Gate. I have watched gleaming brass and steel silently turning the wheels of a paddle-steamer. I have sat perilously on top of the boiler of a steam car, steering not with a wheel but with a tiller, as on a boat. I call it perilous because if it had blown up, which is not unknown, the driver and passenger risked being projected forcefully from their seats. Nothing, however, beat the thrill of being invited to stand on the footplate of a railway steam-engine.

The City of Truro was built in 1913, just after the Victorian era, and was the first engine to break the 100 mph speed record. It still runs majestically across the North Yorkshire Moors from Grosmont through Goathland to Pickering. Occasionally it makes forays further afield to Cheltenham or Bath. Wherever it goes, its driver John Fletcher told me, people still run to the edge of the line and wave, just like the Railway Children, though when the railways began they were more likely to run away. These monsters belching steam and smoke and moving at speeds never before seen must have been terrifying.

The train changed Britain in the nineteenth century as profoundly as the motor car in the twentieth century. It brought town and country closer, allowing city dwellers easy access to the moors or the seaside. It imposed its own discipline. To run efficiently trains need timetables, and timetables depend on the time in Bristol, for instance, being the same as the time in London. Before the railways, different cities had different times. Each town or big house could set its clock by the sun at noon, with a variation that depended on how far east or west of Greenwich the clock was. But if clocks did not all tell the same time, a train leaving London for Plymouth would make up twenty minutes of clock time (roughly the difference between the time of

Boarding the City of Truro to experience the excitement of steam travel.

midday at both places) and would lose twenty minutes on the way back to London – a variation of forty minutes. Standardised train time changed all that, with huge station clocks and the station-masters' watches on their chains all synchronised, from Penzance to Inverness.

Not surprisingly, the railways were controversial from the start. It was not safety that was the issue, though the early safety record was poor. It was their impact on the towns and countryside they cut through. Railway mania was the name given to the bouts of intense speculation that marked the Victorian embrace of the railways.

Thousands of miles of track were laid down in only a few years, and wherever the railway went there were complaints. Landlords objected to the despoliation of their property. Farmers complained that the smoke from the trains was damaging the fleeces of their sheep. Cities such as Oxford originally refused to have a station, because it would be too disruptive, and to this day the line to Oxford is more of a branch than a main line, meandering through bucolic countryside towards Wales. Lines were driven through city centres. In Newcastle they knocked down the castle walls; at Lewes, in Sussex, they built a viaduct over the high altar of the earliest Cluniac monastery in Britain. The magazine *Punch*, taking a jaundiced view of this desecration, suggested St Paul's Cathedral as the best choice for the main-line terminal for London, arguing that once all the railways came right into the city, it would be fit for nothing else.

The novelist William Thackeray described people like himself, born before the railway era, as belonging to another world. The gulf between now and then was so great, he wrote, that he felt as Noah and his animals must have felt coming out of the Ark after the flood to see a new landscape. On the side of change were the great engineers, foremost among them the Stephensons of Newcastle and Isambard Brunel, along with the financiers and the investors who saw the chance to make their fortunes by providing capital for the new enterprises. In 1837, during one of the sporadic bouts of railway mania, the architect George Godwin wrote an 'Appeal to the Public' describing the benefits the railways would bring. Godwin was editor of one of Britain's first and most influential architectural magazines, *The Builder*, which kept up a running commentary on Victorian developments throughout the century. He believed that the railways, with their stone viaducts, bridges and depots, would embellish the country – and how right he was. There is scarcely a Victorian station, whether the smallest wayside halt or the grandest terminal, that is not still a source of delight.

Newcastle, home to the railway, is among the finest. Supported by cast iron, a high curved glass roof was built to protect passengers on the platforms. The railway here cut like a scimitar through the city centre, through the castle beside its keep, and across the River Tyne in two places so that it formed a loop. (To this day it is the best turning place between London and Edinburgh, sometimes alarming passengers who start their journey from Edinburgh

The imaginative use of cast iron for the pillars and the roof allows Newcastle's railway station to curve gracefully through the centre of the city.

Sir Hiram Maxim's magnificent flying machine. He believed that if visitors enjoyed the experience of flying they would back his plans to build a real plane.

facing forwards, as after the train is turned, putting them back to the engine, they think they are on their way back to Scotland.)

The impact of the main concourse, once so elegant, has been slightly spoilt by a shiny black ticket-office opened in 1985, reminiscent of the Kabba Stone in Mecca, and by the little food-franchise booths. The grand entrance hall, meanwhile, with its strong stone classical pillars, stands intact and sends out a clear message: You can trust us. Given that 146 people were killed on the railways in 1853 in just six months, some reassurance was needed. Outside the station is a bronze statue of George Stephenson dressed in a Roman toga. On the plinth around him one figure holds a piece of railway line, another rests on a steam train. A statue of his son Robert, dressed in a frock-coat rather than a toga, stands in Euston Station in London. The Stephensons were the great pioneers of the railway, visionaries who fought off opposition to pursue their dreams, building the first locomotives in the world as well as the first line, the Stockton and Darlington Railway, which opened in 1825.

The fairground and the flying machine

My final stopping-point in search of the Victorian age was Blackpool. Here, on the South Beach, there is a reminder of the Victorian passion for exploring and developing mechanical skills. Sir Hiram Maxim was born in America, where as a young man he invented a reusable mousetrap, but by adoption he was a Victorian. He settled in England, possibly to escape some complex marital difficulties. He was knighted for his invention of the Maxim gun, which could fire over 600 rounds a minute, and which was used by Britain in the Matebele wars, while being wisely acquired at the same time by the Germans, the Austrians, the Italians and the Russians.

In his later years Maxim's interest turned to powered flight. He managed to fly a hundred yards at two feet off the ground with a twin-engined machine, but ran out of funds for developing it further. He decided to raise money by making a captive flying machine, so that the public could enjoy the sensation of flying without its dangers. He made four machines, of which one remains among the gleaming silver and plastic of the fairground in Blackpool. It was built in 1904, which I suppose just removes it from our era, but I include it because it typifies the Victorians' sense of enterprise. I took to the skies in it and whirled round and round, trying not to fall out. It seemed a great deal more exciting in every way than being strapped to a seat and shot a hundred feet in the air, which had my neighbours in the fairground screaming in terror and delight.

Blackpool itself provides one of the great insights into the spirit of the Victorian era. Its tower, modelled on the Eiffel Tower in Paris, was erected in 1896. A revolutionary construction, it served no other purpose than to provide pleasure for the workers of the cities of the north-west who flocked here for Wakes Weeks. These were holiday weeks, when all the factories in a town would close while the employees went to the seaside for a brief respite. Today

215

its exuberant ballrooms, the Empress and the Tower, are still exciting, their gilded ceilings adorned with buxom, semi-naked figures who disport above while couples circle decorously beneath.

I have spent far too much of my life sitting in the gallery at Blackpool listening to aspirant politicians droning away the afternoon at party conferences. But now at last I have taken to the floor and whirled and twirled the foxtrot, leavened by a little modest jiving to the sound of the mighty Wurlitzer organ. A much healthier way of passing the time.

At the end of the century the floor would be full at the *thé dansant*. Blackpool in 1890 only had 7,000 houses, but during a Wakes Week it could squeeze in a colossal 250,000 visitors. The Victorian era, which had begun with such hardship, ended with these first signs of leisure spreading to the working class. Numbers are falling now, despite efforts to rejuvenate the town. It is cheaper to fly to Spain or Florida, and maybe there is something to be said for avoiding the summer gales hurtling in from the Atlantic. Perhaps a time may come, however, when global warming will bring prosperity back to our most famous seaside resort.

The buildings of the Victorian era give the impression of a society gradually coming to terms with the social problems thrown up by the Industrial Revolution and the influx of millions from the countryside to the cities where work could be obtained. The energy and imagination with which the Victorians grappled with the conflicts they faced was impressive. We tend to think of them as stuffy, but in many ways they were far from conventional. We never really enjoyed their inheritance. The upheavals that followed their time – two world wars and the loss of our Empire – meant that we had a new set of problems to face in the twentieth century. In our attempts to deal with them we often floundered, sometimes found original solutions, and frequently ran ahead of ourselves, devising ways of living that many people were not happy to adopt: it was the age of modernism.

The Tower Ballroom, Blackpool, with the Wurlitzer organ playing. The designers wanted to provide luxury for the working classes on their brief escapes from factories and mills.

ELSEWHERE IN VICTORIAN BRITAIN

1837–1901

The Victorians confronted the architectural problems of their age with extraordinary confidence and imagination. They strove to manage the growth of cities throughout Britain, cities that were swelling to unimaginable proportions. They sought to serve the needs of industry, trade and transport through daring works of engineering. Their architectural ambitions gave rise to completely new methods of construction and the use of new materials. The Victorians also made a concerted attempt to understand the architecture of the past, which was meticulously revived in many of the buildings they created. Victorians both rich and poor enjoyed a variety and scale of building unknown to earlier generations.

< GREAT EXHIBITION
LONDON

The Great Exhibition in Hyde Park was intended to celebrate the diversity and achievements of the British Empire. This picture shows the Indian section of the display. It was initially proposed to house the exhibition in a brick building, but the costs were judged excessive. Joseph Paxton, the superintendent of the Duke of Devonshire's gardens at Chatsworth, used the ideas he had developed when constructing a conservatory there to create a much cheaper exhibition building of iron and glass. The building was later moved to Sydenham and burnt down in 1936.

v BROMPTON CEMETERY
LONDON

The nineteenth century saw the creation of numerous huge cemeteries around Britain's major cities. These were filled with funerary monuments of every kind, from the simple to the wildly extravagant, which provide a fascinating insight into nineteenth-century taste and attitudes to death. Sir Augustus Henry Glossop Harris, whose tomb this is, was born in Paris in 1852. He enjoyed a brilliant career as an impresario, and his funeral in 1896 was attended by thousands of people. Sadly, the bust on the tomb was recently stolen.

ST PANCRAS STATION
LONDON

In 1863 the Midland Railway began building their new London terminus, seen here when near completion. The glass and iron train shed had to be raised up above ground level so that trains leaving the station would clear the neighbouring Regent's Canal. In 1865 a competition was held to design the Grand Hotel. This was to form the principal façade of the station overlooking the Euston Road. The winning design was that by George Gilbert Scott for a Gothic-style building, which was erected between 1868 and 1872. Recently St Pancras was chosen to serve as the London terminus for Eurostar.

< HETTON COLLIERY
COUNTY DURHAM

The first shaft of the Hetton Colliery was sunk on 19 December 1820, and the principal coal-seam was struck on 3 September 1822. It was four-foot deep and lay beneath Magnesian Limestone, a discovery that disproved contemporary geological theories about where coal could be found. The mine possessed its own railway served by three locomotives named 'Dart', 'Tallyho', and 'Star' after racehorses. They pulled loads of coal at a speed of about four miles per hour. In 1894 there were 1,051 employees working in the mine and it produced 1,000 tons of coal a day.

< THAMES TUNNEL
LONDON

The Thames Tunnel between Rotherhithe and Wapping was the first underwater tunnel created in the world. It was built using a shield devised by Sir Marc Brunel, father of Isambard Kingdom Brunel. The tunnel was begun in March 1825, but work was fraught with difficulties and proceeded slowly. Two months after this banquet was held in November 1827 to celebrate progress made, a flood of the Thames led to the suspension of work for seven years. The tunnel was finally opened to pedestrians in March 1843. It was subsequently absorbed into the London Underground network and is still in use.

<< RIVER OUSE VIADUCT
BETWEEN BALCOMBE AND HAYWARDS HEATH

The pretty stone viaduct built to carry the London, Brighton and South-east Railway across the River Ouse. From the train the view is spectacular – across open countryside. Each end of the viaduct is marked by a pair of pavilions, just visible at the right of this photograph.

v TERRACED HOUSING
LONDON

Views not unlike this are still familiar to those who commute by train across London. Gustave Doré's engraving of a row of terraces in a poor district of the city was published in 1872. The view vividly captures the atmosphere of urban life in late Victorian London, the terraces of brick houses hemmed in by roaring trains belching smoke. Visible in the walled yards behind the houses are scenes of daily life: children play and washing is strung out to dry. The small shacks with chimneys behind each house are kitchens.

> MAP OF WESTMINSTER
LONDON

A map of Westminster in 1898–9 with the streets coloured 'according to the general condition of the inhabitants'. Black indicates 'lowest class, vicious, semi-criminal'; the blues 'poor areas'; the reds 'moderate and well-to-do'; and yellow the 'upper-middle and upper classes. Wealthy'. Westminster embraced areas of all these kinds, a reflection of its complex development and long history; Buckingham Palace is shown as 'wealthy'. Maps from further east in London are generally coloured blue or black.

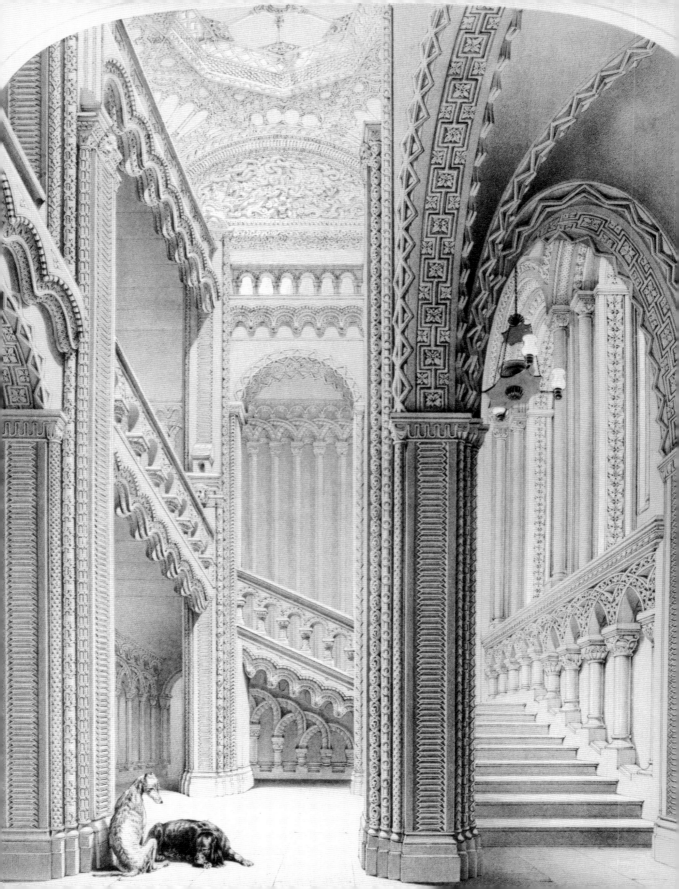

< PENRHYN CASTLE
CARNARVONSHIRE

Penrhyn is a vast residence designed in the style of a Norman castle by Thomas Hopper. This bizarre imitation of medieval architecture was begun in 1819 and continued into the 1830s. The owner of the castle was George Hay Dawkins, a man obsessed by architecture. He was heir to the industrialist Richard Pennant, who used the profits of his Jamaican sugar plantations to develop his estates in Wales. Dawkins diversified into slate quarrying, which also proved successful. From the beginning, the house was open to visits by the public.

∨ CROWN LIQUOR SALOON
BELFAST

The Crown Liquor Saloon in Great Victoria Street assumed its present appearance in the 1880s. At the time, Belfast was one of the richest and fastest growing cities in the empire. The building makes ingenious use of glazed ceramic tiles moulded into complex sculptural forms. Inside, it is also very richly treated, with a long bar and a row of snugs for customers to sit together in comfort and relative privacy. John Betjeman was among those who encouraged the National Trust to restore the building to its late Victorian splendour in 1978.

SUMMER SMOKING ROOM
CARDIFF CASTLE

Thanks to his father's development of Cardiff Docks, the third Marquis of Bute enjoyed the largest fortune in Britain. Both scholarly and an enthusiast for building, the Marquis found in the Gothic Revival architect William Burges the ideal figure to realise his dreams. Between 1868 and 1881 Burges converted the medieval shell of Cardiff Castle into a Gothic residence. The castle interiors are unexpected, lavish and brilliantly designed. Meanwhile the Marquis also had the thirteenth-century Castel Coch outside Cardiff reconstructed as a summer residence.

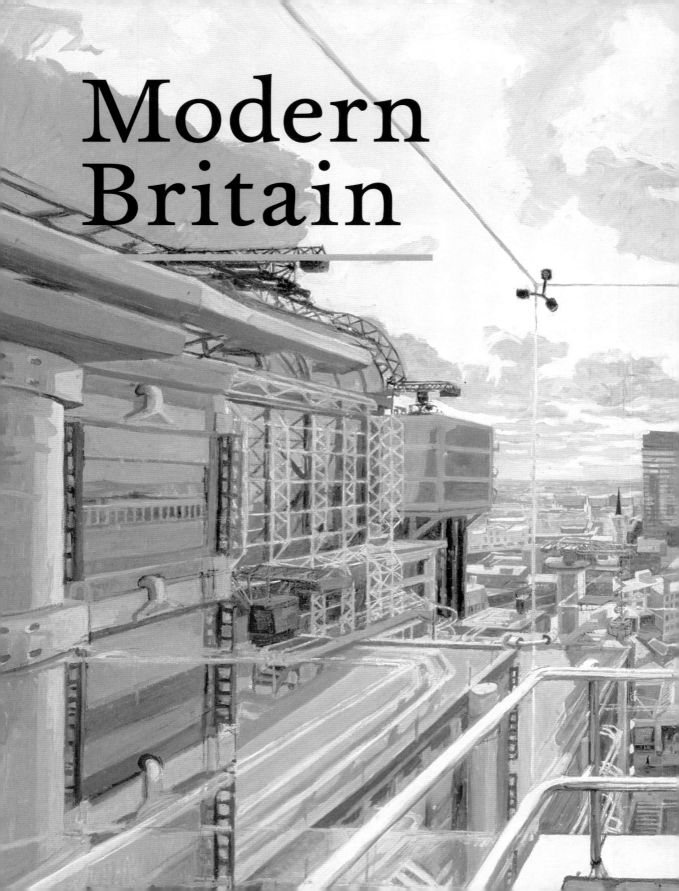

Modern
Britain

The South-east
Dreams of Tomorrow

THE TWENTIETH CENTURY WITNESSED A BATTLE OVER THE KIND OF BUILDINGS WE SHOULD BUILD. It still rages today. In previous centuries we had adopted and absorbed styles that came here from the Continent: chiefly the Gothic style, which Ruskin called simply 'pointed', and the classical from Greece and Rome. Each had created controversy, but each in the end had been accepted and had become part of our own national style. The new invasion, which can loosely be described as modernism, also arrived from abroad. At its most extreme it urged the abandonment of the decorative features of much that had gone before in favour of simplicity: clean-cut buildings, usually recognisable by their straight lines and square or rectangular shapes. They were made possible by new building techniques that used steel frames and reinforced concrete to achieve their effect.

The purists argued that these were buildings designed to fit their purpose with no concessions to style. In reality style was always important. These were buildings with a message. They proclaimed that we were entering a new age, a brave new world in which we would turn our back on the past and fearlessly embrace the future. These new ideas came as a shock, challenging our innate conservatism and threatening our deepest held convictions.

Turning our back on the past does not come naturally to the British. Moreover our circumstances in the twentieth century were different from those of our Continental neighbours. We had not faced social and political upheaval on the same scale as they had, nor had we been invaded. At the end of the First World War our instinct was to continue to build as we had in the past. Classical buildings were still our preferred choice for new public building. As for our homes, they too followed traditional lines.

The buildings that went up during the transformation of the Home Counties in the early part of the century owed little to new ideas about design. The massive expansion of London into the countryside that was seen in the 1920s and 30s owed more to a romantic nostalgia for the past – and a great deal to the railway. With the city once again bursting at the seams, the Metropolitan Railway, which ran a service from the centre of the city towards the west, decided to take advantage of the demand for more houses. In doing so it helped define a new way of living: the suburb.

PREVIOUS
The City of London viewed from the Lloyd's building. This panorama is constantly changing as giant corporations, banks and commercial houses vie with each other for bigger and better buildings crammed into a few square miles.

The essence of the suburb was that it would provide the benefits of country living with the convenience of being close to the city, so that a man (and it was mainly men) could travel by train to work in the noise and grime of the city but come home in the evening to his family and the healthy air of the countryside. The rate of this expansion was astonishing. Within two decades the market gardens of Middlesex disappeared and the open countryside shrank as new houses were built at a speed and on a scale that had never before been seen in Britain.

At Rayners Lane on the western outskirts of London, beyond Wembley and Harrow, is an underground station that typifies the enormity of the change. In 1929 only 30,000 passengers a year, or eighty a day, used its platforms. Within a decade four million passed through, or nearly 11,000 a day. The station itself, unlike the houses built for those who used it, but like many other stations in London at the time, adopted a bold and strikingly original style emphasising its quite unnecessary height with high glass windows.

The name given by its promoters to this new development was Metro-land. Every year from 1915 until 1932 the Metropolitan Railway's publicity department published a guidebook to new housing being built along the line from the outskirts of London to the villages and small towns beyond: Wembley and Harrow, Ruislip and Pinner, Uxbridge and Rickmansworth, Chorleywood and the Chalfonts, St Giles and St Peter.

Each new area for development was described in glowing terms, the virtues that the guidebook extolled being precisely those that the new settlement would itself extinguish. The book was illustrated with pictures of cows grazing in fields, leafy lanes or ducks swimming on ponds. Of Pinner, for instance, 'eleven and a quarter miles from Baker Street', it said, 'Until the coming of the Metropolitan Railway Pinner was just a sleepy little village, living a secluded life of its own.' Of Chorleywood: '... beautiful woods, a glorious open common, and a salubrious atmosphere have attracted many new comers to the favoured locality of Chorleywood.' As for Harrow, its 'residential advantages are specially advanced by the admirable train services. The electric trains are rarely at rest.' The guide listed B&Bs to stay in while looking for the best location, the names of golf clubs and local schools, and the prices of a season ticket to the chosen site. At the back of the brochure came the most important part: the advertisements for houses that were being built by developers along the length of the railway.

Most of these advertisements also stress the merits of living in the countryside. 'Delightful and artistic freehold houses, splendidly built, only the best material being used,' runs one. 'Perfect rural surroundings, lovely views, extraordinarily healthy. Property on this estate cannot depreciate in value.' The houses on offer are often half-timbered properties, detached or semi-detached, with a small front garden and a much larger garden behind. Some of them had garages in which one could fit a car of the period such as the Austin Seven or the Bullnose Morris. A small modern car can still be

233

driven into them, but it is such a tight squeeze that once the car is parked neither driver nor passenger can get out.

There were streets and streets of houses like this built between the two world wars: four million new homes in twenty years, with London and the south-east bearing the brunt of the expansion. By today's standards they were not expensive. In the 1920s £1,000, which is under £50,000 in today's money, could secure a high-quality, three-bedroom semi-detached house. The same house would now sell for £350,000. To put it another way, the acute shortage of housing we face today means that one of these houses costs seven times what it would have cost had supply kept pace with demand.

This expansion of the city into the countryside was controversial from the start and seemed to bring out a rather unpleasant condescension in critics, not just towards the houses but towards those who lived in them. The writer E.M. Forster said that in the suburbs 'nothing had to be striven for, and success was indistinguishable from failure'. A later critic, Ian Nairn, was even more severe. We were 'wrecking the environment so that man can everywhere see the projection and image of his own humdrum Suburban life – mild lusts, mild fears, mild everything'. J.B. Priestley was characteristically more generous. There was a great deal to be said for the suburb, he wrote, because 'nearly all Englishmen are at heart country gentlemen'.

The debate goes to the heart of who we are and what we want. Do we make houses to suit ourselves or do the houses make us? All the evidence suggests that, whatever the critics may say, we build what we want. Speculative developers after all risk their money to construct what they think will sell. If they thought that we wanted something different, they would provide it.

This is not just a hunch. It is borne out by the evidence. The typical suburban houses in Ruislip, for instance, have much in common. The entrance door is under a porch, to shelter against the rain. Inside is a small hall to hang coats and leave umbrellas. There are typically two living-rooms downstairs, sometimes now knocked into one, with a separate kitchen that may be large enough to provide an eating area. Upstairs will be three bedrooms and a bathroom. If the house is semi-detached the walls will be thick enough, in a well-built house, to muffle the sounds from next door, both from living-room to living-room and, perhaps more importantly, from bedroom to bedroom. The design offers privacy not just for the family but within the family, with every member able to go into their own room and close the door behind them.

During the same era in which semis were being built by the million, an alternative way of living was being offered. The modernist architects adopted a rational approach to the problem, studying the way people seemed to lead their lives and designing houses to match rather than offering the kind of houses people thought they wanted. It was a mistake. We are reluctant to sacrifice our idea of the cosy home for the reality of a house designed to suit our needs. Efficient living spaces count for little if what is offered does not look and feel right. Because of this the modernist alternative never caught on.

234

METRO-LAND

PRICE TWO-PENCE

An uncluttered style of living

In a suburban street in Ruislip are three white houses, set side by side, which are at odds with their neighbours. To either side are conventional suburban houses built in the 1950s. These three houses date from 1934 and were built in the modernist style by Connell, Ward and Lucas. The leading proponent of modernism Mies Van der Rohe famously summed up its philosophy as 'Less is More'. The ideas excited the architectural schools. Here was a way of building that used the new construction technique of reinforced concrete and steel. Shapes could be built that would have been impossible in brick or stone. Houses could be designed to look more like abstract sculpture than a conventional home.

The three modernist houses in Ruislip are all straight lines with no curves. The windows are square or rectangular. The walls are pure white concrete with windows and doors outlined in black. Inside there are great panes of glass, letting the light flood in, and big open-plan rooms that are kept in the simplest style. On winter nights sliding doors allow these big spaces to be reduced to make the house more intimate, but there are none of the details relished by the builders of what the cartoonist Osbert Lancaster, a sharp observer of style, called 'stockbroker Tudor'. Brick inglenook fireplaces, mullioned windows, plaster coving where walls met ceiling are all absent. The design is unforgiving. Any attempt to introduce these features would look ridiculous.

A modernist home in Ruislip, designed in 1934 as an antidote to suburban stockbroker Tudor. It didn't catch on.

The simplicity suits those who choose an uncluttered style of living. One resident, Laurence Melford, told me that since he moved in he has found himself drawn by the house into adopting a simpler life-style, ridding himself of knick-knacks and clutter. He also claims that the house has freed him from the drudgery of housework associated with a more conventional home. There are, for instance, no floorboards to gather dust. The concrete ceiling of the living-room provides the floor of the bedroom above.

These three houses were controversial from the start. In 1934 the 'Ruislip Case' was a cause célèbre among architects. Argument raged between the designers and the local council over whether their strange appearance warranted granting them planning permission. When it was granted, the houses stood in glorious isolation on a green-field site. Plans to build similar houses in Ruislip came to nothing. One problem was that the houses were almost twice as expensive as those built of brick. But another reason was that potential buyers did not like their appearance. They were too radical, denying the occupants the opportunity of living J.B. Priestley's country gentleman's life. These houses were strange, foreign looking, austere, un-cosy. Compared with their neighbours they now seem to some eyes, and I include mine, refreshing and exciting. Hundreds of sightseers come to tour them each year during 'London Open House' weekend.

Mathematical modernism

The cost of building has always been a key factor in how we have built Britain. From the earliest days it was the rich who built well, the less well off who had to put up with what they could afford. It was as true of the great houses of Tudor times as it was for the Georgians and the Victorians. The bulk of our housing has always been built down to a price, and there is a price to pay for parsimony. When money was no object, modernism could deliver a spectacular new way of living to make even the experimental Ruislip houses seem very much the poor relations.

The Homewood in Esher is a large suburban house built by a 24-year-old architect in 1938 for his parents. His father called it, wryly, 'a temple of costly experience'. When his parents died, Patrick Gwynne took the house over and continued to change it until his death in 2003. It is a tribute to the originality of the Homewood that it was accepted by the National Trust as an outstanding example of modernist architecture. The design of the house is austere and sculptural. The strictly rectangular façade of white concrete is pierced by huge rectangular windows that look on to a typical Surrey landscape of heather and rhododendrons, azaleas, silver birch and pine trees. The proportions of the Homewood are determined by Gwynne's own formula: a vertical unit of twenty inches and a horizontal unit of forty-eight inches. The dimensions of the entire house are derived from this mathematical ratio.

Gwynne was a man who could afford to indulge his fastidious taste. The house, both inside and out, is simple but luxurious. I am afraid my description

may make it sound vulgar, which it is not. Gwynne used modern materials. There is plastic wallpaper simulating Japanese grass cloth. There are doors of white leather, a leatherette couch, chaises-longues in fake fur and a white vinyl desk. The floor of the living-room is of maple wood and is sprung for dancing. The end wall of this room is made of polished black Levanto marble veined with white, red and green. The back wall is entirely covered with Indian laurel wood, and built into it is a cocktail cabinet and table, both of which fold away out of sight when not in use. The windows have electrically controlled Venetian blinds to shield the room from the midday sun. Behind a screen painted with a bamboo pattern is the dining-room. Here again no expense is spared. The table is of grey tinted glass and is lit from below. The intensity and the colour of the lighting can both be altered. Gwynne used it to provide a different mood for every course.

Running along the back of the living-room was the kitchen. Cooking was Gwynne's passion, and he was constantly changing the design of the kitchen. Those who have tried to design a kitchen for themselves will know how difficult it is to match the space available to all the routes the cook takes when preparing a meal. Gwynne's final design incorporates many of the features that have become standard in a modern kitchen, with a central island for preparing food, and pots and pans hanging from the ceiling above it. Everything that is needed is within reach. Like the whole house, it is a triumph of efficiency achieved at a price.

The Homewood, Esher (1938). Contrasting with the gentle woodland, this modernist house was designed according to strict mathematical proportions (above). The living-room (opposite) has a maple floor sprung for dancing.

Ebenezer Howard's vision of the 'Social City'

The evidence of the twentieth century suggests that although we have become a richer country we have used our wealth to improve the quality of our private lives rather than our public lives. Our cities and our suburbs show a level of neglect by governments, local councils and planners that reflects our own carelessness about our surroundings.

It need not have been like this. At the start of the last century there was an extraordinary experiment, an attempt to build a new and better way of life. Ebenezer Howard was a social reformer with a vision. He wanted to create a new Jerusalem in southern England as a response to the overcrowded and unhealthy slums of the inner cities and equally the hardship and squalor of the lives of most country people. He was particularly concerned about the effects of the migration of so many rural workers to London, in the wake of a slump in farming. 'I am haunted,' he wrote, 'by the awfulness of London ... a tumour, an elephantiasis sucking into its gorged system half the life and the blood and bone of the rural districts.'

His proposal was what would nowadays be called the third way: not town life, not country life, but 'town country' life. His sights were set on an area of farmland north of London. Here the first garden city, Letchworth, was created on the drawing-board of architects Unwin and Parker. The city was to have a spider's web of streets radiating from a central square. There would be houses, shops, libraries, churches and, most important of all, factories, so that the new community could be self-contained and self-sufficient. Howard stipulated that rich and poor should rub shoulders in his new town. Every

'What some people think of us': one of a series of cartoons published by residents of Letchworth, aware that visitors found their lifestyle odd.

house would face the sun. Every house would have a garden large enough to keep its family in fresh vegetables. The houses themselves were built by individual private developers, but had to accord with strict guidelines on style, which gave Letchworth a slightly old-world appearance with many cottage-like homes built in traditional materials and roofed sometimes with tiles and sometimes with thatch.

The idealism behind Howard's new town attracted other idealists: artists, writers, theosophists, early socialists, Quakers and free thinkers of infinite variety. Vegetarianism became fashionable, and in an attempt to emulate rustic simplicity some men took to wearing smocks and open sandals. Letchworth relished its eccentricity, even publishing in its newspaper a series of cartoons entitled 'What some people think of us'. One cartoon shows day trippers looking on bemused at signposts reading 'To the hairy-headed banana munchers' and 'To the sandal-footed raisin shifters'. A stall displays 'Nuts ... for the bald-headed nut peckers', and a boy says to his father, 'Daddy, I want to see them feed.' George Orwell took a dim view of the louche reputation of Letchworth. In *The Road to Wigan Pier* he attributed the failure of socialism to win popular support to its association with communities such as Letchworth,

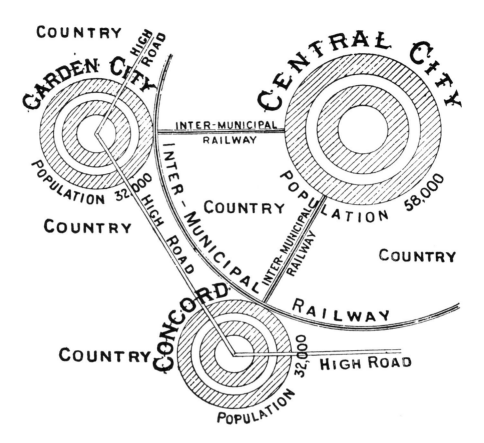

Ebenezer Howard's diagram illustrating the 'correct principle of a city's growth – open country ever near at hand, and rapid communication between off-shoots'.

which attracted 'every fruit juice drinker, nudist, sandal wearer, sex maniac, Quaker, nature cure quack, pacifist and feminist in England'.

Howard's ambitions for his garden city were far bolder than Letchworth's reputation as a slightly cranky socialist community would suggest. His grand plan was for Letchworth to grow until it spawned another garden city, also independent and self-sufficient. This new city would be linked to Letchworth by connections including railways, roads and canals. This in turn would spawn another city and another, until the country was made up of a series of small, interconnecting cities: the Social City. Separating the cities would be swathes of unspoilt countryside under the ownership of the cities and protected by them.

In his time he was mocked by Fabians and socialists who thought the social aspects of the scheme were unworkable. These involved inveigling businesses and tenants of the city housing into sharing their profits for the public good to provide health care and pensions for the elderly. But Howard's vision for town planning lasted long after Letchworth failed to fulfil his dream. At the end of the Second World War, in propaganda intended to show that the fruits of victory would be a better world, the government was still using his model as an illustration of the town of the future, and no one has come up with a better plan since. Milton Keynes, generally agreed to be the most successful of the new towns built since the war, owes much to Howard's vision.

Howard expected small factories to set up around Letchworth, attracted by the skilled labour that would be available. Few came. One company that did, and which only ceased production in the 1980s, was Spirella, making a newly devised ladies' corset which substituted spiral springs for whalebone in its support mechanism. Spirella built their factory in the modern style, using reinforced concrete that allowed for open-spaced floors and big windows.

The factory provided baths for its workers, a canteen, gymnastic classes, a library and a ballroom. 'These conditions,' its owner explained, 'make for efficient, contented, progressive workmen and women. A principle of Spirella's policy has been to instil into its employees right methods of living, right methods of work, and an appreciation of the vital needs of sunlight.' Spirella and Letchworth were not the first to devise better living and working conditions for their work-force in the interest both of their own success and more general social well-being. There already existed the experiments of the Cadbury's at Bourneville, outside Birmingham, and Lever's Port Sunlight, near Liverpool. One grey December day I visited a similar experiment in Essex.

Letchworth Garden City: the much admired thatched cottage style (left); a view of the town laid out to a pre-ordained plan (centre); and Spirella's corset factory (right).

On the flat and dismal marshes just beyond the Tilbury docks on the north bank of the Thames is a company town that embodies all that was right and all that was wrong with the concept of creating a workers' paradise. The route to this isolated spot leaves London travelling east on the dual carriageway. It soars over a land that has been despoiled, where giant pylons stride across the fields of potato and kale, where the fumes from factory chimneys create their own industrial cloudscape. It emerges on to narrower lanes bordering rough pasture. Scraggy horses, never ridden, stand forlorn, their backs towards the feeble drizzle. Old cars rust by rotting sheds.

Just as it seems that the road can go no further, there is an odd sight ahead: a row of little white concrete houses with flat roofs. Beyond them, curving away on avenues, are more little houses. They look like shoe boxes. It is an old joke, because this is East Tilbury, the company town of the Bata shoe empire's outpost in Britain. Following the example of Bourneville it should really have been named Bataville.

Bataville was built in the early 1930s by Thomas Bata, an industrialist with a vision. Bata had founded his shoe business at Zlin, in Czechoslovakia.

243

He had built a workers' town there. When he expanded into Britain he adopted the same approach. To fulfil his ambition to become 'shoemaker to the world' he needed a disciplined, healthy and competitive work-force. Everything about the company town he built at East Tilbury was designed to that end. Bata was a passionate modernist, and the houses he provided were clean-cut and angular. Each had a large garden, as at Letchworth, to allow families to grow their own vegetables. There was a cinema and a swimming pool, sports grounds, a library and a company hotel with a ballroom for dances. It was a workers' Utopia – as long as the workers did not step out of line.

I talked to some members of Bata's staff who had lived and worked here for many years. Their stories were all similar. Living in Bataville was comfortable and enjoyable, as long as you conformed. This was a company town with a strong ethos laid down by Bata himself. 'We want to create in our town,' he said, 'free human beings who have smiles for all the world, but firstly for their neighbours. Men who feel the full pleasure of life. For the right freedom of family life is required a dwelling separated from the neighbours, in a free space of a green garden, air and sun.'

The community was self-contained and highly disciplined. Each year, for instance, there was a competition for the best garden. Joan James, who worked for Bata for twenty-four years, told me, 'If you had a bad garden and it wasn't up to standard you had a letter saying, "Pull your socks up and get back and sort it".' One man planted potatoes in his front garden to clean the soil. When the managing director saw it he ordered him to dig them up and lay a proper lawn.

If a child of a Bata employee misbehaved in the town, his mother or father would be likely to hear about it first through a summons to the manager's office. More serious was the threat that if you misbehaved or were lazy or constantly late for work you could lose your job, and if you lost your job you had to leave your house within two weeks. I asked another Bata worker, Mary Duffess, whether she knew of that happening. 'Oh yes,' she said, 'the man who lived over there was thrown out of his house within the week.' 'What had he done?' I asked. 'Pinched shoes,' she said.

Paternalism is like a cocoon. It can be comfortable inside, but it is restricting. Many people who lived at Bataville were full of praise for the place and its amenities, as well as its constant round of competitive games, not just after work but also during working hours. Each department of the factory was given the name of a football team and scored points for efficiency. The winning department was rewarded with a dinner dance. 'You have to remember that this was the 1950s and 60s. People did not have that much and did not go out often,' said Joan James. Mary added, 'What we had here was lovely. People thought we were snobs because we had the amenities here. We had bathrooms and everything.' Her friend Evelyn Haxell commented, 'Some thought we were a bit cocky.'

The small square white boxes of Bataville look a little incongruous in the Essex marshes, but Thomas Bata's devotion to modernism and his insistence

East Tilbury: the austere modernist design of the 1930s buildings for workers employed by the Bata Shoe Company.

on this kind of building for his company villages at Bata factories in the United States and Czechoslovakia as well as Britain was not just a matter of style. The modernists were not designing in straight lines and rectangles using austere white concrete because they thought it was more attractive than arches and pillars and porticoes and curves and decoration. Theirs was a philosophical approach based on building what was functional and necessary, not what looked pretty, so the starting-point was the use to which the building would be put. It is not difficult to see why a man like Bata, dedicated to efficiency, would advocate such a style. It was efficient but it also satisfied his philosophy of nurturing a healthy work-force. Big windows and sunshine and large gardens were provided for a purpose, to help keep the work-force alert and contented.

A breath of fresh air: seaside lidos

There was another reason for the enthusiasm with which modernism was embraced by architects in Britain. It represented a clean break with the past, and symbolised an age which would put the horror of the First World War behind it, along with the old-fashioned, hierarchical structures of pre-war society. A new approach seemed to warrant new architecture. After both great wars of the twentieth century the exhaustion of the warring nations led to a questioning of attitudes and values and a search for social improvements. The First World War in particular had shown up the feeble physical condition of the young working-class men who served in the army. There were many causes: poor diet, unsanitary housing, and inadequate health care among them. Improvements in the nation's health became an obsession. Rickets, lice and diphtheria were all rife, and sunshine and fresh air were believed to be the cure.

It took some time before the attempt to find practical ways of improving the health of the nation made any real progress. The financial slump of the late 1920s delayed many ambitious schemes. But unemployment itself ultimately promoted public projects when the government gave local authorities the right to carry out schemes on condition that they used unemployed labour. The most striking example of this initiative was the building of seaside lidos. Here modernism at last came into its own.

Modernism first hit the headlines in Britain with a famous building by the seaside at Bexhill. A German Jewish refugee won the competition to design

The De La Warr Pavilion in Bexhill, built in 1935 to cheer up the dreariness of Britain's seaside.

a building that would, in the words of the man who commissioned it, be an antidote to 'the gloom and dreariness of British resorts'. It was the socialist mayor of Bexhill, the Earl De La Warr, who wrote the brief, the first to ask for a specifically modern design for a public building. It had to be simple, light in appearance, with large window spaces, terraces and canopies, using steel-framed or concrete construction.

There were over 200 entries and Eric Mendelson, one of a number of Jewish architects who had fled to Britain to escape Nazi persecution, won the contract. His design, with its great curved balconies and windows providing protection from the wind and rain, was the talk of the decade. When it was opened in 1935 it attracted crowds of visitors, and it became the model for seaside buildings all around our coasts. The sea is a punishing neighbour for any building, however, and the De La Warr Pavilion fell into disrepair until a recent restoration revived it in its original splendour.

In the 1930s a startling 180 lidos were built. One of the grandest was further along the coast from Bexhill, just to the west of Brighton at Saltdean. It was opened in 1938, the year incidentally when all workers in Britain were for the first time legally entitled to one week's holiday a year. I went there on one of those dismal winter days when the wind is bowling up the Channel and the waves have churned up the sea-bed, turning the water brown. The lido looked dejected in its hollow behind the chalk cliffs. On my next visit it was possible to imagine Saltdean in its heyday. It was only February, but the sky

Saltdean Lido. Built on Bexhill's success, Saltdean, near Brighton, still provides the rigorous pleasures of open-air bathing.

was blue and the sun shone warmly. For a moment I could picture the scene as it would have been on a hot summer day in the 1930s. There are two pools, one for children and one for adults. A great apron of concrete invites sunbathers. Behind is the lido building with a small glassed-in pavilion in the style of Bexhill, though more modest, and a terrace leading off it to each side, providing a vantage-point to watch the activities below. Maybe it would be the turn of Fearless Roy Fransen to climb the ladder to the high board and perform his 'sensational dive of death', or for the women to enter the competition for 'Miss Calf and Ankle', 'Miss Lovely Legs' or 'Miss Physical Excellence'.

Behind the innocent fun was an ideology: not just to improve the health of the nation but to change its social outlook. As Sir Josiah Stamp, Director of the Bank of England, explained a little pompously when opening the lido at Morecambe, 'Bathing reduces rich and poor, high and low, to a common standard of enjoyment and health. When we get down to swimming, we get down to democracy.'

The bright lights of the moving pictures

Not all our pleasures were taken quite so earnestly. The 1920s and 30s were the age of the cinema. By the late 1930s over twenty million people were going to the cinema each week. The impact of the pictures, which were mainly American, was so great that there was concern about their effect on society. In the pre-television age, films opened our eyes to a different world. One regular described to me the contrast between her daily life, lived in 'a very dull, dark sort of place', and her weekly visit to the cinema. 'You were in complete darkness, then all of a sudden the screen would light up and you'd see all these marvellous film stars. Everything was bright. I just wanted to go there and be like them.'

Young girls took to imitating the stars. Denied access to make-up, which was still only used by the rich, they would whiten their cheeks with flour and use soot to darken their eyelashes. Moistened red tissue paper was pressed to their lips to simulate lipstick. American slang such as 'OK kid' and 'What are you doing tonight, babe?' was heard on the streets of London. The commentators complained about the phenomenon. The *Daily Express* in 1927 observed that picture-goers were becoming Americanised. 'They talk America, think America, and dream America. We have several million people, mostly women, who to all intent and purpose, are temporary American citizens.' Politicians, clergymen and teachers were all critical, but the cinema industry sat back and enjoyed the boom, building palaces of light and colour to bring the customers flocking in from the drab streets.

The most glamorous of these cinemas still in use, albeit as a bingo hall, is the Granada cinema in Tooting. It was part of a cinema chain founded by Sidney Bernstein. On a walking tour of Spain he had visited Granada and decided not only that the name would add a touch of glamour to his enterprise but that he would build his cinemas in the exotic Moorish style of that city. He engaged an exiled White Russian, Theodore Komisarjevsky, to help him.

Komisarjevsky was a stage designer whose watchword turned the principle of modernism on its head. Not 'Less is More' but 'More is More'. The first cinema he designed for Bernstein was the Granada in Dover, which opened in 1930, but Tooting, which opened the following year, is his true memorial.

I met Doreen Paskell, who remembers coming here every Saturday to the children's cinema club. It cost sixpence and was the one big treat of the week: 'the only time you really ever did anything apart from play on the streets or around the park. It was a few years later till we got our televisions, so it was the only chance to see the outside world. There was nothing about everyday life. It was all just fantasy ... even the [Pathé] news took you to places that you wouldn't dream of because you never went outside your own little area.'

She explained why the arrival of the Granada made such an impact. 'To come into a building like this all those years ago would have been absolutely incredible to the type of people who lived around here ... Just ordinary working-class people that paid their bills and had tick at the corner shop ... To come into somewhere like this would take you into another world, probably a bit like walking into Buckingham Palace now would be amazing for most people.'

To build his flagship cinema Bernstein bought and demolished houses, shops and a pub on a two-acre site in the centre of Tooting called Salvador. It had been one of those small, self-contained communities that can still be found in parts of London, isolated from the noise and bustle of the rest of the city. It was named Salvador after a prosperous Portuguese Jewish family who had arrived in Britain in the eighteenth century and had built a country mansion in Tooting.

The palace commissioned by Bernstein towered over the few cottages then left on the edge of the site. Its entrance façade boasts four massive Corinthian columns, which bore the name of the cinema above them. The grand foyer through which every cinema-goer passed is a medieval baronial hall, the walls painted to look like stone and the ceiling made of imitation oak beams. There are long mirrors and columns decorated with griffins playing trumpets and harps. There are fanciful, high-backed chairs and tables in the Gothic style. A double marble staircase with a stone balustrade swept customers past more imitation marble columns to the cinema itself. Before taking their seats, those who had tickets to the circle could wait in a hall of mirrors, like a miniature Versailles, 150 feet long and lit by imitation candles in ornate brackets.

None of this matches the magnificence of the auditorium. It is difficult to take in all the detail of such a complex and florid design. To each side of the stage are massive pointed Gothic archways, suggesting the entrance to a French cathedral. The impression is strengthened by stained-glass windows lit from behind. For a moment I thought that if I strained my ears I would be able to hear the faint strains of music from choir and organ drifting in. Above the archways the religious is abandoned in favour of the secular. Medieval figures of troubadours and wimpled maidens decorate the arcades. The ceiling is painted to resemble a blue sky flecked with clouds, and the whole place is lit by chandeliers.

EXIT

EXIT

At the centre of the stage is a Wurlitzer organ, something which no self-respecting cinema of the 1930s could be without. It was used to accompany silent films in cinemas too large for a piano to be heard. An orchestra would have cost too much, but the Wurlitzer could imitate many of its sounds. Its organ pipes are concealed below the stage with baffles which open to allow the music to escape. Traditionally, before the film, the organist started playing out of sight, underground. At the throw of a switch he slowly emerged and rose to the level of the stage, playing his keyboard and foot pedals with a flourish. At the end of the performance, with a wave to the audience, he disappeared back into the depths as the curtains opened and the film began.

I tried my hand sitting beside Len Rawle, who has restored the Tooting organ. He is famous for buying the organ from the Empire Leicester Square and rebuilding it in his house in Chorleywood (the organ takes up half the house and his family are reconciled to living in the other half). We tried 'I Love Paris in the Springtime'. It did not sound too good. 'I may not be much of a pianist but I am not this bad,' I thought, until I realised he was playing one page of the tune and I was playing another. No wonder the bingo players looked pained.

Prefabricated housing and the Excalibur Estate

Half-way through the twentieth century all the plans for creating a bold new Britain had to be abandoned. For the six years of the Second World War (1939–45) the story of how we built Britain became the story of how the Luftwaffe tried to destroy it. We emerged from the war impoverished, battered, and suffering from shortages of all kinds including a lack of materials for building. New homes were urgently needed. London and other big cities had suffered massively from bombing raids, and in the latter years of the war London had also been the target of devastating rocket attacks from across the Channel. Swathes of houses in the capital had been demolished, and many more were too badly damaged to be habitable.

The priority was to house as many people as quickly and as cheaply as possible. In the final year of the war the Ministry of Works was already looking for a solution – and found it in the 'prefab', or prefabricated house. The plan was to design a small house that could be built in a factory and assembled on site. This would guarantee a supply of houses that did not require skilled builders and craftsmen to make them, thus bypassing the problem of a labour shortage. Examples of a suitable house were put on show outside the Tate Gallery in London, and a number of companies submitted plans. These all varied slightly but had much in common, particularly the kitchen and bathroom arrangements.

The prefabs were intended to be a temporary measure and had an expected life span of only ten years. Most have now been demolished by the authorities who built them. One large estate does remain, however, in Catford in south-east London. It is so popular with its residents that they are fighting a

Prefabs being assembled in Hackney, 1944. The parts were made in a factory – they could be erected on site without the use of skilled labour.

campaign to have it preserved. Many homes display a poster of a boxing glove with the words 'I am fighting for my home and our estate. Are you?' and the logo 'Save the Original Prefab'. There are over 180 prefabs on this estate.

At first glance they look like mobile homes: low, flat-roofed, with little gardens around them. All kinds of individual touches have been added over the years. Some have mock-Georgian porches and stained-glass front doors. One or two have adopted the Tudor look by fixing wooden beams to the exterior walls. A sign on another reads 'Trespassers will be eaten', though the welcome they give the visitor is far from hostile. 'Do you like our little village?' I was asked after being regaled with the advantages of living here 'right next to the houses'. The 'houses' are part of the old Downham Estate, built on a green-field site by the London County Council in the 1920s. The prefab estate feels itself to be very different, an intimate community where everyone knows everyone else, where the crime rate is low compared with neighbouring estates, and where generous gardens give a feeling of space and airiness denied to the dense building around.

Eddie O'Mahoney is the organiser of the campaign to save the prefabs. He is eighty-six years old now and was one of the first residents. On his return from the war he had been offered a prefab but told the local council, 'I've lived in enough tents and Nissen huts. I want a house.' 'Don't turn it down before you've seen it,' they advised him. 'Take a key and go and view it.' He went with his wife to take a look, and after walking down a rough track made of rubble from bomb damage, they had a surprise. 'It was heaven. My wife was amazed. We came into the hall and she said, "Look at the size of it. We can get the pram in here." We went into the kitchen and there was a New World stove and an Electrolux refrigerator – unheard of in 1946. There was a bathroom and an inside toilet. We'd been used to having a toilet in the garden and never had a bathroom.'

In the early days the Excalibur Estate, to give it its proper and romantic name, was occupied mainly by ex-servicemen who had lost their homes. There was, as Eddie explained, a wonderful atmosphere. 'We were comrades. We had been in the war together. There was that bond. Everybody worked for one another. Our first Christmas there was an electricity failure but we had gas, and my wife cooked three turkeys for people who had no power. I can honestly say if I go out for the day I look forward to coming home. I love this place. My wife died twenty-one years ago unfortunately, but I have lived here since then, sixty years in all, and I've been very, very happy.'

There is still a waiting list of families wanting to move in to Excalibur, and it is not hard to see why. Everyone I spoke to, particularly the older

The Excalibur Estate in Catford, one of the last prefab villages left. The house on the right has been embellished with mock-Tudor beams and a lamp post.

residents, told the same story. The emergency housing, built without any particular attempt to design a community, had succeeded where the urban planners who followed had so spectacularly failed. The preferred long-term solution to the housing shortage was to build high-rise blocks of flats. Eddie is scathing. 'God I wouldn't want to live in a high-rise flat. The people next door to me came from a flat and they said "This is heaven". They used to have skateboards up and down, people above them, people below ...' His voice tailed away at the horror of the prospect.

The Festival of Britain

The first sign of the way the post-Second World War era might develop was the Festival of Britain in 1951. This was intended to be a commemoration of the Great Exhibition of 1851, which had celebrated Britain's industrial and economic strength in the middle of Queen Victoria's reign. The Festival of Britain too had a clear purpose. It was intended to cheer people up after the privations of war and to remind them of the country's achievements and potential. In the words of its guidebook, 'It tells the story of British contributions to world civilisation in the arts of peace ... A story that has a beginning, a middle and an end – even if that consists of nothing more final than fingerposts into the future.'

The future was represented by the Skylon, which became the symbol of the exhibition. It was 300 feet high, a slender, torpedo-shaped structure pointed at each end and apparently floating in the air. It was held in place by cables attached to three steel beams. At night it was lit from the inside. I went to see it and remember being astonished and excited by such a spectacular and improbable construction. The whole exhibition was laid out in a series of pavilions all boasting of the achievements of Britain and the British people. 'The land,' as the guidebook told us, 'endowed with scenery, climate and resources more various than any other country of comparable size, has nurtured and challenged and stimulated the people. The people, endowed with not one single characteristic that is peculiar to themselves, nevertheless, when taken together, could not be mistaken for any other nation in the world.'

Such confidence at a time when there was still food rationing, when the economy was faltering, when the damage of war was still evident across the capital, was breathtaking. The whole South Bank site was taken up by the best architecture, light and clean and uncluttered, a display of the international modernist style on a scale never before seen. Everywhere there were the finest examples of modern sculpture: Epstein, Moore, Hepworth, Chadwick and Butler among them. Eight million visitors came to see it in the five summer months of 1951. When it was over, all the buildings were demolished except the Royal Festival Hall, which still dominates the South Bank site. The Skylon was cut into pieces and sold, it is said, as commemorative ashtrays. My father bought two chairs, their seats made with yellow, plastic-covered springs, which sat in our garden for years until the legs buckled and they had to be thrown away.

The Festival of Britain showed what modern architecture at its best could achieve. Over the years that followed we became used to new and often controversial designs changing the face of our towns and cities. There was inevitably much second-rate building, as the centres of many a town and city rebuilt in the 1960s bear witness. Old towns were destroyed by councils in love with the idea of modernising. Houses were pulled down to make way for new roads. Ugly multi-storey car-parks and bland shopping arcades took the place of streets of shops. But London was protected from the worst. There were far too many buildings of all ages, many of them steeped in the country's history and all jealously protected, for ambitious developments to make much headway. The pleasure of London is its variety and its complexity. The contribution of the modern age to this panoply is distinctive but not dominant, even though some of its contributions may seem out of place.

High-rise tower blocks

Modernism has always had its critics. When it first began to appear among the more traditional neo-classical buildings which predominated in the decade after the First World War, doubts were already being expressed. The painter Paul Nash wrote in 1932 that 'whether it is possible to "Go Modern" and still "Be British" is a question vexing quite a few people today'. It may have been enthusiastically embraced by intellectuals and architects who felt that neo-Georgian buildings were a symptom of cultural decay, or by industrialists and businessmen who wanted to make a splash with spectacular buildings such as the black *Daily Express* headquarters in Fleet Street or the Hoover building on the Great West Road, but home builders still preferred brick and wood. 'There is in this reversion to a traditional material,' commented the architectural historian Nikolaus Pevsner, 'something typically British.'

In London the instinct of most families was to continue to live in the kind of buildings they had been used to before the ravages of the war had destroyed the streets of the East End. The rows of terrace houses may have been cramped and lacking decent facilities, but they allowed a way of life that most people enjoyed: a street safe for children to play in, and back-yards which provided a little private space but also a low wall to lean on and chat to the family next door. The planners, however, decided on a different course. They would re-house thousands of families in new blocks of flats which would be cheap and easy to build. Around them they would provide more open space than was possible where rows of terrace houses backed on to each other.

High-rise flats gave architects and planners a bad name from which they have still not wholly recovered. Yet the idea must have seemed so attractive at first: a perfect solution to the demand for thousands of new homes to be built on limited space. The flats would have all the latest modern equipment, views over the city, and building high would mean that everyone would get some sun. Above all, they could be built cheaply and fast. In the post-war years hundreds of high-rise blocks were built in London and they were generally held to have been a mistake. Sometimes this was the fault of the construction methods. One new technique was known as system building, meaning the prefabrication of walls and windows, which were made in a factory and assembled on site.

There were flaws in the method, highlighted by the Ronan Point disaster. An explosion caused by a gas leak in a corner flat on the eighteenth floor caused one side of the tower block to collapse. Four people were killed and seventeen injured. The subsequent inquiry found that some of the joints which held the panels of concrete together had not been properly fitted. Some were even filled with newspaper instead of concrete. The whole structure had depended on each wall supporting the wall above it. In effect the floors were held together by gravity, and when one panel blew out, those above, now unsupported, fell. The discovery that their homes were no more substantial than a house of cards produced, not surprisingly, a loss of confidence among many high-rise dwellers, even those living in blocks built by more conventional methods.

It was not just the structural problems that led to this disillusion. It was quickly becoming apparent that high-rise flats were creating acute social problems too. There is a famous high-rise block in North Kensington, the Trellick Tower, which dominates the West London skyline. It used to encapsulate all the problems of high-rise. The lifts would break and were not repaired. The walls were covered with graffiti. Light bulbs were not replaced. Worse still, women were assaulted in the dark corridors. Heroin addicts shot up in the basement and left their used needles where children played. It was a story repeated across London and other cities. The architect of Trellick Tower, Erno Goldfinger, who was proud of a building designed along the lines first espoused by the Swiss architect Le Corbusier, was shocked: 'I built skyscrapers for people to live in there and now they messed them up – disgusting.'

Blaming the tenants missed the point. It is true that there were families living in tower blocks with all kinds of social problems. But the real blame should be placed on the councils who built the tower blocks to meet their housing quotas and then failed to look after them. There was no proper maintenance, and no security. The proof of the pudding is in Trellick Tower today. It has become a much sought-after block of flats, with trendy architects and others buying freeholds and living alongside tenants. The difference is that it is now properly protected, almost a gated community, with a twenty-four-hour concierge service to make sure that the residents are not harassed or threatened on their way to their flats and that strangers are kept out.

An even more striking example of how a tower block can work successfully is Keeling House in Bethnal Green. It was designed by Sir Denys Lasdun, the architect of the National Theatre. Lasdun was a thoughtful man with a strong social conscience. When he was commissioned to build Keeling in the late 1950s, he took great trouble to find out what the people of the East End wanted and tried to marry this to modernist principles. He spent hours wandering around the streets photographing the way people lived. His solution,

The Trellick Tower in West London. Built by Goldfinger in 1972, it became a byword for social problems and crime until simple improvements turned it into a trendy desres in the 1990s.

perhaps a trifle optimistic, was to attempt to recreate the atmosphere of a street by setting it on its side and building it vertically. Key to the design was to make each flat two storeys high with an internal staircase, similar to the terrace houses of the area. The front doors all looked in on each other so that tenants could meet. There were drying areas for hanging out washing, like the back-yards of the terrace houses.

In the 1990s a piece of the exterior fell down. The residents were moved out and the council planned to repair the building and return it to the tenants. However, the cost of repairs and the widespread dislike of tower blocks among the tenants led them instead to propose its demolition. Then, just before demolition was due, Keeling was listed as a building of special merit. It was bought by a developer, who renovated the block, put a high fence around it, made an entrance with pools of water and fountains, and installed a foyer with a concierge sitting proprietorially behind a desk.

The flats now sell for a good price, and the people who live there not only feel safe but enjoy some of the finest views over London, stretching from the Dome, past Canary Wharf, to the London Eye. New resident Nikolaus Greig told me, 'I think it's cool. I used to drive past it when it was derelict and it looked absolutely awful. Atrocious. People thought let's pull it down, it looks so ugly. When they restored it, it was like Wow. It's not the same place. It was amazing.' It has not, however, achieved the village atmosphere Lasdun had hoped for. 'We just say "Good morning" to each other. With the gates and everything it is a bit of a fortress, but it's lovely. Home sweet home.'

A cityscape of controversy

In recent years high-rise flats have come back into favour. The flood of money that has swamped London and the extreme constraints on available land has revived high-rise as the glamorous way to live for a new generation of young professionals, and now taller and taller blocks are being built or planned along the Thames and in other regenerated cities too.

For most of the second half of the twentieth century, however, the most successful architects turned to big public commissions or to designing trophy offices for corporations. Here they were freer to express their own convictions about how we should build. What they offered was controversial. In 1984 the Prince of Wales was invited to speak at the 150th birthday party of the Royal Institute of British Architects. Instead of offering a paean of praise, however, he launched into a scathing attack on modernism. 'For far too long, it seems to me,' he said, 'some planners and architects have consistently ignored the feelings and wishes of the mass of ordinary people in this country. Consequently a large number of us have developed a feeling that architects tend to design houses for the approval of fellow architects and critics, not for tenants ... Why can't we have those curves and arches that express feeling in design? What is wrong with them? Why has everything got to be vertical, unbending, only at right angles – and functional?'

261

Professions do not enjoy being taken to task, and architects were stung by criticism from someone they saw as an ignorant amateur. His comments, however, struck a chord with the public, whose hostility to much modern building had found a voice. 'At last,' he continued, 'people are beginning to see that it is possible, and important in human terms, to respect old buildings, street plans and traditional scales and at the same time not to feel guilty about a preference for façades, ornaments and soft materials.' His onslaught successfully blocked a proposed modernist extension to the National Gallery, which he described as a 'monstrous carbuncle on the face of a much-loved and elegant friend', and for a time, it was said, chastened architects would send their designs for new buildings in London to the Prince's office to check whether he would voice objections.

It would not have been possible, nor would it have been right, to have all new buildings in Britain subject to a princely veto. In any case the pressure to build new and more spectacular modern buildings became irresistible as London emerged in the 1980s as a rival to New York for the title of financial capital of the world. Today the city boasts some of the most original buildings to be found anywhere, its ancient and restrictive street layout seeming to stimulate architects into ever more ingenious ways of celebrating their clients' wealth and aspirations. Two of the most spectacular stand side by side: the

Lloyd's building and the Swiss Re Insurance headquarters, which everyone calls the Gherkin. They were built by the superstars of architecture, Sir Richard Rogers and Sir Norman Foster. These architects, at the peak of their profession, command huge fees from clients throughout the world. They have become, no doubt to the chagrin of some of their fellows, the two colossi of building in modern Britain.

Both buildings are controversial. The Lloyd's building is famously designed 'inside out'. All the services that would normally be concealed inside a building, to carry water and air-conditioning and waste, are brazenly exposed on the outside in a maze of stainless steel pipes and tubing. It is as though the building itself were in intensive care, with its life-support systems attached to different parts of its body.

From the moment I saw it I thought it a work of genius and superior to a similar building Rogers had designed in Paris, the Pompidou Centre for the Arts. It enlivens the narrow city streets in which its stands and which determine its irregular shape. The lifts were among the first to be made of glass and fitted to the exterior so that they rise like a rocket from the ground, offering spectacular views over the London skyline, at the price of a little vertigo.

Inside, however, the building does not live up to the expectations aroused by the exterior. It is meant to provide a large open space for Lloyd's underwriters to carry on their business in the same manner that they have used since they first contracted insurance business in a coffee-house over 300 years ago. Underwriters sit at their desks, and brokers sit beside them on stools, discussing the risk involved in an insurance proposal and urging the underwriters to subscribe for part of it. Lloyd's wanted to keep the traditional accoutrements of their trade. There is the great Lutine bell, suspended beneath a wooden canopy, to be rung when major disasters strike. There are bound volumes in which losses of shipping are recorded by hand, and boards for the display of other losses. But most curious of all is the dining-room. Lloyd's insisted on bringing to their new premises the eighteenth-century dining-room which they had bought many years before from Bowood House in Wiltshire.

Fitting this elegant Robert Adam room with its delicate plaster work into his glass tower posed a problem for Rogers. His solution is incongruous but does what the client wanted. On the eleventh floor sits what looks like a huge neo-classical tomb. I tapped a corner and it sounded hollow, like polystyrene. It is in fact made of GRP – glass reinforced plastic. Heavy mahogany doors are set into it and open into the Adam room, moved lock, stock and barrel from its old home in the earlier Lloyd's building – a gesture to the Georgian of which even the Prince of Wales might approve.

The building boasts a huge interior space rising up from the ground floor, over 250 feet of glass. It should make the interior of the building full of light, but there is a flaw. The vast trading floor at street level has no natural light. The side walls which could look on to the street are windowless. 'Even on sunny days', one underwriter, Quentin Prebble, complained, 'it is a gloomy place, lit by artificial light.' Perhaps gloom and insurance losses are natural bedfellows.

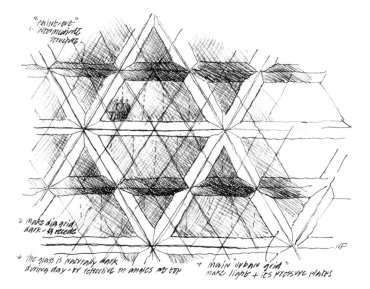

I do not imagine that the Gherkin, just a few steps away, suffers from the same problem. It is a different kind of building altogether, and the product of a revolutionary new architectural technique: the use of computer programs to design buildings. To put it crudely, it is now possible to design a building on the back of an envelope – just to sketch out a shape, and scan it in to a computer. The computer then offers suggestions for constructing what has been drawn. It has given modern architecture the freedom of sculpture. New and ever weirder designs are looming above the skyline of many cities: the Sage Music Centre in Gateshead, silver ectoplasm on the banks of the Tyne, or the Selfridges building in Birmingham, a vast pincushion made up of 15,000 silver discs.

The Gherkin, with its strange, cigar-shaped profile looking like a half-inflated balloon about to escape from the ground and slide up into the sky, is another building made possible by this technique. The Gherkin has been much lauded, but I think it looks too dominant against the London skyline. It makes me feel a little uneasy. Maybe it is because its supposedly friendly shape is not matched by the disposition of its owners. The views from the top, where there is a restaurant and bars, are said to be magnificent, but the public is not allowed in. Entry is reserved for tenants of the building. Any building that thrusts itself on our attention in such a dominant manner should reciprocate by welcoming us in, to share the excitement.

The impact of the present age was summed up for me when I started arguing with a taxi-driver about the merits of the new buildings in the city. Barry Nash spends his working life driving around the city streets, and loves it. Crossing Waterloo Bridge or Westminster Bridge, when bringing tourists in from the Eurostar terminal at Waterloo, he watches in his mirror as their jaws drop at the sight of buildings stretching from St Paul's to the London Eye. He sees no conflict between old and new, no choice to be made. 'The past is

The Gherkin, rising like a half-inflated balloon behind the Tower of London. No prizes for guessing which will last longer.

a wondrous thing, and that's what makes us who we are, you know, but there's no reason why you can't move on. I mean London's an organic place. It changes every moment, day and night.' I said I preferred the Lloyd's building to the Gherkin. He disagreed. 'It looks unfinished doesn't it ... sort of modernistic gone a bit awry?' The Gherkin on the other hand: 'Fantastic. You can see it for miles and miles. It's an amazing building. Phenomenal. Norman Foster's done a good job there.'

It was his final comment, though, which summed up for me the state of building in Britain today. We accept any fantasy we are offered for our public buildings, the more exciting and unexpected the better. But when it comes to the homes we live in, we remain deeply conservative. After we had analysed all the modern buildings we had passed, I asked Barry what kind of house he would live in if he had a free choice. 'I'm not really into modernistic things,' he replied. 'To be honest with you, I suppose if I could really choose it would probably be a chocolate-box cottage.'

The love of the past against the challenge of the new: a battle that will be fought for the rest of this century and beyond. Our era is producing some of the most startling, original and imaginative buildings Britain has ever seen. But their lifespan could be relatively short. Technology has given us the freedom to design as we want but perhaps at the price of no longer building to last. Grandiose as the ambitions of architects may be, their buildings are likely to be outlived by what went before. If so, a hundred years from now historians will no longer be able to trace the story of who we were from what we built.

In Britain today we live in an ever-changing and hugely complex architectural environment, with buildings of every kind around us – new and historic, industrial and domestic. The motor car and the needs of an increasingly urbanised society, combined with the trauma of two world wars, have transformed Britain. Architects and planners have responded in a variety of ways to the challenge of creating new architecture for our needs. Some have tried to ignore or abandon the past, others to mimic, improve or complement it. The public delivers its judgements on all these efforts with increasing bluntness and vigour. Never has the phrase 'I know what I like' been used with more confidence.

SPAGHETTI JUNCTION
BIRMINGHAM

Europe's largest multi-level interchange. The photograph was taken the day after its opening in 1972. Today it would be jammed with traffic. The junction was an ingenious but ill-fated attempt to link the M6 with motorways and local roads into Birmingham. It was designed without traffic lights or roundabouts. The result was this monstrous monument to the tyranny of the motor car, with roads of different widths writhing above and below each other over thirty acres of land. Locals advise drivers not to enter the maze without food and water.

The window of the baptistery of Coventry Cathedral, with glass designed by the artist John Piper. On 14 November 1940 the medieval church of St Michael in Coventry, elevated to cathedral status in 1918, was largely destroyed by bombing. A competition for a replacement was held in 1951 and won by the architect Sir Basil Spence. The new building stands at right angles to its ruined predecessor. Spence wanted to break in some respects from the traditions of cathedral design, and the church is an artistic monument to the late 1950s.

**BRITISH MOTOR
CORPORATION
COWLEY**

A nostalgic glimpse of
industrial Britain in the
1960s. BMC was created by
a merger of Austin and Morris,
once responsible for nearly
forty per cent of British car
production. The shock of
BMC's closure was matched
by closures and mergers
throughout the British
industry. An era of certainty
was making way for a new era
where national prosperity
would depend not on what
we made but on the services
we provided. In building it
has been marked by the
demolition of old factories
housing production lines in
favour of open-plan offices.

Castle Drogo was designed by the architect Sir Edwin Lutyens for the millionaire store owner Julius Drewe. It was built between 1911 and 1930. The building's location and castle form seem to have been intended to celebrate Drewe's ancestral claims. By the time he designed Drogo, Lutyens had already been involved in the restoration of another castle at Lindisfarne, in Northumberland, and the creation of the imperial capital at New Delhi. Although Lutyens was a critic of the modernist theory that the home was a 'machine for living', his interiors can be very austere. This staircase reflects his remarkable confidence in handling volume and his ability to create magnificent effects without resorting to ornament. Castle Drogo was the first twentieth-century building to be accepted into the care of the National Trust.

Holiday camps were once found all around our coasts. In the 1960s there were about a hundred registered camps in Britain, of which Butlins were the most famous. They offered packaged family holidays, organised to provide freedom for both parents and children. Accommodation was in individual chalets, and all-day fun was supervised by the famous 'Redcoats'. Babysitters informed parents when there was a problem (as in chalet R 34). Growing prosperity in the 1970s and 80s led to several camp closures, as families increasingly chose to holiday abroad.

Corby was a village that had produced iron ore since Roman times. In the mid 1930s a combined iron- and steelworks was built, bringing workers to Corby from all over the UK. Its population grew until by 1951 it was one of the largest villages in England with a population of 15,000, and it was designated a 'New Town'. Its population is now 55,000. The closure of the steelworks in the 1980s devastated the town for many years. It has recovered by attracting new industries. The attractive old village of Corby still exists on the fringes of the New Town.

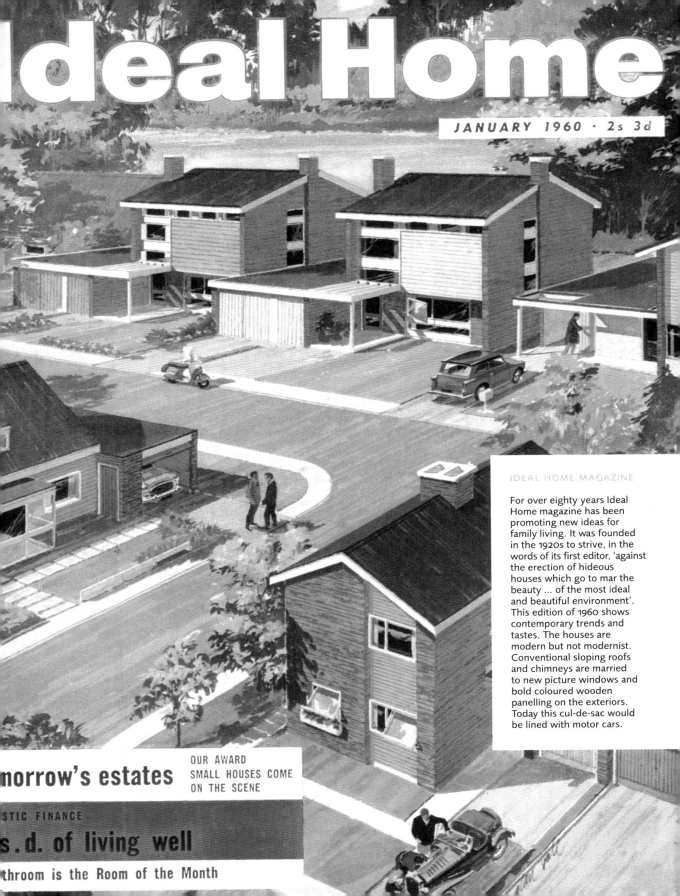

Ideal Home

JANUARY 1960 · 2s 3d

IDEAL HOME MAGAZINE

For over eighty years Ideal Home magazine has been promoting new ideas for family living. It was founded in the 1920s to strive, in the words of its first editor, 'against the erection of hideous houses which go to mar the beauty ... of the most ideal and beautiful environment'. This edition of 1960 shows contemporary trends and tastes. The houses are modern but not modernist. Conventional sloping roofs and chimneys are married to new picture windows and bold coloured wooden panelling on the exteriors. Today this cul-de-sac would be lined with motor cars.

morrow's estates

OUR AWARD
SMALL HOUSES COME
ON THE SCENE

STIC FINANCE

s.d. of living well

throom is the Room of the Month

A Ballistic Missile Early Warning Station at Fylingdales, on the North Yorkshire Moors, built in 1961–2. The globe, which has since been demolished, had a diameter of 140 feet and protected a radar aerial. An officer stands beneath it to convey its scale. Visible for miles around, this was one of three white globes that became locally known as the 'golfballs'. To the architectural historian Sir Nikolaus Pevsner they represented 'the geometry of the space age at its most alluring and most frightening'.

An example of what can be
done with new technologies.
These huge domes set in an
old china clay pit in Cornwall
look from the outside like
spaceships that have just
landed from Mars. They house
all kinds of tropical plants.
The design was made possible
because of computers that
could work out the different
shapes and stresses. The result
is the biggest greenhouse
in the world. It is made of
tubular steel hexagonal panels
glazed with what looks like
clear plastic. The price of this
visual excitement is that it
has a life expectancy of only
thirty years.

SAGE MUSIC CENTRE
GATESHEAD

This spectacular centre for musical performances with two auditoriums and rehearsal spaces was opened in 2004. It stands high up on the bank of the River Tyne facing Newcastle. The whole site is covered by the vast undulating glass and stainless steel roof which is wrapped around it. Designed by Sir Norman Foster, it has been described as a giant caterpillar crawling along the river bank. This detailed photograph shows how the modern architect can make shapes that were impossible to contrive only fifty years ago.

IMPERIAL WAR MUSEUM
NORTH
MANCHESTER

One of the most striking of a number of new museums that have sprung up in Britain. Its architect, Daniel Libeskind wanted to create a building that symbolised the drama of war on land, on sea and in the air. It is composed of three shards or splinters, the two in this picture representing the war in the skies and on the ground. A further shard looking over the Manchester Ship Canal represents battles on the sea. It is a simple, efficient building, but also a work of soaring imagination by an architect whose work knows no boundaries.

Index

Numbers in *italics* refer to illustrations.

279

285

Picture credits

Advertising Archives – p.271

Alamy – p.19, p.21, (Florian Monheim) p.45, p.77, p.103, p.104, (Michael Jenner) p.219, p.246, (Popperfoto) p.253, (Chris George) p.267, (Matt Botwood) p.274 [top], (Christine Widdall) p.274 [bottom]

T & R Annan, Glasgow – p.138, p.139

Arcaid – Richard Bryant p.275

Bayeux, Musée de la Tapisserie – p.48–9

Bridgeman Art Library – p.56–7, p.81, p.93, p.96–7, p.130, p.133, p.142–3, p.149, p.155, (Yale Center for British Art) p.158, p.166, p.180, p.181, p.184–5, p.191, p.228–9, p.230–1

British Library – p.38, p.50, p.91, p.113

Burghley House – p.65

Corbis – p.259, p.272–3

Country Life – p.269

Crown Copyright, 2006, Historic Scotland Images – p.134–5

English Heritage – p.87

Exeter Cathedral Archives – p.90

First Garden City Heritage Museum, Letchworth Garden City, UK – p.240

Foster and Partners – p.264 [left]

Francis Frith Collection – p.132

Getty Images – p.166, p.257, p.270 [all]

Guildhall Library – p.176

Ironbridge Gorge Museum – p.223 [bottom]

London School of Economics – p.225

Manchester Local Archives – p.206

Reproduced by courtesy of the Marquess of Bath, Longleat House, Warminster, Wiltshire – p.94–5

Marquess of Salisbury – p.54

Mary Evans Picture Library – p.46, p.108, p.187

National Galleries of Scotland – p.100–1, p.120

National Library of Scotland – p.136–7

National Maritime Museum – p.180 [top]

National Trust – p.157, p.226, p.227, p.238, p.239

Regimental Headquarters, The Highlanders – p.138

Royal Institute of British Architects – p.247, p.256

Science and Society – p.140–1, p.220–1, p.222

Sir John Soane Museum – p.99

The Art Archive – p.28, p.47, p.51, p.52–3, p.55, p.92, p.98–9, p.124, p.176, p.178–9, p.182–3, p.218, p.222 [top], p.224

Trinity College, Cambridge – p.12–13

Grant Smith/VIEW – p.165

Waterways Archive – p.181 [top]

Elizabeth Zeschin – p.236

Photography on all other pages by Paul Barker.

Thanks

The idea for the television series that formed the basis of this book came from the BBC, and I am grateful to them for a unique opportunity to see places in Britain I had never visited and to explore the story of how and why our country has come to look as it does.

I am grateful to Peter Fincham, Controller BBC 1 and Adam Kemp, Commissioning Editor, who backed the project, and Mark Harrison, Creative Director Arts, who oversaw its conception. Basil Comely, Executive Producer, was a stimulating and provocative overseer of the project, and Julian Birkett, the Series Producer, was generous in his encouragement and penetrating in his criticism.

The directors and researchers are beyond praise. Working to insane deadlines they found ways of telling the story for television, answering my endless questions with patience, and reading and commenting on the chapters of the book in which they were involved. They were also fun to work with. Sally Benton, Jonty Claypole, Nicky Illis, Kate Misrahi, David Thompson and Nigel Walk were the directors, and Krysia Derecki, Naomi Law, Edmund Moriarty and Jon Morrice the researchers.

I was lucky to have as cameraman and sound recordist two of the best in the business in Mike Garner and Dave Williams. They could not make the final film, unaccountably exchanging the excitement of the Middle East for the pleasures of the London suburbs in a wet December. Patrick Acum and Ben Joiner (camera) and Godfrey Kirby and Stuart Thompson (sound) stepped into the breach with equal skill.

The programmes were beautifully edited by Andrea Carnevali, Mark Townsend, Anne Dummet, Jan Cholawo and Kieran Smyth.

The whole project was held together by assiduous work behind the scenes from, among others, Paul Ralph, Jenny Scott, Alison Castle and Emma Fletcher. They juggled a complex filming schedule with my other life as chairman of *Question Time*.

Many others helped with advice and comment. Chief among them was John Goodall, historian at English Heritage, who offered his insights, his deep knowledge of the subject and his boundless enthusiasm to all of us who worked on the project.

I should also like to thank the countless people we encountered along the way, local historians or experts in one or another aspect of British life who accompanied us on location or who were called on for advice and interpretation. Medieval: Leigh Alston, Sophie Cabot, Jayne Bown, Peter Brears, Barry Hillman-Crouch, Anne Mason; Tudor: Fr. Huw Chiplin, Jon Culverhouse, Ian Fletcher, Lt.-Col. Gerald Lesinski, Holly Pomeroy, Gill Smith, Keith Wilmot; Scotland: John Harvey, Lorna Hepburn, Keith Jones, Willie McEwan, Norman Mackie, Mairi Macritchie, Jamie Montgomery, Daphne Rose, Alan Sharp, Aubin Stewart-Wilson, Peter Trowles; Georgian: Paul Bonnington, Michael Casey, Bob Daimond, Ray Knowles, Cathryn Spence, Karin Walton; Victorian: Fr. Sandy Brown, Patrick Fitzgerald, Penny Hartley, Kate Lamb, Eddie Lawler, Dave Lyndop, Olwen McLoughlin, Shemayne Parkinson, Maggie Silver, Bernard Talbot; Modern: Barnabas Calder, Maureen Copping, Douglas D'Enno, Joan James, Rachel Marks, Dr Richard Scarth. I am tempted to turn the conventional caveat on its head and say that any mistakes are theirs, but since the words you read here are mine I must take the blame for error.

My publishers at Bloomsbury rose to the challenge of a tight schedule with flair and alacrity. Richard Atkinson and Natalie Hunt gave me the confidence to tread where I would otherwise have feared to go and created a stunning visual impact for the book. I would also like to thank Lisa Fiske in the production department and the sales, marketing, publicity and rights teams at Bloomsbury. Paul Barker took the special photographs, following in my tracks but at such a distance that although we spoke many times we never met. The other illustrations were found by Anne-Marie Ehrlich, our diligent picture researcher. I am grateful to Steve Dobell for his sensitive editing, Peter Dawson at Grade for the elegant design and Reginald Piggott for his beautiful map.

I am indebted to Michael Sissons and Rosemary Scoular, my agents at Peters, Fraser & Dunlop Ltd, for devising a strategy that would allow both film and book to be completed on time, and for their constant help and encouragement.

My assistant Carolyn Smith, who has worked with me (though neither of us can quite believe it) for the past thirty-nine years, remained as calm as ever, however agitated I became.

And lastly I want to thank my wife Belinda Giles, to whom this book is dedicated. She supported me wholeheartedly throughout. As a former television producer she knows the testing demands that combining a book and a film series like this makes on family life. However demanding my schedule, she never complained but always urged me on. Without her enthusiasm it would not have been the enjoyable and rewarding experience that it turned out to be.